RURAL PROGRESS, RURAL DECAY

Rural Progress, Rural Decay

Neoliberal Adjustment Policies and Local Initiatives

Edited by

LIISA L. NORTH AND JOHN D. CAMERON

Kumarian
Press, Inc.

Rural Progress, Rural Decay: Neoliberal Adjustment Policies and Local Initiatives

Published in 2003 in the United States of America by Kumarian Press, Inc.
1294 Blue Hills Avenue, Bloomfield, CT 06002 USA

Copy editing, design, and production by Joan Weber Laflamme, jml ediset, Vienna, Va.
Index by ARC Films, Inc., Pacific Palisades, California.
Proofread by Beth Richards, Southington, Connecticut.

The text of this book is set in 10/12 Janson Text.
Printed in the United States of America on acid-free paper by Cushing-Malloy.

∞The paper used in this publication meets the minimum requirements of the American National Standard for Information Sciences—Permanence of Paper for Printed Library Materials, ANSI Z39.48-1984.

Library of Congress Cataloging-in-Publication Data

Rural progress, rural decay : neoliberal adjustment policies and local initiatives / edited by Liisa L. North and John D. Cameron.
    p. cm.
Includes bibliographical references.
  ISBN 1-56549-170-X (pbk. : alk. paper)—ISBN 1-56549-171-8 (hardcover : alk. paper)
  1. Rural development—Ecuador. 2. Structural adjustment (Economic policy)—Ecuador. 3. Non-governmental organizations—Ecuador. 4. Rural development—Latin America. 5. Structural adjustment (Economic policy)—Latin America. 6. Non-governmental organizations—Latin America. I. North, Liisa. II. Cameron, John D., 1969–
  HN320.Z9C67 2003
   307.1'412'09866—dc21

                                   2003003742

---

12 11 10 09 08 07 06 05 04 03   10 9 8 7 6 5 4 3 2 1   First Printing 2003

Contents

Part III
Case Studies from the Ecuadorian Highlands

Acknowledgments

The preparation of this volume and the field research on which it is based would not have been possible without generous support from the Social Sciences and Humanities Research Council of Canada (SSHRC). Four of the scholars whose work is presented here—John Cameron, Tanya Korovkin, Louis Lefeber, and Liisa L. North—received grants or fellowships directly from the Canadian SSHRC, and Luciano Martínez was incorporated into the SSHRC-funded project of Lefeber and North. In addition, the University of Waterloo provided financial assistance to Korovkin, and York University and its Centre for Research on Latin America and the Caribbean (CERLAC) lent assistance of many different kinds for the entire project. We are particularly grateful for the multiple services, efficiency, and good humor of CERLAC's former and current administrative assistants, Liddy Gomes and Marshall Beck.

In Ecuador our institutional debts are many. The Ecuadorian seat of the Latin American Faculty of Social Sciences (FLACSO) in Quito provided a home base for the researchers, extending services and opportunities for participation in numerous seminars and conferences that contributed greatly to the development of the project. We would like to thank FLACSO's director, Fernando Carrión, as well as its secretarial staff, librarians, and researchers.

In addition to publishing a volume-related monograph by Luciano Martínez, the Centro Andino de Acción Popular (CAAP) published articles by Victor Bretón, John Cameron and Liisa North, and Louis Lefeber in its journal, *Ecuador Debate*. We owe a great deal to the intellectual support and generously shared insights of CAAP director Francisco Rhon.

The Fondo Ecuatoriano Populorum Progressio (FEPP) assisted North's, Lefeber's, and Bretón's field work in several locations, and we are particularly grateful to FEPP's national director, José Tonello, and to the heads of its offices in Riobamba, Alonso Vallejo and Fausto Sanaguano, and in Guaranda, Edison Silva. In addition to the help of FEPP directors and staff, foreign volunteers at the Fund—Heinz (Enrique) Stachelscheid and Jean Fortín prominently among them—gave unstintingly of their time and offered much astute commentary to Lefeber and North. Field work in Salinas would not have been possible without the cooperation of the Salesian Mission and Father Antonio Polo; the directors, Germán Vasconez and Luis Gonzalez, and the staff of the Fundación de Organizaciones de Salinas (FUNORSAL); the heads, administrators, and workers of the many enterprises that form part of the cooperative system in Salinas; Gina Echenique, the town's dedicated doctor; the administrators and staff of the hostal Refugio; the schoolteachers, especially Aidé Vargas; and the children—Adiran, our guide around town—and all the others, Esther, Paula, and Carmen as well as Jorge and Alejandro.

The heads of the offices of the Instituto de Investigaciones Socio-Económicas y Tecnológicas (INSOTEC) in Pelileo and Ambato, Alba Chavez and Jenny Perez respectively, greatly facilitated North's, Lefeber's, and Martínez's research at those locations; they not only put us in contact but often set up the interviews with textile and small-industry leaders, local politicians, and producers. Roberto Hidalgo, director of INSOTEC's Centro de Estudios y Políticas at its main office in Quito was particularly helpful with establishing and maintaining communication with the NGO's field offices in Pelileo and Ambato, and María Verónica Dávalos and Wilson Araque provided invaluable assistance in the conduct of our first series of interviews at the research sites. And we thank the jeans producers of Pelileo who graciously welcomed us into their homes and enterprises as we visited them over and over again during the period from 1998 to 2002.

The mayors and employees of the municipalities of Bolívar, Cotacachi, and Guamote did a great deal to assist Cameron's research at those sites. At Terranueva, a lively organization that supports participatory processes in Cotacachi and Guatmote, Sara Báez, the executive director, and staff members Jomar Cevallos and Mary García were immensely helpful. Angel Bonilla, Fernando Guerrero, and Ana María Larrea at the Instituto de Estudios Ecuatorianos (IEE) provided extremely helpful information about their work in supporting democratization processes in Cotacachi and Guamote. Hernán A. Valencia, at the Asociación de Municipalidades Ecuatorianas (AME), took time from his very busy schedule to share his extensive knowledge and to lend logistical support for the conduct of a survey on NGO-municipal cooperation. In Bolívar, Henry Romero, president of the Fundación El Arteson and jack of all trades, provided daily encouragement.

At the Comisión Ecuménica de Derechos Humanos (CEDHU), Elsie Monge (director) and Nellie Herrera (archivist) provided North with access to their unique data collection on land conflicts and generously shared their time and knowledge.

The individuals who helped the authors with information, suggestions, comments, contacts, and good conversation are simply too many to name. Nevertheless, a few of them must be mentioned here. All the contributors to the volume have relied on the goodwill and remarkable data collections of Carlos Larrea and on his always informed and enthusiastic support for research on development issues. Juan Maiguashca and Miguel Murmis are our much appreciated colleagues who, way back in 1978, first involved CERLAC fellows and associated students in research on the political economy of rural Ecuador. Manuel Chiriboga incorporated North into his project on FEPP's rural promotion work and introduced her to the NGO and its personnel. Gloria Camacho and Maria Cuvi tried to keep us informed on, and attentive to, the gender issues of development in rural Ecuador. Alberto Acosta, Pablo Andrade, Susana Balarezo, Patricio Donoso, Patricia Espinoza, Jonas Frank, Fernando García, Erika Henekamp, Fausto Jordan, Rafael Quintero, Fernando Larrea, Peter Meier, Mercedes Prieto, Byron Real, Alicia Torres, and Victor Hugo Torres facilitated contacts and offered valuable suggestions and information. Yasmine Shamsie provided research assistance for Chapter 3. Anthony Bebbington, Phillip Stuart Caurnyeur, Cristóbal Kay, Jean Daudelin, David Myhre, Kathleen O'Neill, and Luis Silva provided much-appreciated commentary on earlier drafts of some of the chapters presented here.

The authors are very much indebted to one another, although each one, of course, is responsible for any errors in his or her work. Since the early 1980s, most of the contributors to this volume have been involved in an ongoing conversation with one another, and with Carlos Larrea, about the issues analyzed here. John Cameron translated Victor Bretón's and Luciano Martínez's chapters from Spanish to English; all other translations were made by the authors of the different chapters. Many thanks are also owed to Tim Clark, who assisted in the last stages of the volume preparation in numerous ways, from formatting tables to hunting down the details of incomplete references and preparing the list of acronyms.

Finally, it must be said that several of the contributors passed through very difficult and painful times in the course of this volume's preparation. Liisa North and Luciano Martínez lost their mothers, Rob Koep lost his father, and John Cameron's father faced recovery from a stroke. We take this opportunity to thank our parents for the many ways in which they provided support for our studies and research at home and in distant lands that they never visited.

Acronyms

AIECH	Asociación de Indígenas Evangélicos de Chimborazo (Indigenous Evangelical Association of Chimborazo)
AME	Asociación de Municipalidades Ecuatorianas (Association of Ecuadorian Municipalities)
AoA	Agreement on Agriculture
BNF	Banco Nacional de Fomento (National Development Bank)
CAAP	Centro Andino de Acción Popular (Andean Centre for Popular Action)
CALACS	Canadian Association of Latin American and Carribean Studies
CEAS	Centro de Estudios de Acción Social (Centre for Research on Social Action)
CEBEMO	Central Holandesa de Mediacíon para Cofinanciamiento de Programas de Desarrollo (Dutch Center of Mediation for Cofinancing of Development Programs)
CECI	Centro Canadiense de Estudios y Cooperación Internacional (Candian Center for Research and International Cooperation)
CEDHU	Comisión Ecuménica de Derechos Humanos (Ecumenical Commission of Human Rights)
CEE	Conferencia Episcopal Ecuatoriana (Ecuadorian Episcopal Conference)
CELA	Centro de Estudios Latinoamericanos de la Pontificia Universidad Católica del Ecuador (Centre for Latin American Research of the Pontifical Catholic University of Ecuador)
CEPLAES	Centro de Planificación y Estudios Sociales

CERLAC	Centre for Research on Latin America and the Carribean
CESA	Central Ecuatoriana de Servicios Agrícolas (Ecuadorian Centre for Agricultural Services)
CIAT	Centro Internacional para la Agricultura Tropical (International Centre for Tropical Agriculture)
CODENPE	Consejo de Desarrollo para las Nacionalidades y Pueblos del Ecuador (Development Council for the Nationalities and Peoples of Ecuador)
CONAIE	Confederación de Nacionalidades Indígenas de Ecuador (Confederation of Indigenous Nationalities of Ecuador)
COTESU	Cooperación Técnica Suiza (Swiss Technical Cooperation)
DCTR	Denuncias de Conflicto de Tierra Rural (Rural Land Conflict Reports)
DDP	Derechos del Pueblo (People's Rights)
DRI	Desarrollo Rural Integrado (Integrated Rural Development)
ECUARUNARI	Ecuador Runacunapac Riccharimui (Awakening of the Ecuadorian Indigenous Peoples)
FA	Farmers' Association
FAO	Food and Agricultural Organization
FEPP	Fondo Ecuatoriano Populorum Progressio (Ecuadorian Populorum Progressio Fund)
FEI	Federación Ecuatoriana de Indios (Federation of Ecuadorian Indians)
FICI	Federación Indígena y Campesina de Imbabura (Indigenous and Peasant Federation of Imbabura)
FISE	Fondo de Inversion Social de Emergencia (Emergency Social Investment Fund)
FLACSO	Facultad Latinoamericana de Ciencias Sociales (Latin American Faculty of Social Sciences)
FODERUMA	Fondo de Desarrollo Rural Marginal (Marginal Rural Development Fund)

FOLADE	Fondo Latinoamericano de Desarrollo (Latin American Development Fund)
FTAA	Free Trade Area of the Americas
FUNORSAL	Fundación de Organizaciones de Salinas (Foundation of the Organizations of Salinas)
GDP	Gross Domestic Product
GIEDEM	Grupo Interdisciplinar de Estudios de Desarrollo y Multiculturalidad (Interdisciplinary Group for the Study of Development and Multiculturalism)
IAF	Inter-American Foundation
IDB	Inter-American Development Bank
IEE	Instituto de Estudios Ecuatorianos (Institute of Ecuadorian Studies)
IERAC	Instituto Ecuatoriano de Reforma Agraria y Colonización (Ecuadorian Institute of Agrarian Reform and Colonization)
IFI	International Financial Institution
IICA	Instituto Interamericano de Cooperación Agrícola (Inter-American Institute for Agricultural Cooperation)
IICO	Organización Inter-Eclesiástica para Cooperación al Desarrollo (Inter-Ecclesiastic Organization for Development Cooperation)
ILO	International Labour Organization
IMF	International Monetary Fund
INDA	Instituto Nacional de Desarrollo Agropecuario (National Institute for Agricultural Development)
INEC	Instituto Nacional de Estadísticas y Censos (National Institute of Statistics and Census)
INSOTEC	Instituto de Investigaciones Socio-Económicas y Tecnológicas (Institute for Socio-Economic and Technological Research)
ISI	Import Substitution Industrialization
MAG	Ministerio de Agricultura y Ganadería (Ministry of Agriculture and Livestock)

MAI	Multilateral Agreement on Investment
MERCOSUR	Mercado Común del Sur
MICH	Movimiento Indígena de Chimborazo (Indigenous Movement of Chimborazo)
MPD	Movimiento Democrático Popular (Popular Democratic Movement)
MST	Movimiento dos Tabalhadores Rurais Sem Tierra (Landless Rural Workers' Movement)
NAFTA	North American Free Trade Agreement
NGO	Nongovernmental Organization
NICs	Newly industrialized countries
OAS	Organization of American States
ODEPLAN	Oficina de Planificación de la Presidencia de la República (Planning Office of the President of the Republic)
OGN	Organización No Gubernamental (NGO)
OSG	Organización de Segundo Grado (Second Level Organization)
OTG	Organización de Tercer Grado (Third Level Organization)
PNUD	Programa de Naciones Unidades para el Desarrollo (United Nations Development Program)
PRODEPINE	Programa de Desarrollo de Los Pueblos Indígenas y Negros del Ecuador (Development Program of the Indigenous and Black Peoples of Ecuador)
PRONADER	Programa Nacional de Desarrollo Rural (National Rural Development Program)
SAP	Structural Adjustment Program
SCC	Savings and Credit Cooperative
SEL	Social Enterprise London
SIISE	Sistema Integrado de Indicadores Sociales del Ecuador (Integrated System of Social Indicators of Ecuador)
SNV	Servicio Holandés de Cooperación para el Desarrollo (Dutch Service for Development Cooperation)

SPS	Agreement on Sanitary and Phytosanitary Measures (WTO)
SSHRCC	Social Sciences and Humanities Research Council of Canada
TRIPS	Trade Related Intellectual Property Rights
UCAE	Unión Campesina del Ecuador (Peasant Union of Ecuador)
UCASAJ	Unión de Cabildos de San Juan (Union of Community Councils of San Juan)
UN	United Nations
UNDP	United Nations Development Program
UNECLAC	United Nations Economic Commission for Latin America and the Carribean
UNFAO	United Nations Food and Agriculture Organization
UNIDO	United Nations Industrial Development Organization
UNOCIC	Unión de Comunidades Indígenas de Cacha (Union of Indigenous Communities of Cacha)
UNORCAC	Unión de Organizaciones Campesinas de Cotacachi (Union of Peasant Organizations of Cotacachi)
UR	Uruguay Round
USDA	United States Department of Agriculture
WTO	World Trade Organization

Society may subsist,
though not in the most comfortable state,
without beneficence;
but the prevalence of injustice must utterly destroy it.

—ADAM SMITH,
Theory of Moral Sentiments

Chapter 1

Rural Progress or Rural Decay?

An Overview of the Issues and the Case Studies

Liisa L. North

This volume deals with the nature and impacts of neoliberal structural adjustment programs in Latin America and the degree to which rural development programs, especially those led or assisted by NGOs, can prosper in the context of those programs. Specifically, the contributors assess the developmental consequences of the ways in which SAPs, or so-called Washington Consensus policies of economic liberalization, have transformed the roles of states, markets, and civil societies in the rural areas of the hemisphere, with special reference to Ecuador.

The authors come from different disciplinary specializations, but their conceptual anchors are rooted in a political economy perspective. Although they do not always agree in their interpretations, they share scholarly traditions that investigate development possibilities with attention to the ways in which historically structured relations of power at the local, national, and international levels facilitate or prevent improvements in the social conditions and opportunities of underprivileged sectors. While the authors write from a perspective highly critical of neoliberal economic theory and policy practice, none is ideologically anti-market. Thus they also cast a critical eye on ISI—the state-led industrialization policies that preceded SAPs in Latin America—and on the activities of NGOs and civic organizations.

Although the studies included here concentrate for the most part on productive activities (within their historical political-economic settings), the contributors to the volume do not equate development with economic growth alone. Rather, they understand development as progress toward equity and respect for the full range of internationally recognized human rights—most important, the rights enshrined in the International

Covenant on Economic, Social, and Cultural Rights and the International Covenant on Civil and Political Rights. As Louis Lefeber argues in his analysis of neoliberalism and its consequences in Latin America (Chapter 2), equity is both an ethical *desideratum* and a necessity for establishing the requirements for domestic market growth and development.

The book focuses on equitable rural development, broadly conceived to include rural industrialization and other nonagricultural activities. It does so because the contributors to the volume are convinced that rural social and economic progress is essential to any viable national development process. First, although the majority of Latin Americans today live in urban centers, it is in the rural areas of the hemisphere that the most acute forms of poverty, grievous inequality, and political oppression are to be found (e.g., Plant 1999; Dandler 1999). The majority of the hemisphere's rural population faces a daily violation of the rights enshrined in the various UN covenants and declarations, including the basic right to subsistence. Sustainable national development is not possible without the reversal of these conditions.

Second, these inequitable conditions feed political instability and violence. Indigenous uprisings in highland and Amazonian Ecuador as well as southern Mexico, the landless movement in Brazil, and the civil war in Colombia represent only the most prominent rural struggles that have persisted into the twenty-first century. Although Central America's largely peasant-based civil wars of the 1980s were settled through negotiations, the peace agreements that were signed between 1990 and 1996 failed to deliver agrarian reform and social improvements in the rural areas, thereby threatening new cycles of violence (e.g., Boyce and Pastor 1996; Kowalchuk 2000; Jonas 2000, 167–216). The prevailing social and political conditions in rural areas thus provoke conflict and severely curtail the possibilities of deepening what has been characterized as Latin America's "shallow" or "low intensity" democratization (Kay 2001b).

Third, agriculture in Latin America has failed to create jobs and yield improved incomes, even though it is a sector in which employment opportunities and productivity gains could be generated at low cost. As a consequence, migration to the overburdened cities of the continent has remained high or even accelerated over the past two decades. At the same time, the incapacity of urban sectors to generate reasonably remunerative employment for the large numbers of migrants who are entering the labor market has been demonstrated throughout the hemisphere. Not surprisingly, the spread of urban marginal settlements, poverty, and social violence has also accelerated in many Latin American countries. Clearly, a more equitable distribution of productive assets and investment in labor-intensive rural development would not only relieve deprivation and oppression in the countryside, but it would also make it easier to address the growing social problems of Latin America's cities.

Finally, it should be mentioned that rural progress constitutes the basis for resolving two critical hemisphere-wide problems: illegal migration and the spread of the drug trade.

Although the case studies presented here deal with Ecuador, one of the smaller, poorer, and most ethnically diverse Latin American nations, its political-economic evolution and developmental problems are a prototype of those that prevail in many other countries in the hemisphere and elsewhere in the Third World; that is, Ecuador has been historically characterized by autocratic and unstable governments, weak and corrupt public institutions, high levels of social deprivation, blocked redistributive reform, acute ethnic and class cleavages, and a high degree of vulnerability to international economic forces.

As for the role of NGOs, in the course of SAP implementation, their numbers "exploded" all over the Third World as they became increasingly prominent recipients of funding from IFIs and the development assistance programs of donor nations (Edwards and Hulme 1995). NGOs in Ecuador, as elsewhere, were drawn into a very broad range of activities, but here we deal in particular with those that were involved, first of all, in providing support to various kinds of productive activities and, second, in assisting municipal democratization and social development. In fact, three chapters deal wholly or in part with programs undertaken by one NGO that became particularly notable in promoting rural development in the Ecuadorian highlands—the FEPP.

In-depth evaluations and analyses of the performance of many types of grassroots-based and NGO-assisted rural service delivery and development initiatives are now widely available (Bebbington et al. 1993; Hulme and Mosley 1996; Tendler 1997; Krishna, Uphoff, and Esman 1997; Uphoff, Esman, and Krishna 1998). Nevertheless, we are not aware of works that examine their degrees of success or failure in relation to, first, the implementation of SAPs, and second, the patterns of asset and power distribution within the nations and at the sites (or micro-regions) where such programs were established. This volume attempts to take steps in that direction: that is, to identify relationships between macroeconomic policies and relations of power, on the one hand, and the evolution and viability of local initiatives in rural areas on the other hand. Part 1 provides historically grounded theoretical critiques of neoliberal policies and the international trade agreements under which current processes of globalization are advancing. Part 2 deals with national trends in Ecuador in light of comparative trends in the Andean region countries, other parts of Latin America, and elsewhere in the world. Part 3 presents five case studies that deal with local development initiatives, including municipal democratization and grassroots-based entrepreneurial activities assisted by NGOs. All the case studies, in various ways, address questions of market access, the distribution of assets, and the structures of power at the local level; two of them, in addition, address questions related to the appropriate design of cooperative enterprises.

Below, we provide an introduction to the interrelated themes and issues that cut through the studies included here, beginning with the consequences of the changing roles of states, markets, and civil society under neoliberalism and followed by discussions of international, national, and local power relations; the possibilities of movement toward greater equity through income and asset redistribution and employment generation; and finally, the institutional design of cooperative enterprises and social capital formation in relation to central state policies.

STATES, MARKETS, AND NGOS

Neoliberal Structural Adjustment Programs

When SAPs began to be adopted in Latin America in the wake of the debt crisis of the early 1980s, their advocates in the IMF, the World Bank, and the major donor nations expected a relatively rapid renewal of economic growth, along with or followed by improvements in living standards. Those policies—market liberalization, the reduction of the state's role in the economy, privatization, the elimination of fiscal deficits and balance of payments disequilibria, export promotion, and the creation of conditions to attract foreign investment—were supposed to involve "short-term pain," at worst. However, as growth remained erratic, living standards continued to deteriorate, and deepening social inequalities generated widespread political protest, the 1980s turned into "the lost decade" in Latin America.[1]

In response to these disturbing trends, IFIs and donors began to fund social compensation programs that were initially delivered through public agencies. However, for reasons that included the pervasive corruption of many governments and state bureaucracies as well as the need to gain legitimacy within civil society for the neoliberal economic policy framework, by the mid-1980s donors had begun to channel some assistance through a broad range of civic organizations and NGOs that, in fact, had often been highly critical of the cutbacks in public social spending involved in SAPs. Subsequently, since many NGO-delivered social support programs proved themselves effective in reaching the poorer sectors, and as further "market friendly" reforms failed to generate reasonably remunerated employment or reduce poverty, donor attention in the 1990s turned toward support for NGO-led small and cooperative enterprise programs aimed at fostering what some have called "poor people's entrepreneurship" (Adams and Von Pischke 1992). With the objectives of achieving sustainable improvements in incomes and living standards, NGO-led programs in this area focused on the provision of training, technical assistance, credit, marketing opportunities, and various services.

In the course of these developments, NGOs demanded access to, and step by step became involved in, policy consultation forums sponsored by national development agencies as well as the World Bank and the IDB (e.g., Fox and Brown 1998; Hulme and Edwards 1997). In both the South and the North, NGOs thus came to occupy uneasy and contradictory positions as both critics of SAPs, on the one hand, and implementors of development programs financed by the principal enforcers of SAPs, on the other hand. Despite the contradictions involved in both cooperating with and criticizing the IFIs, by the mid-1990s NGO advocates of poor people's entrepreneurship and local initiatives spanned the entire ideological spectrum (Bienefeld 1988; Petras 1997). In effect, World Bank–associated technocrats, disenchanted Marxists, and NGO activists found themselves in the same camp, inspired by, among other things, certain prominent success stories such as the Grameen Bank of Bangladesh (Bornstein 1996; Holcombe 1995; Todd 1996).

Decentralization, institutional reform, and social capital formation were added to the IFI-sponsored policy mix in the mid-1990s as parts of a broader package of so-called second-generation reforms. Decentralization was intended to make government more accountable and responsive to citizens by bringing it "closer to the people"; reform of judicial and public administration systems was aimed at making governments more efficient and transparent in order to encourage investment (see Burki and Perry 1998); and social capital formation was expected to reinforce accountability, improve government performance, and generate norms of trust and cooperation across society (e.g., Putnam 1993; Evans 1996). Projects specifically oriented to generate social capital—that is, strengthen civil society organizations, including NGOs—thus began to be funded by the World Bank and other donors (e.g., Carroll and Bebbington 2000).[2]

All these trends, taken together, led to what has been described as an explosion in NGO formation and activity across the world (Edwards and Hulme 1995), an explosion that was highly visible in Ecuador, where indigenous organizations also grew rapidly in numbers (Arcos Cabrera and Palomeque Vallejo 1997; Bretón 2001; Chapter 8 herein).

The question is, can poor people's entrepreneurship and local initiatives sponsored by civic organizations prosper and generate *widespread* improvements in living standards in the context of the neoliberal economic policies and entrenched national and international power structures that sustain them? At least three interrelated issues are involved. First, can NGO-led small-scale projects be effectively "scaled up" (Wood 1997) or, as Thomas Carroll puts it, do "these small-scale experiments have a real potential to be expanded to reach larger numbers of beneficiaries"? (Carroll 1992, 120). Second, will NGOs that have developed policy analysis capacities be allowed to influence macroeconomic policy? Third, and this is a fundamental developmental question, are the economic and political conditions that can facilitate the success of large numbers of local entrepreneurial and other types of initiatives in place, or are such conditions being generated by the neoliberal policies favored by donors and IFIs?

Growth and Development in the 1980s and 1990s

The evidence presented in the works included here argues that the answers to all three questions posed above are negative. To begin with the creation of the economic conditions that might facilitate the success of large numbers of local initiatives, Lefeber argues that ideologically rigid reliance in the past on state controls and recently on uncontrolled free markets has led to stagnation and the immiseration of working populations (Chapters 2 and 4). With regard to the results of ideologically driven neoliberal policies, carefully designed studies have found that not only did social progress in the Third Word slow down in the 1980s and 1990s (Weisbrot et al. 2001) but that liberalization failed even in its primary objective of generating growth (Weisbrot et al. 2000). Similarly, the evidence of social, economic, and environmental deterioration under SAPs leads Ricardo Grinspun to argue that the enshrinement of "market friendly" prescriptions in international trade agreements augurs ill for future possibilities of ensuring sustainable growth and responding to the needs of the rural poor (Chapter 3).

Ecuador, the site of our case studies, was among the less successful adjustors in Latin America: in 1998, GDP per capita still stood at its 1982 level, after which it declined by a dramatic 9 percent in 1999. At the beginning of that year the country's private banking system collapsed in the midst of the exorbitant corruption that followed the IFI-mandated financial deregulation that was introduced in 1994. As could be expected under these conditions, poverty levels remained high, increasing to 62.6 percent of the population in 1998. Meanwhile, the distribution of income, in a country historically characterized by profound social inequalities, became even more skewed (Larrea and Sánchez 2002, 14–15, 25, 19).

Deepening poverty was particularly evident in the rural areas, affecting 75.8 percent of the population in 1995 and 82 percent in 1998 (Larrea and Sánchez 2002, 25). Moreover, poverty was most severe among the rural indigenous people who made up about 20–25 percent of the population. Despite significant amounts of compensatory international assistance that was channeled to their communities and to an ever-increasing number of local and provincial indigenous organizations (Bretón 2001;

Chapter 8 herein),[3] in 1995, 73.2 percent of Indians subsisted below the poverty line, and 36.7 percent eked out an existence in conditions of indigence (PNUD 1999, 44). In this context, demand for peasant produced staples stagnated along with the declining incomes of the majorities. As Lefeber points out (Chapter 4), lack of income did not allow a large proportion of the population, concentrated in the rural and informal sectors, to convert their unsatisfied needs for basic consumption goods into market demand.

In his study of neoliberal policy impacts on the peasantry in Ecuador and neighboring Andean region countries, Luciano Martínez found a decline in social, economic, and ecological conditions caused by price instability, lack of credit, cutbacks in public programs (including extension services and education), and the abandonment of state-sponsored agrarian reform (Chapter 5). In these circumstances even a major rural development program financed by the World Bank in Ecuador during the 1990s, PRONADER, failed to yield positive results in seven out of the twelve zones where it was carried out. Martínez also points out that school attendance barely inched up in program zones, undermining the viability of rural development strategies based on the creation of peasant business enterprises, which require high levels of literacy, numeracy, and other skills.

Overall, the lack of progress in PRONADER zones was indicative of the failure of the macroeconomic model within which it was executed. Although it was designed to focus on the minority of relatively well-off peasant farmers who were thought to be economically viable within the framework of market liberalization, it yielded little or no improvement in their lives.[4] No equivalent programs were even attempted to improve the productive and living conditions of the majority of the rural population, that is, the marginal producers whose plight is discussed by Lefeber (Chapter 4).

The case studies provide further evidence of the specific ways in which adjustment programs affected NGOs and failed to create the conditions in which local development initiatives could prosper or, in Carroll's words, be "scaled up . . . to reach larger numbers of beneficiaries." Victor Bretón explains how one of Ecuador's most important rural development NGOs, FEPP, recast its programs in response to the agendas of international donors (Chapter 8). From support to social programs and peasant struggles for land in the 1980s, FEPP's office in the majority indigenous province of Chimborazo turned in the 1990s toward assisting small producers' efforts to engage in commercial production. However, as could be expected in the very unstable and even deteriorating market conditions analyzed by Lefeber and Martínez, FEPP's new orientation yielded mixed results and even led to demoralization among peasants who could not cope with volatile prices.

Similarly, the dynamic growth of family owned textile enterprises, studied by Liisa L. North in the canton of Pelileo, was reversed during the second half of the 1990s (Chapter 11). This happened largely as a consequence of trade liberalization and the incapacity of the state to respond to natural disasters or to regulate the financial system in ways that might have sustained demand among the lower- and middle-income earners who made up the textile producers' market. The IDB-supported NGO that provided services to these producers was unable to counteract the overwhelmingly negative macroeconomic trends of the mid and late 1990s and the impact of the financial system meltdown of 1999. Subsequently, at the beginning of the new century, the sector's crisis reached devastating proportions as the effects of the government's early 2000 decision to adopt the U.S. dollar as Ecuador's official currency led to an overvaluation that favored textile imports from neighboring countries.[5]

In contrast, the FEPP-assisted cooperative enterprises in the parish of Salinas, analyzed by North, largely succeeded in riding out the economic storms of the 1990s (Chapter 10). But it was a combination of not easily replicable factors that explained their relative success. First of all, exceptionally high levels of external assistance—including funding from the IDB—allowed FEPP, together with institutions linked to the Catholic church, to play a state-like developmental role in that isolated microregion where the church had conducted an agrarian reform on its own properties. Second, the parish's principal productive activities were directed to domestic high-income markets and so-called solidarity markets in Europe, neither of which many other peasant producers could access. Nevertheless, even in Salinas, cutbacks in public education, health, and infrastructure spending held back social improvements, and in 2001 administrators of some local organizations were beginning to foresee trouble as imports that competed with their production were made cheap by dollarization.

Evidence from other parts of the world supports the general findings presented here. Examples of NGO-led or assisted projects that continued to prosper or were successfully established in the course of SAPs can be found, but failure was much more common (e.g., Mayoux 1995; Mead and Liedholm 1998). In some cases failure could be traced directly to donor insistence on following neoliberal prescriptions in project design and implementation (Murray 1997; Bebbington 2001); in other cases it could be attributed to the macroeconomic conditions created by such policies and the prevailing relations of power within the state. Bebbington and Carroll, for example, refer to two cooperative peasant enterprises that were undermined by the combination of neoliberal macroeconomic policies and peasant incapacity to obtain state protection. The first, a cooperative of Peruvian alpaca producers, "came to grief" because the domestic alpaca wool market collapsed and the state failed to take remedial action. The second, a federation of seventeen Ecuadorian yuca meal producers descended into crisis when its principal market in Colombia was preempted by Malaysian dumping (Carroll and Bebbington 2000, 445).

Moreover, even the most successful projects benefit only a very small proportion of the socially and economically disenfranchised population. The exceptions, such as the Grameen Bank, which "scaled up" and transformed entire villages and regions, are very few. Despite its success, however, the bank's deputy managing director asserts:

> Government is the most important actor in the development scenario. . . . Even if there were ten Grameen Banks, you would not achieve a significant qualitative change in people's lives without change at the national level. (Quoted in Holcombe 1995, 69–70)

In a similar vein Whyte points out that state policies favored the establishment and consolidation of the Mondragón cooperative complex, which, by the 1990s, included dozens of enterprises and employed more than thirty thousand people in the Basque region of Spain (MacLeod 1997). When its first enterprises were established in 1956, "and for many years thereafter, Spanish manufacturers were protected by high tariffs" (Whyte 1995, 65). Mondragón's manager adds: "If it weren't for the economic situation of Spain when we started and for Don José María [the charismatic founder], the . . . cooperatives would not be here today" (quoted in Whyte 1995, 65). In sum, although all who have studied Mondragón recognize the unique leadership provided by the "red priest" José María Arizmendi, he could work his magic, so to speak, because a state-protected market gave the cooperative enterprises time to experiment and learn.

Second-Generation Reforms

By the mid-1990s, the neoliberal policies had come under critical scrutiny even within the IFIs (e.g., IDB 1996; Birdsall and Sabot 1994), and they were subsequently modified in certain respects. Those modifications resulted from both practical and theoretical concerns. From a practical perspective, the World Bank and others had become increasingly concerned about the widespread increase in social inequality associated with the implementation of SAPs (e.g., Burki and Perry 1998, 1). From a theoretical standpoint the modifications represented the rising influence of the New Institutional Economics and its emphasis on the roles of both formal and informal institutions in economic development. Along this line of thought the failure of neoliberal reforms to bring about improvements in living standards was blamed on the weakness of both formal and informal institutions—that is, respectively, of legal structures and of the unwritten norms of social behavior that make possible cooperation, trust, and reciprocity.

As a result of this theoretical shift, the international banks and major donors placed increasing emphasis on reforms to improve the efficiency of state institutions—the so-called second-generation reforms (World Bank 1997; Burki and Perry 1998)—and on efforts to promote the formation of social capital among marginalized and excluded populations. Nevertheless, it must be emphasized that the new concern with state capacity was limited to improving the functioning of government and certain public agencies so as to create a more secure and attractive investment climate for domestic and foreign capital in order to make liberalization and privatization work. The possibilities of empowering the state to play a directive role in the economy, provide protection from international competition for selected (e.g., employment intensive) sectors of activity, or to address issues of poverty that derived from the inequitable distribution of productive assets—as proposed by Lefeber, Grinspun, and others in this volume—were ignored.

In effect, change in the SAP paradigm took place only on the margins. At the beginning of the twenty-first century, it was still market forces, freed from the "distortions" of state intervention, that were expected to generate economic growth, ensure social progress, and provide the "enabling environment" for local initiatives. At the same time, critics of neoliberal orthodoxy within the IFIs were silenced or forced to resign—the case, most prominently, of the World Bank's senior economist, Joseph Stiglitz (Stiglitz 2002; Wade 2001, 131–32). Accordingly, many previously state-delivered services continued to be privatized or, as Geoff Wood puts it, "franchised" to various private agents, ranging from NGOs to profit-driven corporations, creating what Tanya Korovkin identifies as "new welfare networks" (Chapter 7); or such services were downloaded to local jurisdictions through decentralization policies, as John Cameron found in the case of the rural municipalities that he studied (Chapter 9 herein; Wood 1997).

This ideological context left little room for NGO and broader civil society influence on economic policy. The basic decisions concerning macroeconomic management continued to be made behind closed doors in negotiations between IFI technocrats and government officials who often represented or were tied down by the interests of short-sighted, if not corrupt, national elites and pressures emanating from foreign investors and governments (Conaghan and Malloy 1994). Although civil society consultative mechanisms were set up by the IFIs, the banks showed no willingness to make changes in their macroeconomic policy agenda (Hamerschlag 2001). In Ecuador, the World Bank financed a number of civil society consultations (CELA 2001; Martínez Flores 2001; Zappata 2000), but the basic recommendations that emerged from them were ignored by the Bank and the Ecuadorian government.

RELATIONSHIPS OF POWER
AND THE DISTRIBUTION OF ASSETS

The Historical Legacy

The inequitable rural conditions that hold back social progress, national development, and democratization in Latin America, of course, cannot be attributed simply to SAPs. They are rooted in earlier periods of history, dating back to the region's colonial past, the nineteenth-century agricultural export expansion booms (which led to the dominance of large estate interests), and the limitations of the development model that preceded SAPs—that is, ISI (Thorp 1998, 24, 94–95, 121, 153–57). Of particular relevance for this volume is the fact that ISI was pursued without thoroughgoing agrarian reform, and it was highly biased against the development of agricultural and rural sectors in general (Lefeber 1980; Chapter 6 herein).

The now much criticized ISI-associated state intervention in the economy in fact favored the advance of large capitalist producers—industrialists and estate owners who also invested in commercial and financial sectors. It is they who became the protagonists of the subsequent neoliberal policy model. By leaving the market in charge, SAPs also left in privileged positions the elites that had consolidated market power in previous phases of development in Ecuador and elsewhere in the region—that is, those who controlled the assets and institutions through which market exchange was conducted (e.g., Hewitt de Alcantara 1993; Streeten 1993, 1295).

Landlord Power and Land Conflicts

Since Ecuador's landlords succeeded in blocking the full implementation of agrarian reform laws that were decreed in 1964 and 1973, unresolved land conflicts continued to agitate the Ecuadorian countryside during the following decades. In comparison with the violence that engulfed Peru, Colombia, and much of Central America in the 1980s, Ecuador appeared to be an island of peace and respect for human rights. However, the country's apparent good record does not stand up to close scrutiny. Utilizing data compiled by CEDHU, North, Kit, and Koep describe ongoing land conflicts and landlord violence against agricultural workers and peasants. They also question the possibilities of rural development and democratization without profound changes in the distribution of assets and political power that provoke most conflicts and abuses in the countryside (Chapter 6).

Korovkin documents the truncated agrarian reform and continued struggle for land and related assets in the indigenous highland province of Chimborazo (Chapter 7), one of the provinces where agrarian reform was reputed to have advanced the furthest. Her research demonstrates that most of the land transferred to indigenous communities, in fact, was not suitable for either agriculture or pasture. Indeed, rather than peasant acquisition of land, the most visible impact of the 1973 agrarian reform was the conversion of large-estate production from traditional food crops to livestock raising. This, in turn, had a devastating impact on rural employment. Thus, without gaining access to sufficient land and with fewer employment possibilities, the levels of temporary and permanent migration from Chimborazo increased in the course of agrarian reform. In effect, as Korovkin demonstrates, genuine reform was blocked because representatives of regional power groups staffed the agrarian reform agency while a "legal framework for police action against communities" was created to allow "landlords and their mercenaries" to lead "a wave of violence" against peasants that claimed estate lands.

During the 1980s, FEPP, among other NGOs, supported peasant and indigenous organization and struggles for land in Chimborazo and elsewhere in the country. In the midst of economic crisis and the return of migrants from closed-down construction sites in the cities to their home communities in the countryside, land conflicts heated up, and the indigenous populations staged a highland and Amazonian region-wide, forceful but nonviolent uprising (levantamiento) in 1990. The Catholic church responded by negotiating a debt swap for social programs and land purchases with the Belgian and Ecuadorian governments. As North, Kit, and Koep (Chapter 6) and Bretón (Chapter 8) explain, between April 1990 and June 1996 FEPP provided credit from debt swap funds for the purchase of land by 138 mostly highland peasant organizations that represented 9,235 families, or about 50,000–60,000 persons (Tonello 1997, 146). Although a full-scale evaluation of the program's results remained to be done, the reduction of emigration from about half the communities that acquired land and the defusion of violent confrontations between peasants and landlords, not only in Chimborazo but also in other provinces, represented important progress from the vantage point of FEPP and others (Vallejo, Navarro, and Villaverde 1996, 146).

Bretón, nevertheless, has doubts about the ethics and efficacy of the program. He also questions FEPP's turn toward support for peasant community entrepreneurship in the 1990s, asserting that FEPP and other rural development NGOs in Ecuador abandoned the still necessary struggle for agrarian reform. FEPP defended its actions on the grounds that the peaceful resolution of conflicts had to be prioritized and that its debt-swap-based revolving credit program could be used to provide loans for more land purchases. This volume does not resolve the debate about how agrarian reform might be renewed. However, all the studies presented here corroborate the relationship between access to land and the possibilities of rural progress.

National and International Power Structures

Two pieces of legislation enacted in 1994 merit special attention, given their particularly egregious impacts on social well-being and the ways in which they reflect prevailing power structures. The first of these was the Law of Agrarian Development, which brought redistributive land reform to an end. The second was the earlier mentioned General Law of Financial Institutions, which left the private banking system to essentially supervise itself, setting the stage for the financial debacle of 1999, which, in turn, set the stage for dollarization that was creating havoc among a variety of national industries, including the Pelileo textile enterprises, by mid-2001.

Pressure for the passage of the agrarian law came from internal elite as well as external sources: the IDB conditioned loans for the agrarian sector on its adoption, while USAID and Ecuador's most powerful landowners' associations were its sponsors (Treakle 1998, 247–250). USAID provided funding to the principal "think tank" of the landowning class to contract the studies on which the law was to be based. The conception of agricultural and rural development presented in those studies, Lefeber argues (in Chapter 4), was fundamentally flawed because it ignored distributional issues and the urgent need for policies to generate employment. That same flawed conception, Grinspun holds (Chapter 3), was being enshrined in regional trade agreements that were oriented to furthering the growth of the large-scale commercial and agribusiness sectors.

As for the liberalization of financial markets demanded by IFIs and private banks, the corrupt fashion in which the 1994 Law of Financial Institutions was implemented eventually led to the meltdown of the country's private banking system and a catastrophic economic crisis in 1999–2000. To be sure, the early 1995 war with Peru, the El Niño flooding in the coastal region in 1997, and unstable petroleum markets had taken a toll on the economy and the financial system. Nevertheless, in the words of the editor of Ecuador's leading business magazine, the deregulation law "was an invitation to disaster: a series of unscrupulous bankers concentrated credit in their own real or fictitious enterprises, channelling the savings of their clients to their own personal enrichment" (Ortiz Crespo 2000, 51). And that was not all. According to the estimates of a prominent local economist, Alberto Acosta, in its unsuccessful efforts to keep the financial system afloat, the Central Bank provided private bankers with more than US$2.2 billion dollars, a sum equivalent to 15 percent of the country's GDP (quoted in Saad 2000, 32).

In sum, the distribution of assets and related relationships of social and economic power in Ecuador ensured that legislation and policy implementation would advance the interests of narrow elites rather than responding to the needs of the majorities (Larrea and North 1997). New SAP-related legislation favored elite interests in general, while the state provided protection for specific groups in particular. For example, following dollarization, the government acted to protect and promote the interests of large exporters of bananas and cut flowers from external shocks and to secure trade agreements favorable to them (Carroll and Bebbington 2000). By contrast, peasant organizations could not expect assistance, as the earlier mentioned case of the yuca production federation demonstrates. The case studies presented in this volume illustrate the ways in which NGOs, on some occasions, were able to obtain limited benefits for their constituencies even within the new legal framework (for example, through the debt-for-land swap). However, they were not able to influence the fundamentally exclusionary direction of macroeconomic policies.

THE CASE FOR REDISTRIBUTIVE REFORMS AND POLICIES

Land Distribution and Rural Progress in Ecuador

The importance of progressive land and asset distribution for ensuring social and economic progress is discussed from general theoretical and historical perspectives by Lefeber. Grinspun argues that the proposed terms of hemispheric trade agreements, instead of facilitating, work against the possibilities of redistribution toward the poorest sectors in general and the rural poor in particular. Other contributors to the volume provide evidence that widespread access to land is a necessary although not a sufficient condition for rural social progress.

In his study of the World Bank–financed PRONADER rural development program, Martínez found that the greatest positive impacts were registered in areas where agrarian reform had been implemented in the 1970s (Chapter 5).

Similarly, in his examination of the development opportunities that may emerge from municipal democratization, Cameron discovered that a progressive distribution of land is one of the preconditions for the emergence of participatory and accountable local government with a capacity to promote rural development (Chapter 9).

North arrives at the same conclusion regarding the relationship between land ownership and social progress in her analyses of two highly reputed cases of rural diversification that enjoyed IDB funding channeled through NGO service providers. The widely acclaimed cooperative complex of Salinas took off after the Catholic church sold its estates to peasants in that parish. By doing so, the church laid the basis for the transformation of local power relations in ways that allowed FEPP, the Salesian Mission, and others to assist a new class of small and medium landholders to diversify production, access markets, and benefit from international assistance (Chapter 10).

In the case of Pelileo, as explained earlier, the dynamic growth of family textile enterprises evolved out of relatively egalitarian socioeconomic relations that were deeply rooted in the past. In the absence of a large landlord class, small producers in that canton had gained access to fertile land and experience in production for the market by the last quarter of the nineteenth century (Chapter 11). The role of the IDB-financed NGO that had begun to provide services to the producers in the early 1990s turned out to be marginal to rural diversification and social progress in this canton.

In fact, the importance of a progressive distribution of land for rural social well-being and democracy is confirmed by the economic evolution of other regions of Latin America—like the smallholder coffee-producing central plateau of Costa Rica—as well as by the history of the East Asian Tigers.[6] When the IFIs began to demand neoliberal adjustment programs in the early 1980s, as Martínez points out (Chapter 5), they presented the Tigers—especially Japan, South Korea, and Taiwan—as models of market-driven development, ignoring the highly interventionist role of their states; the implementation of profound agrarian reforms and other redistributive policies; and the massive amounts of international assistance that were provided, for geopolitical reasons, by the United States (Bienefeld 1988; Fishlow et al. 1994; Kay 2001a). Without suggesting that the Tigers provide a model for replication in Latin America, we briefly summarize below the extent and implications of their distributive reforms, with special reference to Taiwan. We do so in order to highlight issues of asset, income, and power distribution, employment generation, and market functioning that the contributors to this volume believe have to be addressed in order to advance toward meaningful development, democracy, and respect for the full range of human rights.

The East Asian Experience and the Evidence from the Ecuadorian Case Studies

In contrast to the Latin American nations, following World War II, both traditional agrarian political power relations and rural asset distribution were profoundly transformed in the course of industrialization in the Tiger economies (Donnelly 1984; Fajnsylber 1990; Evans 1987; Griffin 1989, 164–93; Kay 2001a). All three mentioned above carried out radical land reforms that were accompanied by coherent agrarian and rural development policies that were implemented through decentralized institutions that were responsive to local needs. In Taiwan, these included FAs that provided extension, warehousing, and processing services, and enjoyed monopolies in the marketing of the most important agricultural products of their members (Yager 1988, 133). Consequently, these institutions socialized and redistributed among the new small-scale property holders the gains made from agricultural and other forms of rural growth and diversification (Stavis 1974, 61).

At the same time, in a highly interventionist fashion, the Taiwanese state encouraged rural industrialization that was to play a critical role in expanding off-farm employment and farm family incomes. The state also invested in employment generating public works, especially irrigation and communication infrastructure and electrification, as well as in primary, secondary, and technical education, agricultural research, and rural extension services. Meanwhile, much of large scale industry (and its profits for reinvestment) remained in state hands (Fei, Ranis, and Kuo 1979, 62), and direct foreign investment was insignificant (Evans 1987, 206–209). Taiwan's rapid agricultural and industrial growth and diversification were thus achieved through coherent state action that included profound redistributive reforms. As the economy grew—at a spectacular yearly rate of 8.8 percent between 1953 and 1987—the distribution of income actually improved to become possibly "the most equal in the world" (Griffin 1989, 181).

When economic liberalization measures were introduced in the Tiger economies in the 1990s, as Lefeber points out, they were adopted with caution and by societies in which feudal or semi-feudal agrarian structures had been destroyed and urban-rural balance had been largely achieved. These were also societies in which, by then, coherent and effective public institutions, relatively autonomous of elite control, had been built; strong domestic markets and national capitalist classes had developed; the population was highly educated; and relatively high degrees of social equality and well-being prevailed.

Without engaging in idealization of these East Asian experiences, they clearly left a legacy that contrasted dramatically with the conditions left by Latin America's limited agrarian reforms and distorted ISI—that is, concentration of land ownership along with urban bias; a capital-intensive and low employment-generating industrial structure; weak domestic markets as a consequence of very high degrees of income and asset inequality; generally low levels of investment in infrastructure and in public education and research; weak states that were directly penetrated by elite interests and were not accountable to the broader public; and foreign control of key sectors of the economy. In sum, "market friendly" reforms in Latin America were introduced in the presence of highly exclusionary social and political-economic structures. Neither ISI or SAPs in the region bore much, if any, resemblance to the policies that had led to the East Asian Tigers' success and none at all to the policies that those countries had pursued with regard to their agricultural and rural sectors.

Instead of heeding peasant and agricultural worker demands for completing the truncated agrarian reforms of Latin America, neoliberal inspired donors and national decision-makers insisted that secure property rights and transparent land markets would resolve problems of asset distribution (Kay 1998, 25–27). However, Martínez found no evidence that Ecuador's 1994 Agrarian Development Law was creating land markets or facilitating redistribution, as its advocates claimed it would (Chapter 5). Meanwhile, private institutions, like the Catholic church and FEPP, could only conduct mini–land reforms, so to speak, in some localities (Chapter 6 and 8). Although such mini-reforms defused conflict and benefited sizable numbers of peasants, they clearly could not address an issue that was national in dimension. Moreover, as the East Asian example and North's case studies of Salinas and Pelileo illustrate, making land productive involves access to markets, appropriate infrastructure (irrigation, transportation, electrification, and communications), and services (public health, education, and agricultural extension).

In all these areas it is states and global forces that set the parameters for development and possible redistribution, as discussed by Lefeber and Grinspun in general terms and corroborated by the evidence presented in the case studies. To be sure, NGOs can still play important roles. For example, NGO assistance was critical in the construction of infrastructure and the provision of services in two of the cantons studied by Cameron (Chapter 9), but NGOs do not have the resources to finance such programs in all of Ecuador's poor rural municipalities. Only the Ecuadorian state can do that. Similarly, the Salesian Mission and FEPP did create conditions that allowed the cooperative enterprises of Salinas to sell in upper-income national markets and provided the contacts that allowed them to access both commercial and "solidarity" markets in Europe. However, it was clearly beyond the power and capacity of any NGO to reverse the deterioration in the markets of the family denim-clothing enterprises of Pelileo. Only the state could have done that by providing some protection against used-clothing imports and by pursuing macroeconomic policies that favored the creation of employment and self-employment opportunities for the poorer sectors of the population that formed the Pelileo producers' market. Finally, as Bretón points out, the majority of indigenous rural areas of the province of Chimborazo remained among the poorest in Ecuador even though more NGOs provided support to more communities there than anywhere else in Ecuador.

INSTITUTIONAL DESIGN, SOCIAL CAPITAL, AND STATE POLICIES

Institutional Design

All the contributors to this volume, at one point or another, refer to the importance of cooperative organizations and their potential for socializing the gains from commercial activities. However, the two studies included here that offer evaluations of the institutional design of economic enterprises found that the potential gains from cooperative organization were not realized at all in one case and only partly in a second.

Bretón's study of FEPP's attempt to transfer a modern dairy farm to indigenous beneficiaries of its land-purchase program in Chimborazo (Chapter 8) and North's analysis of the cooperative enterprises that were established in Salinas (Chapter 10) illustrate that institutional design matters a great deal in ensuring economic viability and benefits. In Chimborazo, the Riobamba office of FEPP clearly failed to appreciate the fact that the traditional, indigenous collective practices could not form a sufficient basis for the successful management of a fairly large and modern cooperative enterprise. Similarly, in Salinas, the factory-scale wool-spinning mill that was set up in the late 1980s experienced great difficulties that derived from the complexities of managerial responsibilities and the division of labor within that enterprise. It was the smaller cooperative enterprises and the family enterprises that tended to be most successful.

These two cases, however, should not to be taken as an argument against NGO promotion of cooperative enterprises. NGOs could play an important role in designing such institutions, but it has to be recognized that both in Ecuador and elsewhere in Latin America their expertise lies in the area of social service delivery rather than the design of productive activities. In this respect it bears emphasizing that the successes of the Grameen Bank and the cooperative complex of Mondragón derived from years of step-by-step experimentation with managerial procedures and practices, worker participation systems, and the like (Holcombe 1995; Whyte and Whyte 1988).[7]

While institutional design matters, it is also clear that even the best designed institutions need time to mature in addition to a supportive context of equitable asset distribution and favorable macroeconomic policies. Thus Cameron (Chapter 9) discovered that municipal institutional capacity in Ecuador developed over many years in certain structural contexts characterized by greater equity.

Social Capital Formation

As pointed out earlier, support for social capital formation formed part of the second-generation reforms adopted by IFIs and donors in the 1990s. The concept was derived from Robert Putnam's finding that high-quality regional government policy performance, together with economic development, was associated with high levels of civic organization in northern Italy, while poor performance was associated with a lack of such organization in the south of the country (Putnam 1993). As adopted by the World Bank, social capital was used to refer to norms of trust, reciprocity, cooperation, and mutual help—both horizontal social networks and vertical "bridging ties" between various social divides—that can facilitate economic development (see "social capital" on the World Bank website). The concept was quickly taken up by other major donors who, along with the World Bank, established programs to promote the strengthening of popular civic organizations to administer development projects.

In accord with this new policy orientation, in June 1998 the World Bank signed a contract with the Ecuadorian government to support a US$50 million project "to benefit indigenous groups . . . through investments channeled to their own ethnic organizations." The assistance was directed toward "organizational capacity-building," and it was to be delivered through PRODEPINE, a "council of ethnic organizations, with only minimal official participation" (Carroll and Bebbington 2000, 435). This initiative formed part of the Bank's response to the series of nationwide indigenous uprisings against the SAPs that the Bank and others had demanded; the first of these took place in 1990, and they continued into the twenty-first century, with uprisings in both 2000 and 2001 (Zamosc 1994; Samaniego 2001; Chiriboga 2001).

What kinds of results might be expected from programs such as PRODEPINE? While none of the contributors to this volume systematically utilizes the concept of social capital formation, several provide data and analyses relevant to addressing the issue. First of all, both Korovkin (Chapter 7) and Bretón (Chapter 8) found that very high levels of indigenous peasant social activism and organization in Chimborazo did not result in significant socioeconomic improvement. In the context of truncated agrarian reform and generally unfavorable central government policies, what Korovkin calls the indigenous peasants' "organizational victory" could not be translated into significant economic gains. By contrast, North's study of the textile industries in Pelileo (Chapter 11) found significant social and economic progress without noticeable organizational development. In that case, economic diversification and social progress were facilitated by the presence of certain structural conditions that included longstanding access to markets and to fertile land on the part of small producers.[8]

In fact, in Pelileo the impact of neoliberal policies began to destroy social capital. As the largely SAPs-induced economic crisis of the textile sector deepened during the second half of the 1990s, textile enterprise owners were stuck with bad checks from wholesale merchants with increasing frequency, and the norms of trust and reciprocity that had developed over decades between producers and merchants were being eroded.[9] Similarly, Martínez found that social capital tended to be undercut by a variety of factors related to SAPs (Chapter 5), while North, Kit, and Koep provide data that illustrate the ways in which the powerful attempted to destroy peasant organizations (Chapter 6). Finally, Cameron found that *both* high levels of social organization and local small-producer control over assets were required for the establishment of municipal governments that made significant efforts to incorporate poor rural constituents into decision-making processes (Chapter 9).

In general terms, the increasing rates of both permanent and temporary migration from rural communities described by several contributors to this volume are hardly conducive to strengthening community and peasant organizations. It is difficult to visualize the possibility of consolidating and sustaining strong civic organizations when potential leaders must be absent from their communities for months at a time. Indeed, if the World Bank wishes to promote the development of cohesive horizontal and vertical social networks in rural Latin America, it could begin by encouraging the adoption of policies that allow small-scale farmers to stay in their home communities—that is, to acquire more land, to educate their children there, and to enjoy greater access to services and some protection from imports.

Clearly, civic organization and cohesive social networks—like institutional design—matter for ensuring government accountability and facilitating economic development. However, our case studies argue that it is unlikely that such organizations and networks will develop in contexts without a minimally progressive distribution of assets and relatively secure access to markets. And this leads us back to the role of the state in ensuring the establishment of patterns of asset distribution and market conditions that favor social progress, as discussed above with reference to the East Asian Tigers.

In sum, the macroeconomic policies pursed by the state are critical. Indeed, an effective state and appropriate redistributive policies will allow NGOs (like FEPP) and local institutions (such as municipal governments and peasant organizations) to have greater impact and to work more effectively to promote development.[10] Local institutions and civic organizations can and should be encouraged and targeted for assistance. They are the institutions that are in touch with people's day-to-day lives in ways that the central state is not. However, it is central state policy that creates the general conditions within which local development becomes possible.

CONCLUSION

To summarize the principal conclusions of the volume, it must be stressed, first of all, that states establish the policy parameters for market and other forms of rural development, and that NGOs can be most effective in settings where policy favors employment generation and redistribution to incorporate marginal sectors. Second, while there is no single policy that can generate economic diversification and social well-being in the countryside, widespread ownership of land and access to more or less stable markets appear as critical requirements from the case studies presented here as well as from much evidence from other parts of Latin America (e.g., Waterbury 1999; Winson 1989).

The organization of small and marginal producers into cooperative institutions that can socialize gains and civic associations that can represent their interests—that is, what many now call social capital formation—is to be recommended. However, in the absence of minimally favorable macroeconomic conditions, newly trained cooperative managers and community leaders may decide to use their recently acquired skills and insertion in national and international NGO networks for exit from Ecuador; that is, use their skills and connections for leaving the country in order to support their families from earnings abroad. This was the decision, for example, of some of the leading figures of the FEPP-assisted Centro de Bordados Cuenca, a highly regarded rural artisan cooperative. They joined the ever-growing migratory streams of Ecuadorians who, by the end of 2001, may have represented close to 10 percent of the country's economically active population (Grunfelder-Elliker 2001, 8, 13–15; Jokisch 2001; Acosta 2002).

Finally, foreign assistance through local NGOs can be helpful, as the evolution of the cooperative enterprises in Salinas and of the municipal governments of Guamote and Cotacachi, for example, demonstrate. However, in certain circumstances where peasants have acquired land, market access, and relevant skills, it may be irrelevant. The most important requirement for the continued growth of the family-run textile enterprises in Pelileo was not IDB-financed NGO services but state policies that could provide some protection to the sector and sustain the incomes of the lower- and middle-income groups that formed their market.

Notes

[1] For data on poverty and inequality, see Berry 1997; Berry 1998; Altimir 1999.

[2] The World Bank set up a website on social capital, and in 1998 it created a US$1 million research fund called The Social Capital Initiative.

[3] The number of second level (parish or canton) indigenous peasant organizations increased from 10 in 1974 to 180 in 1998; by then there were 21 third-level or provincial entities and 5 national confederations (Carroll and Bebbington 2000, 438).

[4] For a discussion of the narrowly economic neoliberal vision of "viable" and "non-viable" peasants, see Kay 1998, 25–27. For a conceptualization of viability that takes multiple family income sources, subsistence production, and values into account, see Bebbington 1999.

[5] On dollarization, see Acosta and Joncoso 2000; *Economist* Intelligence Unit 2001.

[6] An in-depth study of forty Grameen Bank members found that those who experienced the most notable improvements in their living standards had invested

in purchasing paddy fields, violating Bank rules that explicitly earmarked the loans for commercial activities (Todd 1996, 215–16).

[7] Kevin Healy provides informative studies of Bolivian NGOs and cooperatives that learned by doing, with support from the IAF and donor-country agencies (Healy 2001). Tanya Korovkin provides a highly informative and policy-relevant analysis of cooperative cotton enterprises in Peru (Korovkin 1990).

[8] The conditions in Pelileo bear a remarkable resemblance to a successful process of agricultural diversification among small-scale producers in Oaxaca, Mexico, which did not receive external assistance. These conditions included "a favorable physical environment," "previous experience with market-oriented farming," a regional marketing system that the peasants could access, and "the absence of large landowners" (Waterbury 1999, 86).

[9] Similarly, Carroll and Bebbington found that the absence of supportive macroeconomic policies resulted in the breakdown of market opportunities for peasant products and led to subsequent financial and organizational crises in peasant organizations (Carroll and Bebbington 2000).

[10] In her study of a reformist state government in the Northeast of Brazil, Judith Tendler argues that effective decentralization and civic organization demand more rather than less central government action (Tendler 1977).

Part I

THEORETICAL PERSPECTIVES

&

Chapter 2

Problems of Contemporary Development

Neoliberalism and Its Consequences

Louis Lefeber

The idea of development, as it evolved after the Second World War, focused almost exclusively on economic growth. It was implicitly assumed that growth would bring about a gradual increase in the prosperity of the low-income communities at large. The unemployed would get jobs, and the workers in low-productivity occupations would be absorbed in higher paying advanced agricultural, industrial, and commercial service activities. Various paradigms of development—ranging from centrally controlled socialism to decentralized planning—were put forward as policy guides. Fifty years later it has become evident that whatever positive results have been attained—in some instances significant improvements in popular welfare—resulted from pragmatic approaches to policymaking rather than strict adherence to any particular ideology.[1]

While some political economists of very different ideological backgrounds have always had their doubts, it took several decades for most development theorists to recognize that policies grafted on the prevailing social-political and economic structures may not bring about development in any sense of the term. The institutions that were created originally for the defense of the established order are inconsistent with the requirements of democratic social and political change. And the believers in traditional wisdom, particularly those of the uncontrolled free

This chapter is based on a public lecture presented at FLACSO, Quito, March 1998.

market variety, still refuse to recognize this, even though the evidence has been flying in their faces.

As the reductionist development doctrines have been increasingly proven to be futile or irrelevant, the idea has gained gradual acceptance that there exist certain unalienable human rights, of which basic economic security is only one, albeit an integral one. The idea was formalized by the United Nations Universal Declaration of Human Rights of 1948. Since then there have been important advances in attempting to make the principle apply in practice (United Nations 1994). Among these are statistical approaches for defining and measuring human welfare in a broader sense of the term (UNDP human development reports). At the same time, the neoliberal tendency toward a hostile undervaluation of the role of governments and the ideological support for the free market are being increasingly questioned. The free market is being recognized not as an instrument of democracy, as the ideologues would have it, but as the means for exploitation by powerful monopolists and multinational corporations, supported by the international financial institutions and the financial authorities of the capitalist industrial nations, with the U.S. government in the lead.[2]

It is with these considerations in the background that this essay attempts to discuss the political economy of poverty and development as it relates to Latin America and the experience of Ecuador.

International political and economic relationships have undergone fundamental changes over the last two decades. In many countries they have had a negative impact on public welfare. The living standards of the poor and the conditions for employment and self-employment have not improved; in many instances they have deteriorated. In countries such as Ecuador, income-earning opportunities have been adversely affected both in rural and urban areas. The freedom of the market has guaranteed access to profits and other huge income-earning opportunities to the already economically powerful groups, multinational corporations, and financial operators. More often than not, the free market policies have excluded participation by the working classes and the low-income populations at large. They have reinforced the wretched state of the most vulnerable groups, such as working-class women, native peoples, and marginal farmers.

International debt obligations have turned many of the poorer countries into capital exporters. Significant portions, ranging from 25 to 40 percent of export earnings, have to be committed to debt service and amortization. The need to obtain the required foreign exchange has led to additional borrowing, conditioned on the acceptance of disastrous domestic policies imposed by the IMF and the World Bank.[3] Among these are measures for lowering domestic import demands through artificially depressing domestic incomes. Other conditions have included the elimination of obstacles to the influx of foreign capital—ostensibly for easing the foreign exchange shortage through long-term foreign investment—and the reduction of government participation in, and control of, markets. Such restructuring has been a component of the process known as globalization.

Under these conditions the freedom of moving capital has become a license for massive speculative activities in foreign exchange markets. The traditional structure and functions of the balance of payments have changed. Foreign exchange rates respond to speculative currency shifts, rather than changes in trade relationships or capital movements undertaken in connection with trade and productive investment. Rate changes caused by currency speculation have had destabilizing effects on trade and have added to the need to borrow for covering import requirements. Correspondingly, there has been a change in the distribution of economic power: it has shifted to bankers and the owners of multinational capital at the expense of domestic producers.[4]

Since the introduction of the neoliberal policies for privatization, marketization, and globalization, there has been a dramatic change in the rate of development in all economically retarded regions. The authors of a most interesting and well documented paper compare the last twenty years of globalization (1980–2000) with the previous twenty years (1960–1980). They find incontrovertible evidence that "for economic growth and almost all other indicators [life expectancy, infant and child mortality, education and literacy], the last 20 years have shown a very clear decline in progress as compared with the previous two decades" (Weisbrot et al. 2001). Using IMF and World Bank statistics, the authors demonstrate that the fall in economic growth rates from the first to the second period was highly pronounced for all countries in the study, which they grouped according to income levels. The poorest group went from an annual per capita GDP growth rate of 1.9 percent in the first period to 0.5 percent in the second. In turn, the middle group (containing mostly poor countries) experienced a sharp decline, from an annual 3.6 percent to less than 1 percent. Progress in life expectancy, infant and child mortality, and education and literacy has slowed down markedly (Weisbrot et al. 2001).

An earlier paper (Weisbrot et al. 2000) gives a regional breakdown. In Latin America, for example, GDP per capita grew by 75 percent between 1960 and 1980, whereas it rose only 6 percent from 1980 to 1988. For sub-Saharan Africa, GDP per capita grew by 36 percent in the first period, while it has since fallen by 15 percent. "These are enormous differences by any standard of comparison, and represent the loss to an entire generation—of hundreds of millions of people—of any chance of improving their living standards. Even where growth was significant, as in Southeast Asia, it was still better in the earlier period" (Weisbrot et al. 2000). Ecuador is no exception. The GDP growth rate for the period 1980–1985 averaged 1.8 percent, and by 1999 fell to minus 9.5 percent.

In per capita terms this translates to a drop from a bad-enough minus 0.9 percent to a staggering minus 11.2 percent (UNECLAC 2000).

At this time the trend toward globalization cannot be readily stopped or reversed. The question is whether it can be tamed to eliminate or to counteract the destructive social and human costs of the concomitant structural changes. As mentioned above, these include the indiscriminate marketization and privatization policies imposed by the IMF and World Bank which, among other things, have resulted in massive losses in public-sector employment. The call for retrenchment in government spending has not been restricted to public enterprises: public education and health programs—including subsidies for basic staple consumption and meals for school children—have also been sacrificed, with untold consequences for current and future social and economic welfare. The opening to foreign investment in production and commercial services has been accompanied by the import of capital-intensive methods of production in both urban and rural areas. The consequent loss in rural employment opportunities and the induced urban migration have not been matched by a corresponding growth in the urban demand for labor. At the same time, with the introduction of new technologies and the encroachment into marginal lands by the rural dispossessed, there has been a progressive degradation of the environment (Lefeber 1997; Chapter 4 herein).

The dynamism of globalization has been primarily in the financial markets, which do not have the capacity to generate employment for the masses of low-skilled or semi-skilled workers. The change in the economic power structure has undercut the capacity of unions to defend already attained wage levels. The imported technologies of foreign investors have eliminated the demand for native skills. Inequality has increased at all income levels. Even in the economically advancing Latin American countries a conflict between structural change and social welfare is evident. In Chile, for example, unemployment remains high, and the percentage of the population living at or below the poverty line is not lower, and may even be higher, than it was thirty years ago. In Argentina the rate of unemployment was about 15 percent even before the crisis that engulfed the country in December 2001. Moreover, it has to be kept in mind that the statistical measurement of unemployment is lower than the rate of joblessness. This is so because those who have given up the job search, due to frustration or for any other reason, are not counted among the officially recognized unemployed.

Population growth, which is not expected to stabilize before the middle of the twenty-first century, has been adding to the rate of joblessness. This has been further enhanced by the burden of interest and amortization payments on the international debt, capital flight, and the profit transfers of foreign investors. In spite of foreign investment, these factors have turned many low-income countries into capital exporters. But it also should be noted that foreign investment has been concentrated mostly in only a few and primarily middle-income countries, and even then it has been largely confined to raw-material extraction, agribusiness, *maquiladora* (assembly plant) production, and even the acquisition of privatized public utilities. The effects of inadequate domestic availability of capital for production for domestic markets and rural reconstruction, the retrenchment in government spending, and the increasing capital intensities in production all add up to an insufficient growth of demand for labor, the supply of which is growing with population growth. The results are increasing poverty and growing inequality, which are bound to lead to various forms of social instability and ultimately to potentially catastrophic consequences.

CAN THE TREND BE REVERSED?

In earlier times the question was whether there could be communism with a human face. Now the question is whether it is possible to have a market economy with a human face. For a positive answer, the institutions of the state—the governments, the private sectors, and the capitalist market organization—would have to change in ways that are not likely to come about in the foreseeable future. Nonetheless, it is important to give at least a brief indication of what stands in the way, so as to gain a better understanding of the nature and rigidity of the obstacles.

The argument is not that markets should be abolished and replaced by some bureaucratic or administrative allocation system. The twentieth century's experience with centrally or excessively controlled economies has shown that social and economic interests could be better served with a judicious interaction of the government sector with a decentralized market organization. But whatever the meaning of "judicious interaction," the prevailing trend to market control by government-backed big-business interests would have to be supplanted by a socioeconomic system that values human rights over market power.[5]

The required changes include fundamentally different attitudes by government and business, both in the industrialized and economically less developed countries. Governments would have to advance the interests of civil societies above particular private-sector interests. Corporations would have to be made to function in a socially responsible way. They would have to recognize that they owe loyalty not only to their shareholders but to the societies that make it possible for them to function. The dominant classes, the members of the higher income groups, would have to recognize the right of the disadvantaged to the same considerations they now reserve for their peers. The military would have to learn to respect civil authority and moderate its exorbitant demands on domestic and foreign resources. The international financial institutions, such as the IMF and the World Bank, which are now closely attuned to the dictates of the US government, would have to serve the social-economic development of the countries in need of support (Stiglitz 2000). The American polity would have to accept that US interests must not be pursued in ways that impede the social and economic advancement of other nations. And the masses of low-income, poor, and marginalized people of the economically and politically underdeveloped countries would have to participate actively and fearlessly in the political process by way of the voting booth and all other democratic means available to them for informing governments and political parties about their concerns and legitimate interests.

None of these problems is unknown to NGOs with long field-work experience. They have contributed to a gradually changing public perception of the nature and levels of the poverty and inhuman conditions suffered by the underprivileged masses. This perception, in turn, has motivated and facilitated many of the projects and programs developed by the United Nations and its associated organizations. At various times and places they also have succeeded in directly motivating social and economic advances, albeit confined primarily to local communities, or in assisting the establishment of microenterprises. But NGOs have had at best a marginal capacity to influence the social and economic policies of national governments and international financial institutions.[6]

At the same time, the younger generations show signs of recognizing the need for change—as demonstrated by the various "Green" movements, the mobilization against the Multilateral Agreement on Investment (MAI), or the protests in Seattle, Washington, Porto Alegre, Quebec, Prague, and elsewhere. But neither they nor the NGOs have at this point a coherent strategic notion as to how to bring about broad-based democratic change.[7] The prevailing power structure is likely to remain entrenched until some major shock to the international economic system clearly indicates that significant social and political changes are called for. One should remember that in the United States the National Labor Relations Act of 1935 (popularly known as the Wagner Act) and related social legislation came about in response to the Great Depression of the 1930s, which discredited the then-prevailing form of capitalism to the population at large, including the capitalists themselves.

Nothing less than a national and international redistribution of incomes would be required. In real terms this would mean corresponding changes in the distribution of consumption and resource use both in the economically developed and underdeveloped countries. It is unlikely that these can be obtained by means of gradual evolution. Even though redistribution need not and could not be a zero-sum change in consumption, the social and economic advancement of the increasing masses of the poor and marginalized people will not be accomplished without massive resource transfers from the economically advanced industrial countries.

Nor will the protection of the environment around the globe—such as water and forest resources, fish stocks, breathable air, and the limitation of carbon dioxide emissions—be obtained without material sacrifice by the economically advanced countries. The transfer of technology could be made relatively cost free, but the same is not true of the redistribution of the use of energy and other scarce physical resources. The political obstacles are enormous.[8]

The currently prevailing resource drain from the economically less developed countries would have to be reversed. This would call for a change in the rules of engagement in international trade and other relationships (Chapter 3). In the meantime, however, the deleterious effects of the drain could be eased directly through debt relief. More generally, as was the case in the nineteenth-century development of North America and other underpopulated regions, the capital flows would have to be directed from the industrialized countries to the economically undeveloped countries. These would have to be mostly unidirectional, that is, the assets and their control would have to remain in the receiving countries or regions instead of being repatriated in the short run. Also, a significant portion of interest and profit incomes would have to be locally reinvested. These are basic requirements for accomplishing the needed international income redistribution (Lefeber 1974a).

As a first step, the relief of poverty calls not for direct interpersonal income transfers but for massive investments in rural and urban public education, housing, and health and sanitation projects, as well as enlarged opportunities for self-employment and increased demand for labor with acceptable minimum wages. In other words, there has to be a change in macroeconomic policies to bring the underprivileged and nonproductive sectors into socially and economically productive activities. Once such policies are instituted, their application must be strictly supervised in order to avoid corrupt and wasteful exploitation of the available resources.

The current self-serving insistence of the capitalist establishment on foreign investment and export-based industrialization needs to be replaced by policies for domestic market development. Foreign trade is a necessity, not for satisfying the neoliberal demand for export orientation, but for supporting the growth of domestic markets. Both the latter and the ethical *desideratum* of raising popular welfare call for sustained increases in public investments and in the enhancement of the political and economic power of the low-income populations.

THE RELEVANCE OR INADEQUACY
OF DEVELOPMENT THEORY

All this calls attention to the limited relevance of the currently dominant economic theories to the development process. Neoclassical economics is based on assumptions that are not rooted in the prevailing social and economic realities. Markets are assumed to be competitive, that is, smoothly functioning and self regulating, at least in the long run. Producers are price-takers who blindly maximize profits while consumers maximize utility. The satisfaction from the pursuit and attainment of power through economic means is alien to the theory. Rivalry leading to monopoly or oligopoly and the reciprocal effects of individuals' decisions on one another, as well as the acts that are not valued by, or are external to, the market are ignored by both producers and consumers. And the concept of utility excludes all pain and pleasure that come from sources other than the most narrowly defined consumer satisfaction. Such behavior patterns imputed to producers and consumers are assumed to lead to full employment and socially efficient resource use (Sen 1977).

But there is more. The critical difference between the time horizons of individual economic actors, which are finite and limited, and those of societies, which are unlimited, is also ignored. Consider how investment decisions are made. The future is uncertain; miscalculations, wars, nationalization, and so forth, can interfere with the realization of expectations. And ultimately there is the finiteness of individual existence. With greater uncertainty the undervaluation of the expected future benefits also increases. The bias, at the expense of long-run interests, is in the direction of shortening the period of the payoff.

In contrast, consider the social point of view. The social risk is always less than the one facing the individual. A bankrupt business leaves behind socially usable detritus in the form of buildings, machinery, technological know-how, and so forth. And unlike individual life expectations, society's time horizon is, if not infinite, very much longer than that of the individual. With lower risk and a long time horizon, society's rate of discounting the future is naturally lower than the private one. In fact, as the late Joan Robinson of Cambridge University once observed, all benefits or costs to society should have the same value, whenever they happen to come. Stated in technical terms, the social rate of discount, that is, the rate at which the future is discounted, should be zero. The implications for the social-environmental consequences of investment decisions should be evident (Lefeber 1992).

Again, the theoretical concept of productivity that is relevant to individual production decisions is not the same as that which is relevant for society. As an example, compare the private productivity gain due to downsizing to the consequent direct and indirect social costs of maintaining the increased numbers of unemployed. Whether these costs are borne by the government or by the community through charity or suffering violence and crime, the social productivity is the sum total of the positive private gain and the aggregate of the various negative social costs.

Another way to look at this is in terms of output per worker. The private concept of productivity is output per employed worker. This is useful for entrepreneurs' profit calculations. In turn, social productivity calculus for social welfare should be output divided by the sum of employed and unemployed workers, that is, the ratio of output to the potential labor supply (Lefeber 1997).

THEORY, INSTITUTIONS, AND DEMOCRACY

The IFIs as well as the national treasuries and central banks are staffed primarily by policymakers and economists who have been brought up in the neoclassical vein. They are committed to a theory that is reductionist in the extreme; they work with a conceptual framework whose assumptions and structural relationships—as discussed above—are unrelated to any social and political reality.

Neoclassical theory, because it has a degree of logical consistency, can be aesthetically appealing. But more important is the fact that it suits perfectly the capitalist ideology as well as the interests of the dominant capitalist classes. Since capitalism is worldwide—albeit not uniform in its various manifestations—the assumption is that the theory's relevance is also worldwide, that it holds everywhere and at any time. It is therefore not surprising that the officials of the capitalist financial institutions insist anywhere and everywhere on introducing free-market policies in which government can have only a restricted role. They prevail because of their enormous economic blackmail power.

The theory's exclusive focus on the market made up of individual or private-sector participants overlooks the fact that the market is just one of the many institutions that constitute the state. Free markets are not a manifestation of democracy, as claimed by the ideologues. Whether or not democracy prevails or can prevail is determined by the nature and interaction of the many and various institutions of the state (Lefeber 2000).

Democracy can be purely formal, in the sense that the government is elected by the vote of the majority that has access or chooses to go to the polls, which frequently does not represent a fair cross-section of the population at large or may even be corrupt. Such formal democracies are typical of most Latin American nations, Ecuador among them. In contrast, essential forms of democracy—that is, forms of democracy that respect internationally agreed upon human rights—would require institutions for popular participation in the determination of laws and rules for the socially just distribution of resources and the benefits from development.[9]

Social justice calls for equity, which is not to be interpreted as absolute equality. The concept has no universal definition; to a large extent it depends on fairness in political and economic power relations. In many ways it may be easier to pinpoint what is not consistent with, or contrary to, the principle. Nonetheless, equity is a fundamental requisite of democracy. Institutions, such as government administration, the armed forces, educational and health organizations, and private enterprise, must be subject to the laws and rules that provide for or protect the principle of equity. It is in this connection that the institution of the market has to be carefully considered.

Given that an effective administrative method for resource allocation has not yet been discovered—at least not for complex economies—markets are a necessity. But the market distribution of income depends, among other things, on the distribution of productive wealth or resources among the participants. This is heavily skewed toward the highest income groups and dominant classes, which is a source of unequal distribution of market power. The built-in bias can change only through wealth redistribution, land ownership being a primary means.

Markets have acquired a deservedly adverse reputation because of monopoly domination and various other practices for the exploitation of individuals, labor, and small-scale enterprises. That such misuses of the markets have become possible is due to the influence of big business on governments, and business power is supported by the cultivation of the mythology of the benefits of unregulated free enterprise, which equates the freedom of the markets with democracy. Most industrial countries have at least some legislation against monopolization and cartelization, but governments are, if not openly supportive, tolerant of monopolies. Worse yet, under the title of intellectual property rights, they have extended, or accepted, patent protection in areas that clearly lie within nature's domain. Various health and basic farm processes have been brought under commercial dominance.

From all this it follows that while monopoly control as well as rules and regulation for observing fairness in commercial relationships and trading practices are necessary, they are not sufficient conditions for bringing markets into harmony with the principle of equity. But market regulation relies on government action. The latter is not an integral or organic part of neoclassical free-market theory. Government participation is brought into it through the back door, primarily for considering the effects of particular policies, such as taxation and expenditures, on the market economy. The theory's failure to integrate the instrumental role of government in maintaining and contributing to a democratic civil society reinforces the capitalists' belief that in well-organized markets there is no need for it because private and social interests coincide. The belief is without rational foundation even in advanced industrial countries, where institutions such as unemployment insurance and other safety nets exist against total destitution. It is even more irrelevant for economically less developed countries where the institutions serve only the interests of the well-to-do.

Free-market ideology is also opposed to communal or community-based economic organizations, because they are against the interests of middlemen, such as market intermediaries with market power ranging from those of landlords, petty traders, and others, all the way to international corporations.[10] Nonetheless, cooperative organizations are not inconsistent with, and usually work through, the institution of the market. Others that are not market but community-based cooperative systems may sacrifice narrowly defined economic efficiency and some profitability for advancing local community welfare. Ecuador provides well-documented examples, including the case studies presented in this volume, but as the experiences of such institutions in Asia, Europe, and elsewhere in Latin America confirm, they can powerfully contribute to the equitable use of resources.

POLICY CONSIDERATIONS

The inadequate, not to say pernicious theories of development on which policies are based have to be reconsidered. At this point there are no general frameworks—and possibly there never will be any—that are capable of covering the total range of social, political, and cultural phenomena. But as a first step, the most important elements of the prevailing theories can be critically reviewed.

First, there is the matter of full employment as a policy goal. As a concept it has appeal and undoubted relevance; nonetheless, it is elusive. What is the definition of *employment?* And who qualifies for inclusion in the labor force? In practice, jobless persons who have given up the search for employment are not considered members of the statistically defined labor force and hence are not considered unemployed. Nonetheless, as soon as improving economic conditions signal a reasonable chance for finding work, most of these jobless begin to seek jobs again. It follows that the measurement of full employment is itself a function of the state of the economy.

Then again, who should be counted as being employed? Does a shoeshine boy or a marginal farmer with an undernourished family count as an employed worker? Statistically, perhaps. But it is more relevant to ask: Does the work provide an acceptable minimum living standard, whichever way the latter is defined? For social welfare it is more appropriate to define employment and self-employment in terms of activities that can yield income for acquiring at least a minimum acceptable market basket of basic consumption items. It follows that employment policies that satisfy socially desirable basic living standards for low-income earners call for actively increasing the demand for labor at corresponding wage levels.

What are these policies? Neoclassical economic theory assumes that pure competition reestablishes full employment through wage flexibility. Even if the conditions for competition existed, there would be no guarantee that the full-employment wage would be high enough to provide an acceptable minimum living standard (Lefeber 2000). In reality, wage flexibility has a downward limit defined by survival requirements. And upward, it is limited by regressive competition offered by the reserve army of the unemployed. Only policies for orderly labor markets could secure wage levels and employment conditions that are within the range defined by the two extremes. This is a necessary albeit complex task, because employment conditions vary greatly among rural, urban informal, and commercial labor markets.

As a substitute for theoretically pure competition, the neoliberal establishment—supported by the World Bank and the IMF—calls for free markets, that is, free trade and free capital movements, with minimal government intervention. The profits and other incomes in the monetized commercial and industrial sectors are supposed to generate secondary benefits to the unemployed and the destitute through a process called trickle-down. And whereas something undoubtedly trickles down, the process does not reach the secondary labor markets with sufficient strength to increase the demand for labor at socially acceptable wage levels. The result, if any, shows up mostly as some additional personal service and informal-sector employment that does not generate sufficient income for basic subsistence. In fact, as discussed below, the processes that are expected to bring about trickle-down may very well cause additional unemployment.

In any case, the idea of trickle-down as the means for advancing socioeconomic justice is unethical and unacceptable. The functional or market distribution of income is not a reward for merit. Relying on it as the means for social justice is a signal endorsement of a social-political system in which the state fails to recognize or abdicates its responsibility for creating and maintaining equity. But the ethical objection to trickle-down does not invalidate the emphasis on suitable policies for employment creation.

The market mechanism discourages private investors from activities that do not promise them adequate returns. In the absence of domestic purchasing power there is only limited demand for domestically produced goods; hence, investors turn to export markets. These are frequently controlled by foreign interests, which have a preference for using relatively capital-intensive technologies imported from their home countries. With that, the induced demand for labor is correspondingly reduced. Worse yet, imports of subsidized staples and other consumer goods and the free inflow of capital can, and have been known to, displace domestic industry and farming. Thus, free-market practices, foreign investment, and substitution of capital-intensive methods of production for more labor-using technologies contribute to unemployment.

The case of Mexico is a good example. Many of the rural workers displaced by the capital-intensive farm technologies of foreign investors have been reduced to marginal farming or searching for occasional work in the informal sectors of the urban economy. Others are looking for employment abroad: They take the risk of illegal emigration to the United States.[11] Furthermore, quite a few of the domestically owned enterprises have also been taken over or displaced by foreign investors with a preference for capital intensive technologies. Thus, the displacement of workers has not been confined to the rural economy. Even though foreign investment does create new job opportunities, the rate of growth of these opportunities does not seem to be commensurate to the rate of displacement. And the wages of workers in the capital-intensive sectors do not reflect their productivity, because regressive competition by the earlier mentioned reserve army of the unemployed keeps wages at subsistence levels (Lefeber 1997).[12]

In contrast, the production of basic goods and staples required by low-income consumers frequently has rather simple technical requirements. Such production is suitable for labor intensive production; it generates that income and purchasing power that are needed for acquisition. Certain services, such as water, sanitation, education, health, and even urban low-income housing can be provided effectively by government. However, food and other low-income consumption goods present complex distributional problems that are not readily solved by direct government action. Bureaucratic approaches to decentralized distribution of goods are too cumbersome; there is no readily available substitute for markets. But markets require demand to absorb the supply, and investment in the domestic economies requires the growth of demand for domestically produced goods and services. It must be remembered, as it frequently is not, that market demand is made up of two components: desire or need for a particular good or service, and purchasing power to acquire it. The question is, What are the sources of the latter? As discussed below, income from employment and self-employment must be a primary source.

SOURCES OF LOW-INCOME PURCHASING POWER

In countries where the distribution of income is highly unequal, income redistribution is not only a matter of social justice but also a requirement for domestic market development through the provision of purchasing power for domestically produced and imported goods. It can have dramatic effects, as shown by the socialist experiences in Cuba and Chile.

Moves toward greater equity brought about in both countries' shortages of consumer goods and inflationary pressures, not because of inefficient socialist supply management—as critics from the right would have it—but because demand expanded faster than production for domestic consumption. After the Pinochet policies reverted the Chilean economy to the earlier highly skewed income distribution, the availability of consumer goods increased visibly, the so-called Chilean miracle, not because of a greater efficiency of supply management but because of the induced drop in demand. The miracle was brought about by increasing the level of poverty.

The question is, What are the feasible and effective means for income redistribution? Direct income transfers that require tax/subsidy schemes are politically and administratively difficult to implement. And in spite of the large income differentials, the redistributable margins are relatively small. This does not mean, however, that the alternative should be trickle-down, which is, as mentioned above, the neoliberals' favorite approach to poverty relief. If the required "favorable market conditions" for private investment and production bring about increases in national income, the resulting distribution of the income increments—neoclassical arguments to the contrary notwithstanding—does not necessarily turn into increased low-income purchasing power. Given that the underlying implicit assumptions have no real-life counterpart, there is no *a priori* reason to assume that they should.

There is, of course, the real possibility of productive wealth redistribution, the primary means being land reform. This will be discussed below. But as far as increasing the demand for employment is concerned, public-sector employment in productivity-enhancing public works, such as water control (irrigation and drainage) and transport or communication systems for rural market development, must be primary. These, combined with relevant education, credit, and health programs designed for aiding the dispersed small-farm sectors are the required policies for rural development. At the same time, in selected industries and mining enterprises, but not in farming, an increase in the demand for labor can be motivated by payroll subsidies based on the number of workers employed. If this policy is financed through profit taxation, the increase in the demand for labor can be obtained through the market mechanism. This too runs very much against the ideas of market theorists, who insist on subsidizing the use of capital relative to wages, thereby motivating increases in capital intensity (Lefeber 1968).[13]

In this connection it may be useful to refer briefly to the evidence of economic history. Simon Kuznets's claim that the early stages of development bring about adverse changes in income distribution (Kuznets 1955) and the various superficial references to the successful development of the East Asian economies overlook some fundamental factors. Most neoclassical students of economic history have ignored the effects of government spending and international migration on income distribution. The massive government expenditures on military and naval supplies and transportation were key factors in motivating the Industrial Revolution. In turn, the consequent increase in the demand for labor yielded corresponding increases in low-income purchasing power. The international migration in the eighteenth and nineteenth centuries, which treated the European surplus labor and the landless to rich, cultivable lands overseas, had similar effects (Lefeber 1974a, McNeill 1998). In the case of East Asian development the income distributional effects of land reform in Japan, South Korea, and Taiwan have also been overlooked or insufficiently appreciated. Both the European migrants and the East Asian rural populations had already been experienced farmers and artisans, who knew how to take advantage of the economic opportunities offered by land grabs or land reforms (North 1997; Bienefeld 1988). Their enhanced income status made it possible for them to become buyers and consumers of agricultural and industrial products.

TRADE AND DISTRIBUTION

As discussed above, the growth of low-income purchasing power is a fundamental requirement for development. This, in turn, raises some complex questions about the relationship among trade, markets, and income distribution. The introduction of free trade in most Latin American countries has brought about the restructuring of production and, with it, unemployment. Traditional industries working with labor-intensive technologies have frequently been displaced by imports of cheap foreign goods, which arguably could have benefited the low-income populations if the assumptions of the neoclassical economic model held. But they do not. There is no short-run—let alone instantaneous—transfer of displaced workers to higher productivity employment. This is particularly so because foreign investment, which frequently replaces domestic production, has shown a strong bias in favor of capital-intensive techniques in both manufacturing and agriculture. Free trade and foreign investment cause an income distribution problem that, in the absence of workable means for compensating the losers from the gains from trade, calls for selective protection.

Consider the case of Mexico. Free trade and uncontrolled foreign investment in agriculture displaced domestic grain production with export crops, such as fruits and vegetables. The country has become dependent on grain imports, so that the cost of living has become a function of exchange rate variations. With the sequence of drastic devaluations over the last two decades the cost of basic food staples—the cost of survival of the low-income populations—has precipitously increased. As a consequence, the already poor low-income consumers have been further impoverished (Lefeber 1997). In such cases protection amounts to social risk aversion.

Protectionism, as practiced indiscriminately in the so-called import substituting drive for industrialization, has caused much damage and is not what is called for. In contrast, an across-the-board nondiscriminating system of tariffs, which is matched by corresponding domestic commodity taxation, does not qualify as protection and may be the only way to raise revenues. But selective protection (or prohibition of specific imports) may also be necessary for protecting the livelihood of domestic artisans and other small-scale producers, at least in the short run. Farmers of staples for domestic consumption may have similar needs. As the Mexican example illustrates, the absence of protection against the destruction of the domestic food production capacity can have drastic consequences on popular welfare. However, given the rigidities of economic structures, the short run may need to have a long time horizon.

With free trade, and under the various strictures of trade agreements, there is no legal defense against destructive intrusions into the domestic economies. The claim that free trade is necessarily beneficial for social welfare is not made even by neoclassical economic theory. It limits the argument to the statement that "some trade is better than no trade." But this is not the neoliberal position.

The impact of free trade in creating poverty and unemployment is evident all over Latin America. For example, in Colombia, after the elimination of tariffs during the 1980s, cheap Japanese and other imports reduced the large artisan class (leather workers, weavers, and so on) into unemployed wage workers. In Ecuador a vigorous labor-intensive garment industry (made up of small-scale producers) has been damaged by the import of used clothing. As a consequence, large numbers of skilled workers have become unemployed (Chapter 11).

This, of course, also raises some difficult questions about income distribution, for which there are no easy answers. Cheap imported goods—such as staples subsidized by the exporting countries (for example, grains from the United States), plastic sandals, or used clothing—are undoubtedly more affordable for low-income earners than the more costly domestic artisan products. But the low-income earners, poor by our standards, who can afford to be in the market, are not as badly off as the unemployed or the marginal farmer. So the question arises: What is or what should be the balance between the loss suffered by the low-income consumers due to selective protection and the poverty caused by imports that destroy or significantly lower the income-earning capacity of domestic artisans or small-scale farm producers?[14]

These are fundamental problems relating to trade and foreign economic relationships. Here it is sufficient to point out that trade policies too must recognize that income from employment and self-employment is a primary means for poverty relief, and that selective protection may be needed as defense against the immiseration of large segments of the low-income population. Protection in these cases is not only risk aversion, as discussed above, but also a form of income redistribution between any income earner (low or high) and the potentially destitute. The argument that protection "ultimately" harms the poor assumes that there are short-run remedies, such as compensation for the losers from the gains from trade or rapid transfer to alternative productive employment. Such remedies do not exist, not even in economically advanced, industrialized countries.

Government policies for basic poor relief and employment creation are severely curtailed by the IFIs' insistence on adopting WTO and other trade agreements. As things are, they serve only international corporate interests; for bringing the marginalized classes into the development process, these agreements would have to be renegotiated. This is not an argument against trade, but rather a call for a basic change in policy orientation. Trade is an important contributor to domestic market development, but not a goal in itself, as it is in export orientation. There is no possible alternative to domestic market development that is structured to encourage vigorous domestic production with corresponding growth of domestic employment and absorptive capacity. And in countries with large and impoverished rural populations, this must begin with the reconstruction of the rural economy. It is the only feasible way to resolve the problem of unemployment and poverty.

RURAL DEVELOPMENT

Rural poverty in the Andean regions has reached appalling levels (Larrea et al. 1996; Larrea in Berry 1998). Unemployment, underemployment, and poverty are self-perpetuating. As things are, only two alternatives are open to the unemployed poor: They can try to subsist on marginal lands that are unsuitable for cultivation, or they can join the exodus from rural regions. Some choose to migrate abroad, legally or illegally. But those who remain, the majority, become net additions to the already prevailing unemployment or underemployment in urban shanty towns. The urban sectors are incapable of providing the migrants with activities that can produce minimum acceptable living standards. Thus rural misery translates into urban poverty concentrated in ever-growing slum communities and shanty towns.

Relief from these socially and humanly unacceptable alternatives is a moral imperative. But there are also techno-economic reasons that make the economic uplift of the poor all the more important. This is where the establishmentarian policies for development—neoliberal prescriptions adopted by the prevailing power structure—are not just ineffective but totally counterproductive. One has to reemphasize the frequently overlooked point that in market economies the poverty-driven need for better nourishment and some basic consumer goods cannot be satisfied without creating low-income purchasing power. For this, the primary means is rural development. It can provide income-earning opportunities in farming, rural small industries, and local services. It also offers opportunities for non-inflationary rural public works (Chapter 4).

Rural development begins with land reform, that is, with the replacement of estates and other large landholdings with small-scale, family-size farms. It may also call for the consolidation of dispersed micro-holdings into more efficient production units. In either case, assistance for the adoption of appropriate technologies is a basic requirement.

It has long been established that productivity of land is inversely related to size of holding (Sen 1964). The reason is that the labor intensity of cultivation increases on smaller farms. And as shown by the Ecuador experience, even very small units, particularly when combined with small industrial enterprises, can become economically viable (Chapters 10 and 11). These, along with community-based, rural, small-industrial enterprises, can generate not only employment and self-employment, but also the means for the absorption of production for low-income consumption both at the local and the national levels.

Examples in the Ecuadorian experience confirm the feasibility of local, community based, social-economic development. In some instances it can come about in response to local and individually managed initiatives. In other instances the support of NGOs and other aid agencies or charismatic leadership may be required (see Part 3, Case Studies). In all cases, however, the reorganization of the rural economy needs new institutions that are specially created to serve the purpose. The existing ones were created to protect the traditional ownership structure and the established commercial relationships. Since institutions do not reform themselves, they must be replaced. But this is easier said than done. Institutions reflect the power structure; therefore, institutional change requires an underlying change in power relations.

The neglect of the rural sectors is a reflection of the prevailing power structure. Even though a significant part of the Latin American low-income populations is rural, and agriculture's share in the national products is disproportionally low, the resources devoted to rural development—as opposed to the support for estate agriculture—are totally inadequate. The resources are used in sectors and activities in ways that satisfy the demands of the dominant social classes. But there also is a residual belief in the primacy of industrialization in the process of development, which is based on the superficially understood historical evidence of the examples of rich, industrialized countries. The fact that agriculture also played a fundamental role has been systematically overlooked (Lefeber 1974a).

There is the additional difficulty that the sector's regional diffusion, and the lack of adequate rural institutions make the implementation of policies for rural development difficult. This has led to the conclusion that the economy may be better controlled if concentrated in centralized locations. For example, the designer of the urban focus in Colombia, the late Lauchlin Curry, was a typical advocate of the concentration of resources in urban activities.[15] But even those scholars who have deplored the urban push, such as Michael Lipton, would only go as far as to leave the development of the rural sector to what they believe to be constructive market forces guided by the price system (Lipton 1977). This leaves the rural poor, the marginal farmer, and the worker displaced by mechanization at the mercy of the forces that maintain the prevailing economic order.

The lack of resources has been most detrimental in the small-scale farm sectors, made up of minimal-size family and marginal farms. Larger-scale commercial farms, estates in particular, have frequently benefited from various forms of government subsidies and have obtained capital for the importation of mechanized, labor-displacing farm machinery. Furthermore, foreign investment by multinational agribusiness corporations has also tended to substitute capital for labor. The process has significantly contributed to the growth of rural unemployment and poverty. It negates one of the basic tenets of the theory of comparative advantage, which is that in relatively labor-abundant economies trade brings about increased specialization in labor-intensive production, so that the demand for labor correspondingly increases. The experience does not support the theory.

CONCLUSION

Economic development has to be integral to the process of creating a civil society in which human rights prevail. Even though the current obstacles seem formidable, in time they may be overcome by peaceful means. The question is whether there is enough time left for a transition that is not motivated by violence or other forms of catastrophic events. The dominant classes and the institutions of the status quo will have to recognize that it is also in their interest to participate in building communities in which justice prevails. In spite of its disappointing conclusion, the World Bank's recent experiment with an open platform for the discussion of poverty is an indication of a growing awareness of the need for change. And popular manifestations of widespread dissatisfaction are being attested by various protest movements in both industrialized and less developed countries, as well as by the resurgence of revolutionary forces of various intensities around the globe. The civil war in Colombia, which the United States hopes to suppress by military intervention, is not about the drug trade but rather civil rights and equity. In Peru the very violent Shining Path movement may be reemerging. The privatization of public services—such as water supplies—and its effect on the poor populations has been a source of restlessness and popular protest in Bolivia. Ecuador, a country with a large poor population and a remarkably nonviolent past, is surrounded by regions where violence and protest movements of various intensities are the order of the day. At the same time, Ecuador also has its share of the indigenous populations of the Andes, a population that is pressing for equity and civil rights. The recent mass movement to unseat the government—initially supported by the military—is evidence that the time for peaceful protest may be nearing the end. In all these cases the ultimate threat is social disintegration and loss of that human security that only a well-organized democratic state can provide.

It is important to study the causes of poverty and exploitation, the forces that maintain them, and the means for change. As was the case of the Bourbons, those who do not learn and do not forget, come to a tragic end. And as Adam Smith, the much misrepresented but enlightened humanist observed in his *Theory of Moral Sentiments*, unless society's foundation is justice, "the prevalence of injustice must utterly destroy it."

Notes

[1] Both India and China eliminated famines by changing from rigid adherence to ideologically dictated controls. In India, the inefficient bureaucratic controls on industrial development and agriculture were eliminated, and resources for new agricultural technologies were provided. However, the undeniable advances brought about significant adverse changes in income distribution. In China, the catastrophic consequences of the "great leap forward" motivated policy changes to the commune system, and after their liquidation, increasing market orientation. In contrast to India and China, in the so-called Asian Tigers, in particular South Korea, Taiwan, and Singapore, market orientation was tempered by wealth distribution (land reform) and strict government controls on trade and investment.

[2] Even capitalists are beginning to be concerned about speculative foreign exchange movements and the free market's adverse distributional effects (Cassidy 1997).

[3] For a history of the debt, see, for example, Miller 1986 and Lefeber 1990.

[4] A very few countries, such as Chile and Malaysia, have imposed limited controls over capital movements. In the United Nations and among others concerned about the deleterious effects of globalization there is a continuing discussion of instituting the so-called Tobin tax, which is strongly opposed by international and US financial establishments. Without an international control agency there may be no effective means for implementing such a tax.

[5] I hesitate to use the term *market socialism*. Even though it is not necessarily an oxymoron, it is an ill-defined concept that, among other things, does not indicate the nature and degree of ownership of productive resources and respect for human rights.

[6] "Social capital" formation, as emphasized by the World Bank (Chapter 1 herein) could only contribute to social and economic development if it were accompanied by major institutional changes. This is due to the way in which the horizontal and vertical linkages of social capital function are determined by the prevailing institutional structure.

[7] The Nader candidacy in the 2000 US presidential election was a strategic attempt to motivate change. It conceivably could have worked in a parliamentary system, in which power brokers can have a decisive role, but in a two-party system it was bound to fail.

[8] Consider, for instance, the April 30, 2001, statement about energy by the vice-president of the United States, Dick Cheney, to the managing editors of the Associated Press. Cheney explicitly called for an energy policy that is suitable for maintaining the lifestyle in America. "Conservation may be a personal virtue," he said, "but it is not a sufficient basis for a sound, comprehensive energy policy" (Kahn 2001, 1). The subsequent *National Energy Policy: Report of the National Energy Policy Development Group* (US Government 2001) places the entire emphasis on expanding fossil-fuel supplies (coal, gas, and oil) with only lip service to limiting demand.

[9] The case of Cuba is particularly interesting. Electoral choices do not exist, and the government permits only very limited expressions of opposition. At the same time, a significant degree of equity has been achieved, as attested by the spectacular increase in educational and health standards. The drastic improvements in social welfare place Cuba way ahead of other so-called democratic Latin American countries. This was recognized in a speech by the president of the World Bank during the April 2001 IMF/World Bank Washington meetings (Lobe 2001).

[10] For example, in the coffee-producing regions of Oaxaca, Mexico, the traders—popularly referred to as coyotes—are bent on destroying the small coffee producers' cooperatives, whose independent marketing they consider detrimental to their interests (Canadian Broadcasting Corporation/CBC, 6 P.M. news, May 8, 2000). Similar cases exist in Ecuador and in other parts of Latin America.

[11] Migration abroad eases the domestic unemployment problem. It is also noteworthy that in Mexico emigrants are the third largest source of foreign exchange (Thompson 2001). There is a flow of legal and illegal migration from El Salvador and also Ecuador, among others. The strength of these flows is attested by the significant contribution of emigrants' remittances to the balance-of-payments current accounts of the countries of origin.

[12] Regressive competition becomes ineffective against wage levels maintained by so-called labor aristocracies. These are powerful unions associated with highly capital-intensive foreign investments, primarily in the mining and petroleum industries.

[13] An interesting example of profit/subsidy policies is the case of Puerto Rico, where rewarding the use of capital through profit tax exemptions resulted in high capital intensities, high unemployment, and mass emigration.

[14] Food aid provides an interesting point. If given to relieve short-term shortages caused by a bad harvest, it can be beneficial. If it is a substitute for domestic production, it is detrimental.

[15] See Lauchlin Curry's "Plan Colombia" and "Plan of Four Strategies," discussed in Sandilands 1990 and Lefeber 1993, respectively.

Chapter 3

Exploring the Links Among Global Trade, Industrial Agriculture, and Rural Underdevelopment

RICARDO GRINSPUN

Decisive steps were taken during the 1990s to institutionalize a global trade regime with the backing of a strong multilateral organization. The World Trade Organization (WTO), established in 1995 on the basis of the 1994 Uruguay Round (UR) multilateral trade agreements, was given broad powers to promote the liberalization of trade and investment on a global scale. In addition to freeing up the movement of goods and capital across borders, measures were taken toward eliminating non-border barriers to international investment and trade and ensuring state compliance with the new rules (Clarke and Barlow 1997; Shrybman 1999). Bilateral and regional trade agreements were negotiated to regulate trade and investment in particular regions and to set the tone for multilateral frameworks. Such was the case of the North American Free Trade Agreement (NAFTA) and the proposed Free Trade Area of the Americas (FTAA), modeled after NAFTA. These new international legal and regulatory regimes, as well as the determined application of neoliberal economic programs in many countries, gave a new impetus to the post–World War II expansion of global markets. This expansion saw a threefold increase in world exports of goods and services (in real terms) and a sevenfold increase in foreign direct investment from the 1970s to the late 1990s (UNDP 1999, 30–31).

Recent innovations in trade agreements and institutions, as well as the expanding role of international business, particularly agribusiness, have had a major impact on rural societies and economies. This chapter

This chapter draws in part on earlier work done with the assistance of Yasmine Shamsie (Sreenivasan and Grinspun 2002).

46

examines the impact of the global trade regime on processes of rural transformation. In particular, it raises the following questions: How is this global trade system affecting small-scale farmers, food security, and the viability of family-based and community-based enterprises? How are trade rules and institutions affecting the opportunities for diversified and sustainable rural and local development in Latin America? Given the scope of these questions and the vast literature that exists on the topic, my effort here is necessarily synthetic, that is, to identify key themes and trends and to sketch some basic propositions.

A desirable rural policy scenario would promote economic viability as well as environmental and social sustainability among impoverished rural populations. This requires, as several chapters in this volume argue, control over productive assets, access to education and health, the formation of entrepreneurial capacities, and new institutional arrangements—such as cooperative or associational marketing and input purchases—among small-scale producers and their families. It also demands investment in nonagricultural income and employment-generating activities along with the promotion of sustainable agriculture; the nurturing of local and domestic markets; and the generation of employment on a large scale, for example, in irrigation and transportation infrastructure (as proposed by Lefeber in Chapter 4). It requires active government institutions and NGOs to improve rural education, health, and infrastructure services and to implement rural development programs in coordination with local level beneficiaries. To achieve such progress, it is first necessary to understand the impact that national and regional programs (that is, rural development, social welfare, education, health) and international forces (that is, new trade and investment regimes) have on fragile rural societies. A complementary set of supportive policies for rural development is, of course, a far cry from the reality of policymaking in Latin America today. There are no integrated sets of policies to promote food security, local economic development, rural diversification, and ecological sustainability. Rather, we are witnessing the implementation of an international business and trade model, enforced at the national and international levels by a neoliberal and free-trade regulatory framework, which is detrimental to those goals. This is, in a nutshell, the argument of this chapter.[1]

There are two principal channels through which the international trading system affects the opportunities for sustainable rural development. The first involves the impact of the global trading system on the role of the state and its capacity to regulate and intervene in the marketplace on behalf of rural dwellers and organizations. It has to do with the willingness and capacity of the state to secure access to basic services needed by small-scale producers such as water, health, schooling, rural extension, and credit. It also has to do with enacting macroeconomic policies to address socioeconomic imbalances, trade policies to support integrated domestic development, and the political will to implement redistributive measures that would benefit disadvantaged social sectors.

Here I focus on the second channel, which relates to the impact of international trade in agricultural and other products on economic restructuring in the countryside. Section one of this chapter argues that the expansion of global markets for rural products, along with the aggressive introduction of industrial methods and export orientation to rural economies, are undermining smallholder and subsistence farming as well as nonagricultural family enterprises. They are also creating new barriers to the efforts of small-scale rural enterprises to diversify their agricultural and nonagricultural activities. Section two focuses on the WTO's Agreement on Agriculture (AoA) and the other principal trade agreements that have an impact on rural restructuring. The AoA serves as a major tool for advancing trade liberalization in agricultural products and primarily reflects the interests of large exporting countries and related transnational agribusiness corporations. The implementation of the AoA, still short lived, already threatens to harm food, employment, and income security for vulnerable rural populations. Section three presents some concluding thoughts about possibilities for shifting toward an international trade and investment regime that would promote sustainable rural development.

INDUSTRIAL AGRICULTURE AND RURAL RESTRUCTURING

Despite urban industrialization and migration, the rural economy is still vital for developing countries (see Chapter 1). Moreover, although cases of rural diversification can be found (see Chapters 10 and 11), agriculture (broadly defined) remains the pillar of rural economies, almost universally.[2] Mainstream economic analysis relates to agriculture as if it were just another sector of the economy, and thus not deserving of distinctive treatment (see, for example, Schott 2001, 86–87; Chapter 5 herein). Much World Bank analysis still measures the welfare impact of trade liberalization in agriculture exclusively in terms of neoclassical measures of terms of trade and "dead weight loss" effects (Ingco 1996).[3] These views, however, ignore the various economic, social, and ecological roles that agriculture plays in both industrialized and rural societies.

Benefits of Small-scale Agriculture

European proponents of the *multifunctional role* of agriculture stress that agricultural production can create positive externalities and produces intangible public goods in addition to its food-supply function. These include environmental stewardship, agro-biological diversity, the economic viability of rural areas and scattered populations, food safety and quality, cultural heritage, and especially, food security (FAO 2001, section III). They argue that the attainment of these policy objectives cannot be guaranteed by market mechanisms alone and that support to agriculture is therefore necessary, including special protection in trade agreements. Latin American authors have harnessed the concept of multifunctionality to argue for a real strategy of sustainable rural development, which will require significant shifts from current approaches to development (Gudynas 2001). One major shift involves the recognition that in developing countries agriculture and small-scale farms in particular contribute to the public good in a variety of ways (Ritchie et al. 1999; Rosset 1999).

Smallholder agriculture provides considerably more employment and food staples in less developed countries than do larger commercial farms (Oxfam GB 2000). Small-scale farmers who produce basic grains are critical to the domestic food supply and hence to food security. They contribute to social and biological diversity (through, for example, multiple cropping systems) and thus to sustainable development. The social organization of small-scale farming may promote empowerment and community responsibility through equitable opportunities and decentralized land ownership. Indeed, small-scale farming is often the social basis for community organizing and for locally based development initiatives, required for rural diversification and other community goals. Moreover, in contrast to the prevailing neoliberal orthodoxy, it has been found that small-scale farms are economically more efficient than large-scale operations in terms of resource utilization and productivity (for example, output per unit of area) (Ritchie et al. 1999, 3). Small-scale farming and local small-scale, value-added enterprises are the only foreseeable alternatives to prevent massive migration from the countryside to peri-urban slums and the consequent social and economic burden this process imposes on underdeveloped countries.

Despite its importance, small-scale agriculture is seriously endangered by current neoliberal policies, and the implications for rural poverty, food security, and urban migration are far-reaching. Rural stagnation and impoverishment are not, however, a new phenomenon in Latin America. Their origins go back to post–World War II economic policies that consistently favored urban-based industrialization at the expense of rural areas. Thus, one should not idealize the rural structures that predate the introduction of industrial agricultural methods on a large scale or the rural conditions that prevailed prior to the late 1970s and early 1980s, when neoliberal policies were first applied. My argument is that the current model of international agribusiness and technological fixes, and the international trade agreements and structural adjustment measures put in place to advance that model, are part of the problems that we must address today. They are not part of a solution that incorporates community participation as well as equitable, sustainable, and diversified development. Recent neoliberal policies—market-oriented reforms, structural adjustment, and most recently, trade-induced restructuring—have, instead of alleviating the problem, made it worse.

Rural Restructuring

A central component of the prevailing orthodoxy has been to promote rural restructuring and a shift toward large- and medium-scale commercial agriculture that requires resources generally far beyond the reach of small-scale farmers and community-based enterprises. Indeed, a central feature of globalization has been the expansion of industrial agriculture to countries in the South and an accelerating encroachment on subsistence and locally oriented agriculture (Ritchie et al. 1999, 1–11). Those who have a stake in such expansion, such as the USDA, assert that feeding the world's growing population depends on furthering global markets for agricultural products (Trueblood and Shapouri 2001, 1). However, most of the world's food is still produced for local and national consumption, and international trade in food and agricultural products is only a small fraction of total world production. Even in the most food-insecure countries, domestic production accounts for about 90 percent of food consumption (Shapouri and Rosen 2001, 1). Concerted economic, technological, and political pressure is being applied to change this situation. The pressure is for new and expanding agricultural export sectors in Southern countries to join a growing global industrial food system, primarily oriented to serve domestic urban elites in the South and the vast market demand of rich, industrialized countries.

Once the modernization of agriculture has reached an advanced stage in particular regions and countries, the destiny of rural populations becomes intimately tied to commercial estates and export operations in their vicinity. Such is the case with agro-*maquila* industries in northern and central Mexico, the fruit industry in Chile, and the cut-flower industry in Ecuador—all of which are dependent on stable access to Northern markets. Rural wage laborers—many of them destitute and landless—as well as small-scale farmers and sharecroppers who want to supplement the family income become increasingly dependent on this type of generally precarious employment. Thus, they gain a stake in those conditions that make such industries viable, including inflows of foreign investment, freer trade, and continuing access to markets in the North. One should emphasize, however, that their interests are not identical to those of their employers, since workers also have a stake in the improvement of working conditions and in measures that will make such productive activities socially and ecologically sustainable.[4] Such measures would include improved labor laws and higher environmental standards, as well as the more effective insertion of those industries into a broad approach to integrated *local* development.[5]

In spite of corporate agribusiness claims about combining science and efficiency, the reality of the neoliberal restructuring of agriculture is one of large inefficiencies that cause serious social, economic, and ecological harm.[6] Industrial agriculture leads to the concentration of wealth and decision-making in a few corporate and individual hands, thus hindering the efficient allocation of resources as prices become controlled through corporate collusion and the prevailing subsidy programs of a few industrialized agricultural exporters.[7] Consumers are misinformed and disempowered by large food distributors integrated with the food conglomerates. These distributors join together with the marketing and advertising industries to promote brand-name allegiance rather than real consumer choice.

Major inefficiencies also result from the systematic "externalization" of ecological and social costs. In economic analysis, *negative externalities* refer to costs of production not borne by the firm, such as pollution of air and water, or the environmental and health impacts of pesticides. The drive to lower production costs results in ecological damage with implications for current and future generations of humans and other species.[8] There are growing health costs from altered diets based on animal fats and processed foods, and from foods polluted with agro-chemicals. Monocultures and the increased reliance on biotechnology also threaten biodiversity. Industrial agriculture has tied the fate of farmland (supposedly a renewable resource) to that of fossil fuels (a nonrenewable one), thus further threatening the sustainability of food production (Shrybman 1999, 46). The large-scale processing, packaging, and transportation systems that are part of a global system of food production require enormous energy, leading to increased use of fossil fuels and a substantial contribution to global warming. The expansion of agribusiness operations is thus contributing to environmental and social erosion in rural areas in many different ways.

Advocates for this industry argue that economies of scale will result in lower costs (that is, a decline in unit costs of production as output rises). The traditional view is that large-scale operations have access to bulk purchasing of inputs, capital intensive technologies, investment in infrastructure, and other means to lower costs that are not available to smaller units. However, as noted above, costs are also "lowered" by shifting them onto others (for example, using large quantities of insecticides to raise plant productivity but increasing the health risks and costs to workers, consumers, and governments). Agribusiness also creates new costs that do not exist in sustainable, small-scale agriculture, such as loss of biodiversity. Thus, arguments based on the benefits of economies of scale should be assessed critically rather than accepted at face value.[9]

Vulnerable rural populations also suffer from the social and economic costs of neoliberal restructuring. As cheap products flood local markets (sometimes as a result of dumping[10] by Northern countries), debts of small-scale farmers' escalate, sources of credit dry up, and livelihoods are destroyed. Trade liberalization and large-scale imports of low-priced products, such as food and clothing, can drive local producers out of business. They can also hold back or destroy efforts toward economic diversification, as was the case with rural "blue jean" producers in Pelileo, Ecuador, who suffered from liberalized imports of used clothing (Chapter 11). In short, rural restructuring is creating a context in which small-scale local actors lose power and control over markets and institutions because only large-scale economic actors have the economic and political clout to extract benefits from new opportunities (Chapter 5). However, even those commercial and cooperative enterprises that can benefit from export markets are struggling with protectionist agricultural markets in the North and unfair competition from the large exporting countries (more on this in the next section).

Impact of Trade Liberalization

One important aspect of trade liberalization is its potential impact on growth, employment, distribution of income and wealth, and, as a result, the alleviation of poverty. While mainstream economists have recognized that some groups will be hurt by trade liberalization and have even suggested specific programs to assist such groups, they continue to argue that trade liberalization is good for growth, and growth is good for the poor (McCulloch, Winters, and Cirera 2001, xxi). As critics point out, however, the evidence does not support such general claims (Rodrik 2001). Over the last two decades rapid market liberalization has been accompanied by slower growth for almost every Southern region. The growth that did occur was concentrated in the rich, industrialized countries and a few newly industrializing countries. For example, in Latin America GDP per capita grew by 75 percent from 1960 to 1980, whereas from 1980 to 1998 it rose by only 6 percent (Weisbrot et al. 2000). Moreover, the growth that has occurred has not sufficiently increased the demand for labor to decrease the rate of joblessness, thus contributing to an increase in poverty and inequality, particularly among rural populations (Lefeber 1997).

Whether trade liberalization and growth will result in broad-based poverty reduction and improvements in human welfare depends critically on the initial conditions of inequity. Even the World Bank recognizes that "most groups have gained from overall growth roughly in proportion to their initial share of the national pie" (Demery and Walton 1998, 9). That this assessment does not go far enough is evident from the widening gaps in income between the poorest and richest people and the poorest and richest countries during recent decades (UNDP 1999, 36). Furthermore, the World Bank acknowledges that positive change will require "action by the state to support the buildup of human, land,

and infrastructure assets that poor people own or to which they have access" (World Bank 2000, 7). However, trade liberalization has become an instrument for weakening the regulatory capacity of the state in a way that limits its ability to support vulnerable and impoverished social groups.

The question of rural employment following trade liberalization remains crucial. If imported products are part of a core consumption basket (such as basic foodstuffs and inexpensive clothing), the fall in prices resulting from liberalization should benefit low-income consumers both in rural and in urban areas. This is a traditional argument harnessed in favor of trade liberalization. But the other side of the coin is the employment that is often lost as a result of such liberalization. If there is structural unemployment in the economy, those workers who lose their paid jobs or self-employment as a result of competing imports may not find alternative employment. This may result in a conflict between the interests of the low-income consumers (those who have a minimum income to be buyers), and those workers whose jobs are imperiled by the imports. The perspective put forward in this chapter agrees with the one advanced by Lefeber (in Chapter 2) and favors maintaining certain trade protections at the expense of the low-income consumer on the grounds that the primary distributional question is not between high-income and low-income earners, but between *any* income earner and the unemployed.[11] In particular, this would apply to protection against imported products that compete with the peasant and artisan economy, as discussed in the next section.

Migration

Displacement and migration are common consequences of freer trade and encroaching large-estate commercial enterprises, particularly when they are implemented in the absence of policies that will effectively spread the benefits and protect those at risk. Experience demonstrates that urban centers and commercial agriculture are ill prepared to absorb the vast number of poor people in the countryside (Bailey 2000). World Bank economists predicted in 1992 that NAFTA-mandated liberalization of US corn imports into Mexico would cause an increase in migration from rural to urban areas of 700,000 peasants during the following decade (Levy and Wijnbergen 1992). Massive rural-urban migration can only be stemmed by rural development and, in particular, strategies that make it viable and attractive for small-scale farmers and rural workers to remain on their land—quite the contrary to the actual effects of "market-friendly" rural policies.

Food Security

Food security is a major concern in this context. In a world where 800 million people suffer from one or more forms of malnutrition (55 million in Latin America and the Caribbean), the issue of food security is paramount to rural development policy (FAO 2001, table 4). Those who advocate for industrial agriculture and freer markets, such as the USDA, believe that "trade liberalization has the potential to enhance developing countries' food-security position and reduce their food gap" by lowering world price levels and increasing export earnings (Trueblood and Shapouri 2001, 1–2). Thus, the question of food security is reduced to one of an adequate aggregate supply of food for a country, with food imports playing a key role in maintaining that supply. This approach is inadequate because it ignores the crucial role of subsistence and small-scale farming, locally and community-oriented economic activities, diversified rural employment, low-income purchasing power, and centrally administered food distribution in maintaining food security—all of which are undermined by neoliberal measures. This approach also fails to provide any protection against volatile changes in the costs of food imports. Once a country becomes dependent on food imports, it has no defense against sudden upward shifts in costs—for example, a sudden rise in oil costs will be reflected in higher transportation costs for agricultural commodities— all of which are ultimately passed down to consumers.

A recent international meeting of civil society organizations brought forward a different conception of food security:

> We recognise food security as the physical and economic access to adequate safe and healthy food by all people at all times in dignity. Key factors in realising food security are the issues of who produces food, where it is produced, what food is produced, how it is produced, as well as who controls trade and key productive resources, such as land, water, and biodiversity. Food Sovereignty to our countries and communities means having the democratic right and power to determine the production, distribution and consumption of food, according to our preferences and cultural traditions. Food security implies securing the livelihood of food producing communities.[12]

Needless to say, this conception leads to a skeptical evaluation of the impact of neoliberal policies and industrial agriculture on food security. Indeed, the accumulated experience of implementing such policies (some of which are summarized below) indicates that such policies have diminished the food security of impoverished rural populations (Madeley 1999, 2000).

It wasn't supposed to be that way. In the Rome Declaration on World Food Security (FAO 1996), the attending heads of state "reaffirm[ed] the right of everyone to have access to safe and nutritious food, consistent with the right to adequate food and the fundamental right of everyone to be free from hunger." In the Plan of Action these leaders recognized that "poverty eradication is essential to improve access to food" and that "poverty, hunger and malnutrition are . . . causes of accelerated migration from rural to urban areas." They also acknowledged the "need to reverse the recent neglect of investment in agriculture and rural development and mobilize sufficient investment resources to support sustainable food security and diversified rural development." Thus, the heads of state recognized the link between rural underdevelopment, poverty, and malnourishment, and the need for concerted action to improve the lives of rural dwellers, particularly in developing countries.

Unfortunately, the same heads of state undermined these efforts as they signed on to the UR agreements that created the WTO. These trade rules are creating an international regulatory framework that weakens state capacity to engage in such concerted action on rural development and food security. They are also having a direct impact on rural restructuring, as discussed in the next section. Many of these heads of state also engaged in neoliberal restructuring at the national level and placed higher domestic priority on protecting agribusiness interests than on protecting the livelihoods of rural populations. All these actions hamper the food security of both urban and rural populations. Thus it is not surprising that current trends are not propitious for achieving the goals of the World Food Summit, including the (unacceptably limited) goal of halving the number of undernourished people by 2015.

TRADE AGREEMENTS

A large number of international trade agreements were signed during the 1990s. Many of those agreements have an overall coherence of method and purpose, thus contributing to the articulation of a new regulatory framework for economic activity that is embedded in international treaties and hence insulated from parliamentary and other forms of democratic accountability. As noted above, this regulatory framework discourages the kind of policies that are required to deal with rural poverty and to achieve equitable and sustainable progress. The WTO's institutional features and its agreements reflect well the interests of those promoting an agribusiness model, as the negotiation process, rules, and dispute settlement mechanisms favor the large transnational actors. Moreover, because of the way they were negotiated and structured, the WTO agreements tend to disadvantage smaller and less developed countries, which had little say during the UR negotiations, as well as locally oriented small-scale producers, who simply cannot compete under the new trade arrangements. They also discourage rural diversification, which is mostly based on access to local markets, equitable landholding, and a flourishing economy of small-scale and community-based producers (Chapters 10 and 11).

Among the UR agreements, the Trade Related Intellectual Property Rights agreement (TRIPs) is particularly important. It compels signatory countries (following a transition period) to establish a US-style patent regime that is enforceable with trade sanctions (Shrybman 1999, 111–19). Serious concerns have been raised about the lack of recognition in TRIPs of the rights of indigenous and farming communities to genetic and biological resources held in common. Critics have also assailed its rules as authorizing the appropriation without compensation of traditional knowledge, for example, about medicinal plants. The TRIPs has also played a role in undermining efforts to regulate international trade in genetically modified organisms. Finally, concerns have been raised regarding adverse effects on the diversity of cultivated crops and on farmers' food security in developing countries.

The WTO's Agreement on Sanitary and Phytosanitary Measures (SPS) also deserves mention. It deals with laws and regulations regarding food and safety, covering pesticides and genetically modified organisms as well (Shrybman 1999, 50–52). In fact, the SPS has been a useful device for diluting government regulations that are unpopular with transnational corporations. Based on the SPS, the WTO has held that the *precautionary principle* is not a justifiable basis upon which to establish regulatory controls. This principle allows taking precautionary action to protect the public and the environment when risks warrant, even in the face of scientific uncertainty about the extent and nature of potential impacts. In the case of pesticides, the SPS has served to limit the allowable scope of protection and regulation, thus potentially endangering farmers, consumers, and others who come in contact with such substances.

Beyond the WTO, a host of bilateral and regional trade agreements are having an impact on agricultural trade and rural restructuring. The impacts are highly differentiated according to the specifics clauses of the agreements, and even within a country one must distinguish among regions and social groups that are affected. A common problem that crops up in even the "successes" of such agreements (generally referring to a successful experience in boosting exports) is low-cost imports or competition from corporations and large estates that destroy the livelihoods of small-scale producers. This has been the case in the Department of Santa Cruz in Bolivia, which has been favored by the Andean Pact with preferential tariffs that have helped to increase soybean and cotton exports but have diminished the food security of the population (Madeley 1999, case 8). Uruguay, in turn, has become a base for transnational food companies such as Parmalat and Nestlé that want to capture the large MERCOSUR market for dairy products. In the process, small-scale dairy producers in the west and south of Uruguay have been hurt (Madeley 2000, 44). And, as mentioned earlier, NAFTA has had a ruinous impact on corn growers in Mexico.

The WTO's Agreement on Agriculture (AoA) merits special attention. Adopted in 1994 under heavy US influence during the UR negotiations, this agreement has been a principal instrument for advancing trade liberalization in food and other agricultural products. It is an unbalanced agreement, with rules that seem designed to benefit a small group of transnational corporations and the large exporting countries. These corporations and nations benefit from a system of managed trade rules that selectively deregulates trade, liberalizes exports and imports, and allows the continued maintenance of export-support programs that favor them. There are three components to the AoA: domestic support, market access, and export subsidies.[13]

Domestic Support

The overall intent of this aspect of the AoA is to reduce, although not eliminate, government support for agriculture.[14] It calls for a 20 percent reduction in an Aggregate Measure of Support[15] within six years for developed countries and 13.3 percent over ten years in developing countries.[16] In theory, the reduction in domestic support should have been a significant victory for the developing countries. Their ability to compete has been continually undermined by expensive support programs to farmers in industrialized countries, particularly in the United States and the European Union, which have allowed Northern farmers to dump products on world markets.

In reality, a complex set of exemptions labeled the Green Box and the Blue Box have prevented any genuine liberalization or the building of a level playing field. These two "boxes" are lists of support programs for agriculture that are exempted from the reductions specified in the agreement. Inclusion of a program in that list means that governments can continue to maintain it without restrictions and without the threat of challenges from other countries. Green Box exemptions include programs that are most relevant to farmers in industrialized countries, such as some direct payments and income supports to producers that require significant fiscal expenditures. The Blue Box was created specifically to exempt direct payment programs with high levels of support in the United States and the European Union, such as the EU's Common Agricultural Policy.

All forms of support not exempted under the Green and Blue Boxes are subject to reductions in accordance to the percentages noted above. The reductions happen only if their level of support exceeds a certain threshold (the allowed "de-minimus" exemption). The impact of these restrictions on allowable agricultural policies for developing countries (and thus, for smallholder farmers in the South) is serious. These countries did not have the clout during the negotiations to protect their most important programs under the Green Box (in fact, they were largely marginalized from the negotiations for this Box).[17] Moreover, many developing countries claimed zero levels of support in the base year for domestic support (because they didn't have the resources to subsidize their agriculture, or their domestic support programs were cut under structural adjustment), thus permanently forfeiting policy discretion in this area.[18] This is the reason for the argument that the AoA reflects an imbalanced and "managed" trade—it institutionalizes existing agricultural support programs in the industrialized countries while prohibiting the future establishment of similar programs in developing countries.

Market Access

The AoA seeks to liberalize import regimes. In general, agricultural markets have been highly protected in both developed and developing countries. The AoA seeks to increase market access by

- *Reducing import tariffs:* All existing tariffs are bound (cannot be increased), and a global decrease in import tariffs is programmed: 36 percent for developed countries over six years and 24 percent for developing countries over ten years, with required minimum reductions for each product (tariff line).
- *"Tariffication" of all non-tariff barriers:* All non-tariff barriers such as import levies and import quotas are to be converted into simple tariffs, to which import tariff reduction rules will apply.
- *Tariff rate quotas:* Tariff rate quotas ensure a certain minimum level of market access. For each protected product, the tariff rate quota forces a country to offer a reduced tariff for a quantity specified in the AoA, so that imports can actually enter its market (Phillips 2000, 10–12).

The impact of these measures has been very uneven (Einarsson 2000, 13; Phillips 2000, 10–12). Developed countries in general have minimized the required reductions in border measures through clever positioning in the negotiations and by taking advantage of loopholes. Thus, producers from developing countries have not gained significant access to markets in developed countries. In fact, these countries have continued to restrict market access severely for agricultural products from the South—particularly those that compete with their own subsidized farm products.

Meanwhile, many developing countries lack negotiating capacity and have been hit with large inflows of low-priced imports, as explained below. Some of these countries have not even taken advantage of the existing rules; for example, many have allowed themselves to be bound with very low or zero tariffs (even when they were not required) and have thus forfeited policy choice in the future.

Export Subsidies

Export subsidies are government incentives to promote exports. The AoA requires a general reduction in export subsidies, with reductions of 36 percent in terms of expenditures over six years for developed countries and 24 percent over ten years for developing ones. The AoA also requires smaller percentage reductions in the quantities of subsidized exports over the same periods (21 and 14 percent, respectively) (Einarsson 2000, 13; Phillips 2000, 15–17). In practice, these reductions have had a very limited effect. For example, the European Union, the largest user of direct export subsidies, managed to make the reference point for its reductions the period from 1986 to 1988, when EU subsidies reached a historical high point. Moreover, the AoA only regulates *direct* export subsidies, exempting other forms of support that have the same subsidizing effect.

The general WTO position is that all export subsidies are unfair trade measures that should be prohibited. However, a noticeable exception was made for agriculture, where the AoA actually institutionalizes high export subsidies in the United States, the European Union, and other industrialized countries, keeping international prices artificially low. Export dumping has had a disruptive impact on developing countries and their food security, as we see next.

FAO Studies

The FAO conducted sixteen country case studies to document the experiences of developing countries with the implementation of the AoA and other UR agreements that affect agriculture (FAO 1999, 1–10).[19] Given the significance of this report, it is worth summarizing it in some detail.

The sixteen country studies demonstrated a close connection between neoliberal structural adjustment and the application of trade rules. They "revealed that none of the countries had to reformulate or re-instrument their domestic policies in order to comply with the . . . AoA." For a majority of countries, "the reform process under the AoA was a continuation of earlier reforms they had adopted under structural adjustment programmes (SAPs), regional agreements, or unilateral liberalisation programmes" (FAO 1999, 2). Thus, rather than introduce new policies, the AoA is serving to congeal post-SAPs agricultural policies, and, in practical terms, make them irreversible. This closure of democratic decision-making space for alternative rural policies is characteristic of the AoA and other trade treaties. We should not lose sight of the fact that these treaties are legally binding and have strong enforcement mechanisms behind them.

With regard to agricultural exports,

few studies reported improvements . . . in the post-UR period—
the typical finding was that there was little change in the volume
exported or in diversification of products and destinations. This
was perhaps to be expected in view of the gradual phasing-in nature of the AoA commitments on market access. (FAO 1999, 3)

In fact, traditional exports of the sample countries continued to follow
past trends. But many studies considered that prospects were good for
nontraditional products, notably fruit and vegetables.

In contrast to the export picture, "food imports were reported to be
rising rapidly . . . in the post-UR period" (FAO 1999, 4). In Guyana, for
example, imports of food and live animals almost doubled between 1994
and 1998. There is a concern that, without adequate domestic market
protection and appropriate agricultural development, local production
of many commodities in Guyana will be hurt and the domestic diet will
increasingly shift toward greater dependence on imported food products.

In summary, there was an asymmetry in the experience between growing food imports and slow-moving agricultural exports. Significant sup-
ply-side constraints prevented many countries from taking advantage of
increased global market access. WTO actions also contributed to the
closure of some markets. For example, Jamaica experienced a significant
increase in agricultural imports as liberalization evolved during the 1980s
and 1990s. However, the most dramatic impact on Jamaican agriculture
came from the WTO rulings that undermined the EU banana regime,
which was based on the preferential arrangements of the Lomé Convention that allowed Jamaica to export its bananas to Europe at prices above
those that prevailed in the world market.[20]

In terms of the overall economic results, the 1999 FAO study stated
that it is still too early to assess fully the long-term impact of the AoA.
Common reported concerns, however, were consistent with issues raised
earlier, such as a general trend toward the concentration of farmland in a
wide cross-section of countries. "While this [liberalization] led to increased productivity and competitiveness with positive results, in the virtual absence of social safety-nets, the process also marginalised small-
scale producers and added to unemployment and poverty" (FAO 1999,
4).

Implementation

Despite the claim that the AoA was a balanced agreement that required
concessions from all groups of countries, the actual experience since 1995
demonstrates that costs and benefits have been highly skewed in favor of
the rich and the large exporting countries. As discussed earlier, many Southern governments implemented SAP measures to liberalize agricultural

imports and dismantle protection for domestic agricultural production; now they are set permanently in place by the AoA. Thus, the trade treaty has served to forfeit essential policy options for poor countries.

In contrast, the practice of export dumping by rich industrialized countries has continued unabated despite the AoA. Large domestic support and export subsidies in those countries promote the dumping phenomenon because they allow their farmers to sell produce at such low prices. In the OECD countries, state support for the agricultural sector exceeds Africa's entire GDP. And the combined domestic support in the United States, the European Union, and Japan accounts for about 80 percent of the world total. The expectation that the AoA would bring drastic reductions in such subsidies was never realized; rather, what has happened is that rich countries have moved to adapt their support programs to make them more compatible with AoA requirements. The US 1996 Farm Bill and the reform of the EU's Common Agricultural Policy both took steps in that direction. In the meantime, support continues to grow; such is the case with the so-called emergency assistance to US farmers that rose from $1.8 billion in 1998 to $7.6 billion in 2000 (*The Economist* 2001). In the ensuing policy debate, there has been no recognition that the resulting international prices are highly skewed as a result of such subsidies and dumping.

Protectionism in the wealthier countries remains an exasperating issue. As *The Economist* recognizes, "The market access they [developing countries] were promised after the Uruguay Round has not materialized" (2001). Japan's duties on most grains average about 63 percent, but a recently installed rice tariff is closer to 1,000 percent. In the European Union the prices of lamb, butter, rice, and sugar are all at least twice the world market price. These price differences (and the subsidies that make them possible) are not inconsequential—poor countries would benefit each year by more than three times the amount of all overseas development assistance if they were to be eliminated (*The Economist* 2001). Developing countries complain that market access to large Northern markets for their products continues to be hindered by tariff "peaks" and "escalations," as well as other forms of protectionism such as anti-dumping and "safeguard" measures.[21]

These concerns are part of a broader problem of imbalances and asymmetries that have characterized what developing countries see as the one-sided implementation of the UR agreements. The agreements have imposed large costs, particularly on food-dependent less developed countries, which have seen jumps in their bill for rapidly rising food imports, while benefiting little from expanded market access in the North. These are generically referred to as the "implementation issues" that Southern countries are pursuing, without much success (Smith 2000; Bridges 2001).[22] Moreover, the WTO is moving ahead with new negotiations on agriculture. The AoA is part of the WTO's so-called built-in agenda, which includes new negotiations that started in March 2000 aimed at achieving an expanded agreement. Many developing countries, which only recently have begun to understand the impact of the earlier round, are not prepared to face a new round of negotiations. Given the shortcomings of the 1994 agreement, it is essential that an evaluation of its implementation be carried out, focusing on its impact on subsistence agriculture, food security, poverty, human development, and ecological sustainability, and on the least developed countries in particular.

There have been numerous proposals from developing countries for substantial changes and additions to the AoA that would address problems of poverty, sustainable development, and food security. One proposal has been to create various derogations for developing countries. Referred to as the Food Security Box or the Development Box, the measures in question would be aimed at improving the ability of developing countries to protect their domestic food production and markets. For example, measures would include exemptions from tariff reductions and minimum market access requirements, as well as the right to increase internal support until a higher level of self-sufficiency is achieved. The Development Box idea was formally tabled in the WTO Committee on Agriculture by a group of developing countries. NGOs, including many from developed countries, have supported this proposal.[23] The WTO ministerial meeting in Doha, Qatar, in November 2001 was extremely disappointing for developing countries and civil society organizations, since the proposal for a Development Box was basically ignored under pressure from the industrialized countries. With the launch of a new round of multilateral negotiations following Doha, the agricultural negotiations have become a key component, under conditions that are not propitious for positive reform of the AoA.[24]

CONCLUSION

Deepening rural poverty in many parts of the world represents one of the most important failures of public policy today. Vital problems that attract policymakers' attention—such as food insecurity, social unrest, environmental degradation, urban poverty, drug trafficking, marginalization of indigenous peoples, illegal migration, deteriorating human security, and civil wars—all have common roots, in one way or another, in rural poverty and underdevelopment. The most important development goal, endorsed in September 2000 at the UN Millennium Summit, was to halve the number of people living in extreme income poverty in the world by 2015. But, as the UNDP has recently warned, we are not on track to meet even this modest goal, in large part because of the failure to improve the conditions of the most vulnerable rural dwellers living in the poorest countries (2001, 23).

In this chapter I have focused on international trading arrangements and their negative impact on inclusive and sustainable rural advancement. The intent has been to explore the intricate international interface of rural development policies. In the first place, I have argued that new multilateral trade rules—and also some regional trade agreements—are being negotiated in an exclusionary fashion, without considering the interests of, and impacts on, the majority of the world's population. The trade and investment regime is becoming an important addition to the various conditionality frameworks that are restricting the scope of public policy by intruding into areas that until recently were considered strictly domestic and by giving additional power to transnational capital (Grinspun and Kreklewich 1994). New regulatory frameworks, such as the General Agreement on Trade in Services, are attempting to reshape the role of the state, reducing its ability to provide public services and to enable local development initiatives. In doing so, those agreements are redefining public policy in ways that are detrimental for the possibilities of socially and environmentally sustainable development.

In the second place, a set of rules for agricultural trade institutionalized in the WTO, primarily the AoA, are creating the conditions for the expansion of a global food and agricultural market dominated by a group of corporate giants. Corporate agribusiness, with its technological know-how, financial acumen, and powerful national and international allies, is intent on strengthening its foothold in less developed countries and accelerating the restructuring of the rural economy. The agricultural negotiations in the WTO embody everything that is wrong about the current trade regime—secretive negotiations, undue influence from powerful economic interests, and the dominant role of selected Northern countries. Meanwhile, the interests of developing countries, with the exception of a few large exporters, are ignored. Despite serious concerns about the impact of the AoA on developing countries, new negotiations are under way to strengthen this trade treaty, rejecting the calls for an evaluation of its implementation to date. The aggressive effort in Doha and since Doha to launch a broad round of multilateral negotiations ignores the concerns of many developing countries, and it is likely to hurt the interests of rural populations in the South.

There is a great deal of evidence concerning the impacts of SAPs, "free trade," and "market friendly" policies on rural conditions, that contradicts the rosy scenarios promoted by the centers of power in the North. Currently, an additional layer of conditionality is being promoted through new trade rules, whose negative effects are just now becoming evident. Governments in the South, NGOs, social movements, and critical academics have responded with detailed proposals for reform that have been put forward in almost every area of international policy, such as the earlier mentioned Development Box within the context of the renegotiation of the AoA in the WTO. These proposals are based on a recognition of the limits of both markets and states, and in the belief that rational reform of global institutions is feasible, so that trade, investment, and other international rules of behavior become facilitators and not obstacles to shared development goals. These proposals embody a vision of rural society that is distinct from the one advanced by agribusiness interests, one that recognizes the role of food security, small-scale farms, diversified economic activity, community involvement, appropriate technology, and sustainable development. It also calls for active governmental support through an array of policies, including trade protection, land reform, public works, public health and education, and appropriate macroeconomic policies.

Notes

[1] I am not proposing that trade arrangements and neoliberal policies are in each and every case a determining factor of rural progress or decay. The actual processes of change in rural society are complex, as multiple influences and forces (local, domestic, and international) mix and interplay.

[2] The analysis in this chapter is mostly relevant to crop and livestock production, as well as to rural economic diversification (small-scale manufacturing and value-added operations, such as food processing). The emphasis on agriculture should be placed in proper context, as most peasants (at least in highland regions of the Andean countries), may obtain less than half of their income from agriculture (see Chapter 5).

[3] These effects have to do with relative prices of agricultural products, as well as with efficiency considerations in terms of the allocation of factors of production.

[4] The foremost demand of peasant families remains access to and ownership of productive land. But in a context of failed agrarian reforms and of increasing concentration in landownership, access to employment—any type of rural employment—remains essential to survival.

[5] Agricultural production for export, under appropriate institutional arrangements, can contribute to an integrated approach to rural development. Such is the case with "fair trade" conducted by organizations that sell coffee produced on an associational basis by small-scale farmers in the South (SEL 2001, 32; Waridel 2002, 99–104). Thus, a critical evaluation of the current structures and rules set up to manage international trade does not constitute a rejection of international trade as such and is certainly not a call for autarchy or economic isolation (Lefeber 1992).

[6] This paragraph and the next one draw on Ritchie et al. 1999, 5–9.

[7] Price competition promotes economic efficiency only in abstract neoclassical models, under highly unrealistic assumptions (Lefeber 1992, 216–17).

[8] Small-scale farmers also create pollution and salination, but they do not have access to large quantities of polluting chemical substances (pesticides, herbicides, and fertilizers).

⁹ Some beneficial economies of scale can be achieved through the cooperative organization of small-scale producers.

¹⁰ "Dumping" is the practice of exporting products at a price below production cost, which severely undercuts the price of local products in importing countries.

¹¹ Of course, this is a trade-off that must be evaluated in each case according to the circumstances. For further discussion of the relationship between trade liberalization and rural employment, see Lefeber 1997.

¹² The *Zeist Declaration on Trade Liberalization and the Right to Food*, quoted in Madeley 1999.

¹³ This schematic presentation of the AoA is based on Einarsson 2000, 13, 23–25; Shiva 2000, 103–108; and particularly Phillips 2000, 10–17.

¹⁴ This discussion of domestic support draws on Phillips 2000, 12–14.

¹⁵ The Aggregate Measure of Support includes all domestic support mechanisms. Based on the so-called PSE (Producer Subsidy Equivalents) measure, it is a method of translating all forms of agricultural support to a monetary equivalent. Critics have argued that it provides a poor measure of actual government support to farmers (Einarsson 2000, 23).

¹⁶ The "least-developed countries" are exempt from most AoA provisions, but they still have suffered indirect impacts.

¹⁷ Programs that are important to address food security and to preserve the viability of rural employment include subsidized credit and input subsidies for low-income and resource-poor producers. These and other measures that support small-scale producers, as well as increased domestic production of staple crops for domestic consumption, were largely omitted from the Green Box and thus are not protected by the agreement (Priyadarshi 2001, 7).

¹⁸ If a country has claimed a zero level in the base year for domestic support, it cannot establish new forms of support in the future beyond the de-minimus level, with the exception of certain investment and input subsidies (Josling 1999, 8).

¹⁹ The countries surveyed were Bangladesh, Botswana, Brazil, Egypt, Fiji, Guyana, India, Jamaica, Kenya, Morocco, Pakistan, Peru, Senegal, Sri Lanka, Tanzania, and Thailand.

²⁰ The Lomé Convention provides preferential access to the European Union for a group of more than seventy former colonies (referred to as African, Caribbean, and Pacific Group of States).

²¹ Tariff "peaks" are relatively high tariffs on "sensitive" products. Tariff "escalation" refers to higher import duties on semi-processed products than on raw materials, and higher still on finished products. "Anti-dumping" measures provide protection in cases where foreign dumping causes serious injury to domestic industry. "Safeguard" measures provide protection in cases where the cause of injury is a significant rise in imports.

²² Most important is the 1994 Marrakesh Decision in which developed countries agreed to offer assistance to least developed and net food-importing countries that might face negative effects from the implementation of the AoA. That assistance became more critical as food-import bills rose, but, in practice, the decision was not implemented.

²³ Evaluations of the AoA and proposals for ongoing renegotiation of this agreement can be found in several sources (Phillips 2000; Ritchie et al. 1999; Einarsson

2000; Shiva 2000; Stevens et al. 2001; Green and Priyadarshi 2001). However, not all believe the AoA can be reformed. During the Seattle protests, Via Campesina, a broad North-South coalition of farmers, called for taking agriculture out of the WTO.

[24] In the Doha ministerial declaration there was only a token acknowledgment of the need to review implementation issues, and although there was some language on the phasing out of agricultural subsidies, it was watered down by pressures from the European Union (Bello and Mittal 2001).

Part II

POLICY CHOICES, POLICY IMPACTS: ECUADOR IN COMPARATIVE PERSPECTIVE

∾ ∾

Chapter 4

Agriculture and Rural Development

A Critique of Establishmentarian Policies in Ecuador

Louis Lefeber

The approach to neoliberal stabilization in Ecuador has been essentially similar to that adopted elsewhere in the hemisphere: reduction of the public sector and the deficit, freeing markets from government controls, privatization, liberalization of capital markets, devaluation, and movement toward free trade. The supporting arguments rest on their supposed beneficial economic effects, the implicit assumption being that whatever promotes economic growth also advances democracy and social welfare. These are strongly ideological arguments, which are further reinforced by an underlying dualistic, not to say, Manichean principle: market-based decisions and policies that promote outward or trade orientation are intrinsically good, and market controls and policies for the promotion of inward, or domestic market orientation, are intrinsically bad. In other words, the neoliberal position places an all-pervading emphasis on trade orientation. Export based development is assumed to have a trickle-down effect, which would naturally benefit the working population and lower income classes. The argument continues to live on, even though some of the original promoters of this ideology, the World Bank in particular, have by now qualified their ideas in this respect.

This paper is based on an earlier version published in Spanish in *Ecuador Debate* (Lefeber 1998) and as a chapter in Martínez 2000c. As such, it refers to a period preceding the dollarization of the Ecuadorian monetary system, which has further aggravated the already manifest problems caused by structural adjustment programs.

The neoliberal argument covers a broad range of macroeconomic and microeconomic policies, but in what follows, I concentrate on those issues that relate more directly to what I believe to be the basic policy problems of agricultural development in Ecuador. I should also point out that even though I disagree with assigning a central role of export orientation in promoting development, or any downplaying of the importance of the role of governments and market controls, I recognize that some of the concerns about the inefficiencies of certain economic policies cannot be dismissed just because the neoliberals are also critical of them. My disagreement is not with the view that there are problems in need of solution, but with the particular neoliberal approaches to a solution.[1]

Focus on the development of domestic markets should not imply a neglect of trade. Policies for encouraging exports are important for generating foreign exchange for needed imports and meeting debt obligations. One also has to recognize the adverse effects of the excessive and frequently contradictory set of controls that has characterized the Ecuadorian economy in general and its agricultural sector in particular. Some of these controls were instituted because of an inadequate understanding of the workings of the economy, and others for the explicit or implicit defense of particular interests. Furthermore, there can be no rational justification for the type of import substitution that followed from a misapplication of the Prebish/Singer thesis of development, or those subsidies for public services and other activities that are provided not for enhancing the productivity or the improvement of social services, such as education, public health or public housing, but because of a lack of both interest and political will to resist pressures from particular interest groups.

It also has to be recognized that markets have a positive socioeconomic function in the organization of the economy but, to paraphrase the late Indian economist Sukhamoy Chakravarty, markets must not be the masters but the servants of the public interest. This calls, among other things, for government action actively to raise the purchasing power of the lower-income classes and intelligent uses of controls, as was done first in Japan and then South Korea and Taiwan (Lefeber 1992).

THE EVIDENCE OF ASIAN DEVELOPMENT

The suggested prototypes of successful export-based development, Korea and Taiwan, have actually developed under conditions that included trade orientation as only one component of a complex set of initial factors. Primary among these was the improvement of income distribution, that is, growth of low-income purchasing power, brought about by conscious government policies, such as land reform. In Japan it was the breakdown of the highly concentrated feudal landownership and incomes corresponding to its military-industrial economic structure that made possible the postwar change to a broadly based domestic market and trade development. This has been reinforced by subsidies provided for the maintenance of the traditional sectors, which continue to make up a significant part of its economy.

An important lesson is how changes in ownership patterns and income and wealth distribution change the socioeconomic power structure. They undercut the economic and political power base of the landowning and other dominant classes that hinder democratic development processes. They also change the structure of demand from luxuries to basic mass consumption.

Japan and the successful so-called Asian Tigers have made effective use of the market while also maintaining strong direct and indirect controls on trade and investment (see, e.g., Bienefeld 1988; Evans 1987). In Japan and South Korea, and to some extent also Taiwan, the financing of economic development has been essentially from domestic sources through state-supported credit. And even though the recent market collapses have affected all the Asian market economies, those that failed to improve their skewed income distributions and did not develop institutions for maintaining effective controls on investment and trade—for example, Indonesia and the Philippines—have experienced greater difficulties in rebuilding their economies than those that have solidly established domestic markets. Of course, the conditions for financial support dictated by the IMF—austerity and dismantling domestic market controls—have further aggravated the current problems of the Asian economies.[2]

Even with the prevailing trend to globalization, the primary source of demand has to be domestic rather than international. This is because domestic demand is subject primarily to domestic controls and domestic purchasing power rather than uncontrollable international demand fluctuations.[3]

THE EVIDENCE OF ECUADOR

The initial moves to liberalize the Ecuadorian economy—in particular, efforts to liberalize trade—were instituted during the Borja presidency (1988–92). But it was under the Durán Ballén government (1992–96) that major macroeconomic and sectoral reforms were undertaken, even though they did not quite measure up to neoliberal expectations. Nonetheless, it was claimed that the economy responded favorably.[4] The rate of inflation diminished by 60 percent over the period between 1992 and 1996, while the economy grew at an average rate of 3.2 percent between 1988 and 1995. Exports, with growing participation by industrial and nontraditional agricultural products, increased at a rate of about 13 percent during the period. But the bulk of this growth continued to come from primary agricultural products, representing nearly 50 percent of total exports.

According to the indicators of the World Bank's *World Development Report 1997* (table 11) the annual growth rate of agriculture was 4.4 percent for 1980–90 and 2.5 percent for 1990–95. It is noteworthy that *the average annual growth rate of agriculture actually fell* in the period in which SAPs were introduced. There was a notable growth of certain activities, such as flower exports and processed foods, but that reflects the fact that in absolute terms both started from very low initial levels.

The sectoral growth of agriculture improved in 1995, a fact that neoliberals attribute to the beneficial effects of liberalization. It is more likely, however, that it was a previously depressed market's response to a rapid increase in US import demand and the broadening of the Andean markets. In any case, neither the growth of flower exports and processed food nor 1995's better performance affected agriculture's relative share in the distribution of GDP: the sector's value added was 12 percent of GDP in 1980, and was still 12 percent in 1995 (World Bank 1997, table 15). This, taken together with the available population and labor statistics, is an indication of a fundamental policy failure.

While the population increase was an annual 2.5 percent during 1980–90, and 2.2 for 1990–95, during the same periods the labor force grew by 3.5 and 3.2 percent, respectively. However, the corresponding increase in labor-force participation rates cannot be ascribed to increased employment opportunities. The statistics of poverty suggest that the growth of the participation rate was most likely indicative of a need to search for additional income-earning opportunities by persons (family members) who previously had not been members of the active labor force.

Per capita incomes have increased marginally, but overall productivity, measured by the ratio of total labor force to output, did not. Furthermore, in 1994 the above cited 12 percent of agriculture's share of GDP was produced by 37.8 percent of the total labor force. At the same time, the proportion in the informal sector was 25.7 percent of the total labor force. Taking the two sectors together, 63.5 percent of the labor force was engaged in low-productivity activities; hence, the median had to remain significantly under the per capita income level.[5]

The statistics of income and consumption distribution confirm this conclusion. In 1994, with a Gini index of inequality of 46.6 percent,[6] the share of consumption of the lowest 10 percent of the population was 2.3 percent, and that of the lowest quintile 5.4 percent of the national total (World Bank 1997, table 5; see also Larrea et al. 1996; Larrea 1998a). Given that most persons in the lowest income groups are rural residents, the level of rural poverty, as confirmed by the World Bank's *Ecuador Poverty Report*, has been significantly worse than the poverty in urban areas. Not surprisingly, the excessive hardship of rural life motivated a high rate of migration to urban areas. This is confirmed by the rapid rate of urban population growth between 1980 and 1995. This was at an annual average of 3.9 percent, a figure that is significantly higher than the average growth rates of the population over the same period (World Bank 1997, table 9).

Even under the best of circumstances urban development could not advance at a sufficiently rapid rate to absorb this level of rural migration in reasonably high-productivity activities. Without adequate income-earning opportunities, unemployed or underemployed migrants were bound to become financially dependent on family, wards of municipal governments or, as the growing urban crime rates indicate, in some cases criminals. Accordingly, the failure to develop a broad-based program for rural development has had a significant social cost. That social cost, which is measurable, should be taken into account in policy decisions concerning resource allocation between urban and rural areas (Lefeber 1997).

The continuing social and economic problems are not due to the government's failure to implement fully the so-called stabilization program that was first promised by the Durán Ballén government. Doing so would have amounted to a shock treatment, the hardship of which would have gone much beyond the tolerance of any democratic polity. The consequent destruction of traditional forms of rural and artisan production would have caused very great, possibly explosive increases in joblessness and underemployment. The resulting social instability could have turned into class war, with unpredictable consequences.

In reality, such policies could be implemented only by totalitarian means, as was the case in Chile, where social protest was suppressed by military and police power. In any case, the social costs of drastic neoliberal restructuring are immediate and very high, and the initial economic repercussions may very well be negative.[7]

It is undeniable that for broad-based social and economic development the structure of Ecuador's economy needs to be changed. Change is called for, if for no other reason than that the current structure is not conducive to growth with equity, that is, growth that is compatible with the betterment of basic living standards. The prevailing less than 1 percent annual growth of the per capita income would take over seventy years to double. If the relationship between per capita and median incomes were to remain unchanged, the median too would require the same amount of time to double. But, due to the effects of neoliberal policies, the gap between the two can be expected to widen over time.

This is obviously unacceptable. Growth has to be accelerated, and the relationship between per capita and median incomes must be changed in favor of the latter. In other words, massive income redistribution is needed.

Effective change will not come about by completing the implementation of the Durán Ballén government's originally proposed reform package. This is not to say that the elimination of certain types of subsidies and socially regressive government expenditures does not merit consideration. In the longer run, per capita and median incomes cannot be increased, and social stability cannot be maintained by democratic means without a sustainable relationship between productivity growth and budgetary and trade deficits. If the productivity growth is sufficiently high, the economy can, as it were, grow out of temporal deficits of both kinds. The question is, then, how to generate equitable productivity growth on a sufficiently broad scale to bring about the desired result.

The neoliberal prescription—the Washington Consensus—calls for a rapid move toward deficit elimination and other unemployment creating reforms as prerequisites of productivity growth. The corresponding causal sequence would lead to instant economic depression, which is the polar opposite of what is required for development with equity.[8]

Instead, the approach to restructuring would have to permit a gradual transfer of labor from low-productivity to higher-productivity activities without destroying or undercutting the limited economic base of the lowest income groups. The latter being made up primarily of rural or rural-urban migrants, the effort would naturally have to focus on rebuilding the rural economy. This, in turn, would require an understanding of the interaction among the various sectoral social, political, and economic factors, and first and foremost, on political will (Lefeber 1974a and 1974b).

THE PROBLEM OF AGRICULTURE

Agriculture plays an important role in the Ecuadorian economy, a fact that is also recognized by neoliberal policy critics.[9] The sector straddles the coastal (Costa), the mountain (Sierra), and the low-lying eastern (Amazonas) regions. It employs about 40 percent of the labor force, generates nearly 50 percent of foreign exchange, and produces a wide range of goods for domestic consumption and industrial use. Nonetheless, with some exceptions the sector's efficiency is not commensurate to its importance for the economy. As mentioned above, its value added has been 12 percent of the country's GDP.

Evidently the combined effects of population growth and poverty have placed great pressure on the availability of even marginally suitable land for farming and/or animal husbandry. The areas cultivated have increased to the point where by 1990 practically all high-quality land as well as most marginal lands were brought into production.

The extension of cultivation to marginal lands—including protected public lands—has had high social costs and low average yields. Among other things, the government has had only very limited control over the use of protected public lands. The private costs of colonization and exploitation of public lands have been small relative to the costs of increasing the productivity of the already cultivated lands. However, the social costs in terms of the damage caused to the ecology have been much higher.

Compared to other Latin American countries, overall productivity has been low in a broad range of farm outputs. Yields have primarily increased in production for export markets (banana and coffee), while with some exceptions they have diminished for products for domestic consumption. The increases of 1.4, 0.8, and 1.9 percent in rice, potato, and hard corn production were below the population growth rate.

Most of the growth in staple production has come from the extension of cultivation to additional lands instead of productivity growth. This has not changed with the introduction of neoliberal market policies. It is a fact that the earlier, more restrictive macroeconomic and sectoral policies had resulted in low prices and significantly reduced incentives. But even after the introduction of neoliberal reforms, the scientific base has remained inadequate, and farmers have only limited access to improved techniques. There has been insufficient investment in research, extension services, and human capital.

POLICY CONSIDERATIONS
FOR COMMERCIAL AGRICULTURE

All these important facts call for careful consideration. In the process, one must differentiate between the conditions and requirements of commercial-farm sectors and those of marginal farming. In what follows, I classify as commercial all those farms that sell a substantial part of their outputs in the monetized, commercial markets, and consider all others as marginal farms.

The neoliberals are not alone in recognizing that in a market economy the commercial-farm sector requires a price policy that ensures sufficiently high real returns to motivate producers to undertake the investments needed for increasing productivity. The real terms of trade between the industrial sectors (including imported inputs) and agriculture would have to favor the latter. In reality, the outcome has been the reverse.

Furthermore, the returns would have to be high enough to provide a margin of security against the risks and uncertainties caused by the vagaries of both nature and markets. The capacity to bear risk increases with the size of the farm operation and access to credit. But the adoption of new technologies that may require increased use of capital and industrial inputs, that is, the willingness to bear risk, is a function of expectations with respect to profitability.

The adoption of new technologies may be a two-edged sword. The demand for labor may not increase commensurately with productivity growth, and in many instances it may even decrease.[10] If urban-industrial development is not capable of absorbing the growth of rural surplus labor, and if there are no suitable government policies for employment creation, then unemployment, underemployment, and the marginal-farm sector are bound to increase.[11] Marginal farmers have, of course, neither capital nor capacity for risk bearing; hence, they cannot be counted on to undertake investments based on their own resources.

In reality, in response to the SAPs of the Durán Ballén government, real returns to commercial farmers fell significantly. Between 1993 and 1995 the prices of fertilizers increased precipitously, while prices for a broad range of farm products declined. Prices of products for domestic consumption were particularly affected. While price decreases for tradeables contributed to increasing exports, commercial-farm production for domestic consumption suffered. Hence, output increases—whatever they amounted to—were mostly due to the expansion of subsistence farming to marginal lands.

THE NEED FOR IMPROVED INCOME DISTRIBUTION

The sources and strength of the demand for domestic staple consumption are the crux of the matter. Even the neoliberal Whitaker report recognizes that the fall in prices of products for domestic use reflects the low rate of income growth and the low income elasticities of staple consumption. But the low income growth has been a consequence of the type of SAPs that have significantly augmented unemployment and the immiseration of the already poor working classes. The demand for domestically produced staples is a function of the purchasing power of the low-income population. It was undercut by the policies for the specific purpose of restricting domestic demand. Here lies a dilemma that neoliberal policymakers cannot resolve.

The income elasticities of demand for staples, as measured over all income classes, appear to be low only as long as the current inequality of income distribution remains unchanged. The middle classes and workers in stable employment have indeed relatively low income elasticities for basic farm products. Policies that increase the incomes of stable income earners will not translate into significant increases in the demand for staples. But this is not the case for the impecunious poor, who are badly in need of improving their basic nutrition. Give them purchasing power and they will become buyers of staples. Their income elasticity for staple consumption is, if not one, near to one.

The development of commercial agriculture is evidently a central concern of the Ecuadorian government and its domestic and foreign advisers. Hence, the Ecuadorian policymakers and their advisers will have to confront this fundamental reality: There is no price policy that can maintain stable market prices for staples, and adequate market returns to staple producers, without first ensuring adequate demand by domestic consumers. Lest this statement be dismissed as one that is ideologically motivated, it is a basic proposition that conforms to the theoretical analyses and empirical observations of the workings of any and all types of market economies. And the problem of absorption cannot be ignored even in socialist economies.

Of course, stable floor prices that guarantee minimum acceptable returns and protection against the vagaries of markets can be maintained by the government. That would motivate increased levels of commercial staple production for domestic use. But that raises again the question of absorption, which cannot be resolved without improved access to the markets by the undernourished poor.[12] It follows that, one way or another, income distribution lies at the heart of the problem. Expectations based on shop-worn ideas of trickle-down theories only delay the application of policies that would put purchasing power in the hands of the needy.

POLICY CONSIDERATIONS
FOR THE MARGINAL-FARM SECTOR

The problems of marginalization and the marginal-farm sector require direct government intervention. The neoliberal ideological commitment to minimizing government expenditures and direct intervention in the economy does not recognize that policies that may advance the development of commercial agriculture are mostly irrelevant to the marginal farm sector.[13] Nor does it recognize that the adoption of new technologies in commercial farming may cause displacement of labor. This has been the case in Mexico, for example, where the intrusion of multinational companies into export-oriented farm production has resulted in increased capital intensities and reduced employment (Lefeber 1997). In alternative cases, where high labor intensity has been retained by advanced commercial producers, for example, in the consolidation of the Chilean fruit-export sector by the multinationals, low wages, unstable seasonal work with no benefits, and high incidence of agro-chemical poisoning has kept the workers (fruit pickers) at the margin of existence (Swift 1977).

Whether it is substitution of capital for labor or unacceptably adverse working conditions, the advancement of commercial agriculture may very well lead to, or be paralleled by, a process of marginalization. This is not an argument against suitable policies that encourage the growth of the commercial-farm sector, but a recognition of the need to institute measures that counteract the deleterious side effects of the growth of commercial agriculture, such as the indiscriminate use of chemical inputs and labor displacement due to highly capital-intensive technologies.

Marginalization, the extension of subsistence farming into marginal lands with unstable soil conditions and the consequent destruction, can be reversed only by effective policies for the improvement of income distribution.

The prevailing tax system and the implementation of tax laws can undoubtedly be made more efficient and also more equitable. Nonetheless, the primary means for the improvement of income distribution are not direct transfers of income. They consist of wealth redistribution in the form of land reform and various measures that increase the demand for labor in wage and self-employment with acceptable minimum earning power. Access to credit, technical support, education, and health services has to be part of the package.

LAND REFORM
AND COOPERATIVE RURAL DEVELOPMENT

For establishing the preconditions for rural development, land reform has to play a central role. This is particularly true for Ecuador, where, in spite of several past land-reform efforts, the distribution of landownership has remained shockingly skewed. In 1994 the Gini coefficient of land operated in the rural areas of Ecuador was a very high 0.86 (and 0.89 in terms of land owned). In the Sierra 1.6 percent of the farms occupied 42.9 percent of the land, and in the Costa 3.9 percent commanded 55.1 percent of the land (World Bank 1995, 2:105–6). In view of the continuing increase of marginal farming, the statistics of land distribution could not have improved since then.

Even though the neoliberals recognize the existence of unemployment, poverty, and the private and social costs of encroachment on marginal and protected lands, they roundly condemn the Borja government's efforts in 1991 and 1992 to break up some of the large landholdings (Whitaker et al. 1996). At the same time, they also dismiss collective and cooperative farming as relatively unproductive.

The Borja government's efforts can indeed be faulted, but for reasons other than the neoliberal arguments against land reform. The intention was correct, but the planning and execution were faulty. The invasions, forcible occupations, and sales of some large estates, and the resulting insecurities, were the consequence of delays and inadequate plans for redistribution, as well as ineffectual implementation. It should have been understood that if the expectations of the landless are raised and then frustrated, the natural consequence is a disorderly and potentially violent response.

Plans have to be properly prepared and implemented without undue delay if disorder is to be avoided. Furthermore, the necessary infrastructure and basic capital must also be provided along with transfer of land-ownership to the beneficiaries, that is, to individual (family) owners or, depending on specific local conditions, some form of cooperative organization.[14]

The experience in various parts of Ecuador indicates that small landownership structures are also conducive to, or even a precondition of, rural small-industrial development. If some of the returns can be secured for the establishment of communally owned and operated enterprises, or the land can serve as security to lenders and/or a hedge against the potential failure of some small industrial investment, the income from farming can be supplemented with industrial employment (Chapters 10 and 11).

As with the case of land reform, cooperatives also have to be planned carefully and structured according to the particular purposes they are expected to serve. They work best in areas that have already established commercial experience, which is the case in most areas in the Sierra and the Costa. Nonetheless, their initial organization may require strong and dedicated leadership. If well organized, cooperatives can be very successful. In Hungary they turned the country into the bread basket and tourist center of the former Warsaw Pact countries. In turn, the subsequent liquidation of the cooperatives resulted in a drastic fall of productivity and output. The successes of the cooperatives in the district of Comilla in the former East Pakistan is well documented. Mondragón in the Basque region of Spain is justly famous. But there are also others, as in Taiwan, or in the Indian state of Maharashtra, to mention a few.[15]

In this connection it should also be emphasized that cooperative organizations or movements are not inconsistent with market-based development, even though they work outside the framework of the rampant individualism characteristic of North American capitalism. Incidentally, the institution of the Ecuadorian *gremios de productores agropecuarios* is just one step removed from cooperative organizations, and many of their actual and potential functions overlap with the latter. Curiously, and quite inconsistently, neoliberal critics of cooperatives who are against cooperative organizations favor strengthening the institution of *gremios*.[16]

Whether the beneficiaries of land reform preferred to farm as individual family units, or within a cooperative framework, the reform itself would significantly contribute to the relief of poverty and unemployment. It has been well established that labor intensity and productivity are inversely proportional to size of landholding (Sen 1964). Unemployment would decrease even if the heightened labor intensity were to be mostly due to the employment of family members, because they would cease competing for work in local or urban labor markets.

PUBLIC WORKS

Neoliberal policymakers do not subscribe to the use of government for employment creation. And they would be entirely in the right if such government expenditures amounted to nothing more than "make-work" for political or even humanitarian purposes. Public works for pyramid building, while not recommended, can nonetheless be acceptable under Keynesian conditions of market failure, when the means (capital and other resources) exist for full-employment production. But in cases of surplus labor, when the private sector does not have the means for employing the potential labor force, public works for productive investment is the only alternative to sustained rural unemployment.[17]

Agriculture in general, and the subsistence-farm sector in particular, provide ample scope for productive public works, including community projects for a wide variety of locally generated productive services. But in the narrow technical sense, the primary requirement for crop enhancement is water control, that is, terracing, irrigation, and drainage. These are infrastructure works that enhance productivity and directly contribute to soil conservation. The measure of enhanced productivity is the increase in the output of the farms or regions targeted by public works.

To the extent possible, the use of imported inputs of the agro-industrial variety needs to be limited. It is even more important that these infrastructure works be built with local or regional surplus or marginal farm labor and with labor-intensive methods. This is to be emphasized, because on various past occasions rural infrastructure construction in Ecuador was done by construction companies and workers with heavy equipment contracted in, and brought to the site from, Quito or Guayaquil. In other words, instead of local labor and labor-intensive methods, capital-intensive technology was used with imported labor. Such practices defeat the purpose.

Labor-intensive public works contribute to employment and low-income purchasing power for basic consumption. If the resulting increases in farm production match or exceed the real cost of the wage consumption of the workers engaged in rural infrastructure construction, the corresponding government expenditures and additional demand for basic consumables are not inflationary.[18]

SCIENCE AND TECHNOLOGY

In spite of the recent cuts in funds for education by the World Bank, even neoliberal policymakers recognize the need for improving the base for development and technological know-how. Clearly, the educational system from elementary to advanced university levels has to be strengthened, and the schooling of the rural populations must be tailored to the requirements of farming. The curricula must not be direct copies of those in the advanced industrial countries. The orientation has to be toward the type of knowledge that is most relevant to the resolution of the country's primary problems. This goes as much for technology as for the study of social sciences, including economics.

As to technology, given the relative abundance of labor, labor-intensive approaches to farming are desirable. It is doubtful, however, that larger-scale commercial farm units can be motivated to employ production methods that do not necessarily serve their particular interests.[19] The important question is whether there are technologies that are particularly applicable to small-scale and marginal-farm sectors. Here neoliberals have nothing to contribute. Suitable forms of farm technologies have to be based on specific and technically competent studies of the conditions prevailing in the various regions and rural sectors. The required technical competence can be obtained with the help of such organizations as, for example, the CIAT, Cali, Colombia. Policy planners and government officials concerned with rural and marginal land development could benefit from establishing working relationships with such institutions.

CONCLUSION

The neoliberal conviction that an unregulated free market has the capacity to bring about a democratic and just development process is wrong and morally unacceptable, because free markets lead to the exacerbation of the already-existing social and economic inequalities. Equally wrong is the focus on export orientation and related foreign investment, with their assumed trickle-down benefits for the poor.

There is no development without the growth of domestic markets. To bring it about, the rural economy has to be reorganized, with special attention to the requirements of the micro- and marginal-farm sectors. If the prevailing need for better nourishment can be combined with growing purchasing power, the marginal populations and other low-income earners can generate the necessary market demand for the absorption of a growing staple production for domestic consumption. Land reform and productivity enhancing rural public works can provide the growth of rural production and income earning opportunities so that the supply of and the demand for food grow at an equal rate.

The advancement of the commercial sectors is also important, subject to the earlier mentioned caveats with respect to input use and capital intensities. Nonetheless, for a very long time it cannot and will not generate sufficient employment with minimum acceptable living standards. Direct government intervention in areas other than the commercial sector is a necessity for increasing the rate of employment and productive self-employment in the large and poverty-stricken rural and urban marginal sectors.

Given the tradition of corruption and mismanagement, controls have to be instituted, not only for overseeing the private sector but also to ensure the adequacy of the government's contribution to the country's social and economic organization. Mismanagement and wasteful resource use by both the public and private sectors create unsustainable imbalances in the economy, which, in turn, undercut the capacity for social and economic development.

But attitudes will also have to change. The dominant social and economic classes, such as high-level government officials, estate owners, managers of banks and enterprises, and other members of the high-income groups, will have to recognize that their privileged social and economic status does not justify their extravagant use of domestic and foreign resources, their luxury consumption, and the subservience of the underprivileged masses. The current attitudes, which to a large extent dominate the Ecuadorian political process, lead to redirecting and, one way or another, appropriating the resources that should be used for advancing the welfare of the poor and marginalized populations. Whether this is done by legal or illegal means, it amounts to nothing less than social corruption.

Only the exercise of a strong political will can protect against such misuses of power.

Notes

[1] For example, I strongly disagree with the use of incomes policy—austerity—for improving the trade balance. Instead, I would favor limiting the imports of luxury consumer goods and farm products subsidized by the exporting countries (the United States, the European Union, and others). Rice and various other grains, for example, can be efficiently produced domestically.

[2] Interestingly, in this case the World Bank has not been in favor of the IMF demand for austerity measures.

[3] It is notable that the World Bank's *Ecuador Poverty Report* (1995) lists vulnerability to external shocks—along with low domestic savings rates, lack of technological innovation, and low returns to investment—as an explanation for "Ecuador's dismal record of past growth" (1:vii).

[4] Whitaker et al. 1996, 2:11. This two-volume report, an extensive neoliberal analysis of the Ecuadorian economy and agriculture, was prepared for the Ministerio de Agricultura y Ganadería and the IICA, with financial assistance from the IDB, PL 480, and USAID, and the collaboration of the Fundación Instituto de Estrategias Agropecuarias. It is an overview of the changes in the Ecuadorian economy since 1992, a year in which certain harsh policies for stabilization were initiated or accelerated. Because of the high-level sponsorship and

the wide use of statistical information in support of neoliberal arguments, the work has influenced political-economic policy design.

[5] For 1980 and 1990, respectively, the World Bank (1997) gives 40 percent and 33 percent of total employment in agriculture, and 20 percent and 19 percent in industry. The remainders correspond to services and the informal sector. The implication is that during the decade there was a 20 percent increase in service and informal employment.

[6] The Gini coefficient is an index of inequality in the distribution of socially significant items, such as income, asset ownership, or, as in the above case, consumption levels. Its value can range from 0 to 1 (or in percentages, from 0 to 100 percent), that is, from the total equality to the total inequality of the relevant item's distribution among persons or enterprises.

[7] For example, in Chile the per capita incomes have regained their 1973 level only in the 1990s, that is, more than twenty years after the imposition of military rule and neoliberal restructuring. Furthermore, since many of the Allende government's wealth and income distribution policies were reversed, it is a reasonable conclusion that the median income in Chile is still below its pre-coup level.

[8] The meaning of *productivity* and *productivity growth* needs clarification. The productivity of *employed* workers may very well increase with the introduction of relatively capital intensive industrial and agricultural techniques, and employers would benefit. But if this were to be accompanied by increased unemployment or underemployment, as has generally been the case, social productivity—as measured by the ratio of national income to total labor supply (that is, the sum of employed and jobless labor)—would decrease. If then the private and public costs of maintaining the increment of jobless persons were to be included in the measurement of productivity change, it would signal a catastrophic economic loss.

[9] The statistical information in this and the following section is taken from Whitaker et al. 1996, 1:58ff.

[10] In fact, that was the case in Ecuador. Even during a period of rapid economic growth, between 1974 and 1982, both urban and rural employment fell in percentage terms. And agricultural employment diminished even absolutely (PNUD 1999, 39).

[11] An Ecuadorian landowner's comment goes to the heart of the matter: "The importance of industrialization is to relieve the estates of unwanted labor." While the share of agriculture has remained constant, industry's share in Ecuador's GDP declined from 38 percent in 1980 to 36 percent in 1995 (World Bank 1997, table 12). So much for industry's capacity to absorb labor.

[12] Absorption through direct government purchases is a possibility. But without means for non-market disposal—such as direct distribution—storage facilities, complex administrative arrangements, and transport systems are required. As to long-term storage—as, for example, a hedge against crop failures and famines—without significant initial capital investments in silos, elevators, and other requirements, it is very wasteful, as was discovered by the Indian government during the 1970s.

[13] I use the term "mostly" in recognition of the fact that marginal farmers—the landless and unemployed labor—who manage to take some small proportion of their product to commercialized or monetized markets would also benefit from better prices.

[14] In Chile, for example, there was a well-prepared plan for land reform, which was legislated but only partially implemented by the Frei government. By the time the Allende government implemented the plan, the patience of the potential beneficiaries was exhausted and a disorderly land occupation ensued. The process also suffered from a less-than-adequate transfer of animal and other productive capital to the beneficiaries.

[15] There is ample literature on the subject. For a list of references, prepared in connection with the project from which this volume emerges, see Cameron and North 1997.

[16] The term *gremio* means "guild," "union," or "association." For their roles in Ecuador, see Flores 1996.

[17] On the experiences and problems with the organization of infrastructure works by two rural municipal governments in Ecuador, see Chapter 9 herein.

[18] Labor-intensive public works could also be used to generate local employment and income in connection with the reconstruction of the devastation caused by natural disasters, such as *el Niño* in 1997–98.

[19] For example, commercial farmers may prefer technologies that substitute chemical instead of labor-intensive weed control. Furthermore, for various reasons, such as fear of labor unrest, claims for land redistribution, and so forth, owners of estates and larger-scale farm operations have a preference for minimizing reliance on labor.

Chapter 5

Endogenous Peasant Responses to Structural Adjustment

Ecuador in Comparative Andean Perspective

Luciano Martínez Valle

The implementation of SAPs in the 1980s and 1990s resulted in increased levels of poverty and social inequality throughout the Andean region. Although the GDPs of the countries in the region did grow during that period, the standard of living of the majority of their residents deteriorated significantly. This decline was especially notable in the countryside where poverty increased even more than it did in urban areas, resulting in a visible pauperization of the majority of rural producers and rural indigenous producers in particular.[1]

Throughout the Andean region the rural sector in general and the agricultural sector in particular faced difficult conditions. The population of the rural sector declined, the contribution of agriculture to national food markets fell, and the share of agriculture in the GDP stagnated. Connected to this were processes of agricultural modernization that served the interests of large-scale agribusinesses and marginalized small-scale peasant farmers. As a result of these trends the rural sector rapidly became characterized by a sharp division between a small elite sector of large-scale agribusinesses that produced for world markets and an immense peasant sector that was rapidly being driven out of agricultural production altogether.

In light of these conditions, we need to ask whether the peasant economy of the Andean countries remains viable. As a result of economic globalization, adjustment programs, the termination of land

---

This chapter is a revised and updated version of an earlier work, Martínez 1999.

redistribution, the general withdrawal of the state from rural development, and the already precarious economic situation of the majority of peasant producers, the margins of viability for peasant producers have become very narrow. It is in this context that the future of small-scale peasant producers must be examined.

THE IMPACT OF STRUCTURAL ADJUSTMENT ON AGRARIAN POLICIES IN THE ANDES

The implementation of SAPs in the Andean region was highly uneven with regard to both the timing and depth of the reforms. Moreover, SAPs were implemented without any consideration for the socioeconomic conditions of the rural sector. Initiated at the beginning of the 1980s, SAPs concentrated on three basic mechanisms to stabilize and reactivate economic growth: liberalization, privatization, and deregulation. These policies had a series of particularly harmful consequences for agricultural policies and the rural sector.

It is important to begin by explaining that SAPs were most thoroughly implemented and their resulting shocks were the harshest in countries ruled by military regimes. In the case of Ecuador, a country ruled by elected civilian governments after 1980, SAPs were pursued in the face of strong social resistance and in the absence of the hyperinflation that had helped to create a stronger political consensus in favor of adjustment in neighboring countries (Martínez and Urriola 1994). In fact, in Ecuador SAPs were implemented later and still remained to be completed at the turn of the century—most notably in the conflictive area of privatization (see Larrea 1992, 295; Thorp 1998, 263–64).

Second, stabilization and adjustment programs do not present answers to the problems of the rural sector. As the FAO argued, the full impacts of SAPs are not only not evident in the short run, but they are also incapable of generating sustainable growth and development (FAO 1995). The immediate results of SAPs may be promising from the perspective of macroeconomic stabilization. However, stabilization based on neoliberal policies is unlikely to contribute either to improvements in agricultural production and productivity or to a decline in rural poverty.

Third, in the Andean region SAPs were implemented without any accompanying support policies for the agricultural sector. The absence of such support policies was particularly devastating for small-scale peasant farmers. Initially, adjustment programs were focused on dismantling the so-called distortionary elements of state-oriented development policies (Cismondi 1994, 3). Although specific initiatives for the agricultural sector were eventually formulated, they were designed in complete accordance with the dominant neoliberal macroeconomic framework, which resulted in policies that were oriented toward neither sustainability nor equity (Cismondi 1994, 4).

Fourth, adjustment programs drastically reduced the role of the state in rural development. The shrinking of the state most seriously affected small- and medium-scale peasants engaged in production for domestic markets, since they were left without access to credit and other critical resources that markets failed to provide (Escobal 1994). In general terms, only those peasants who were able to diversify their production or who became involved in nonagricultural activities were able to maintain their livelihoods.

In Ecuador, adjustment has been viewed from a market perspective as an important step toward the consolidation of modern large-scale agriculture without considering either the social costs of adjustment or the incoherence of agricultural policies. From a macro perspective, the negative impact of SAPs appeared to have been mediated by reasonably good levels of agricultural growth, 2.9 percent per annum between 1988 and 1995 and 3.6 percent in 1995. However, those figures primarily reflected the growth of agricultural exports (Whitaker et al. 1996, 5–6), not an expansion of small- and medium-scale production (Chapter 4). SAPs were implemented in Ecuador without any consideration of the problems facing poor, small-scale producers. The rapid deregulation of prices, privatization of public enterprises, and development of private land markets quickly led to increased poverty and a decline in the supply of food for the internal market, the majority of which was grown by small-scale producers.

The mainstream solutions that were proposed for confronting the growing rural crisis focused on deepening the macroeconomic reforms that were already under way: privatizing what still remained in the hands of the state, eliminating all barriers to foreign investment and trade, increasing agricultural exports, and further liberalizing financial markets. Accordingly, the agricultural policies in place circa 2000 were designed purely from a market perspective. They included the development of technological-scientific support for large-scale private agriculture, the creation of private systems of credit and marketing, the strengthening of rural land markets, and the privatization of water. Sectoral policies were thus aimed at strengthening a highly competitive private sector on the basis of scientific management, high-yielding varieties, and industrial inputs (Whitaker et al. 1996, 32)—a strategy that consisted of little more than combining a market approach with green revolution technology. What is perhaps most objectionable is that the advocates of this model also presented it as an environmentally sustainable alternative to peasant production, which, they argued, was characterized by exploitation by poor, small-scale farmers lacking appropriate scientific and technical knowledge.

Comparative research reveals tremendous contrasts between the neoliberal agricultural development policies that were implemented in the Andean region and the strategies adopted by countries in those parts of the world where rural livelihoods improved over the second half of the twentieth century. The contrast is especially stark with respect to the Southeast Asian countries, where economic development resulted from the state's active role in promoting profound agrarian reforms, a relatively equal distribution of income, and the development of strong internal markets (Evans 1987; Fishlow et al. 1994; Kuo, Ranis, and Fei 1981). By contrast, in the case of Ecuador, average agricultural growth rates and incomes fell and levels of rural poverty increased as neoliberal stabilization policies were pursued. As Lefeber argues (Chapter 4), mechanisms such as employment-creating rural public-works programs aimed at reactivating demand among the popular sectors could be much more effective for stimulating peasant production than the supposed miracles of the market. However, as the experience of the Southeast Asian countries makes clear, the success of such mechanisms requires that state intervention be directed toward the majority peasant sector, a strategy that the market-based model rejects.

THE DIFFERENTIAL IMPACT OF ADJUSTMENT ON THE RURAL SECTOR

To date, no comprehensive evaluations have been conducted that measure the impact of adjustment programs on the highly diverse population of small-scale agricultural producers, either at a national level or for the Andes as a whole. There are, however, various studies that examine the impact of SAPs on specific geographic areas and identify key tendencies that are likely to be present in other areas with similar conditions. Here, I turn to the principal findings of these works.

First, throughout the region, SAPs led to a growth in rural poverty in the context of an increasingly concentrated structure of agricultural landholdings. Poverty increased in the region both as a direct result of SAPs, and also because these policies effectively blocked the access of peasant farmers to the key resources needed for agricultural production. Most important, in Ecuador, data indicated a declining availability of agricultural land: the number of small-scale farms grew while the total quantity of land available for purchase actually shrunk. At the opposite extreme, extensions of land larger than 100 hectares grew in size and controlled over 40 percent of available land (Martínez 2000b). Indeed, the World Bank explicitly noted that the overall concentration of land in Ecuador changed little between 1954 and 1994, and that the Gini index for landownership remained at the astounding level of 0.89 (World Bank 1995, 2:105–6).[2]

Second, the implementation of neoliberal-inspired agrarian laws destabilized rural indigenous communities, which had already represented the poorest sector of rural producers. It was precisely these communities that were most threatened by neoliberal reforms, which undermined communal land-tenure patterns and blocked the possibility of redistributing land through agrarian reform. Indeed, the term *agrarian reform* itself was vilified and replaced with the concept of *land markets* as the central element of the new paradigm for agrarian development in the region. Ideologues of the new agrarian laws emphasized the need to make land markets more efficient by establishing strong regimes of property rights and land titling (e.g., see Whitaker et al. 1996, 7–8) but without considering the highly restricted capacity of small-scale peasant producers to access credit and to purchase land through the market. From this perspective, Ecuador's 1994 Agricultural Development Law clearly worked against the interests of the majority of peasant producers. Although the leaders of Ecuador's principal indigenous and peasant organizations were invited to participate in drafting revisions to the law following massive nationwide protests against the original version of the law, their input was manipulated by the Chambers of Agriculture (the representative organizations of large-estate owners) to create the impression of a consensus around the law rather than making any substantial changes to it.[3]

Third, depending on their levels of productive diversification, peasant producers responded differently to SAPs. In Ecuador, both the volume and profitability of production for the internal market declined (Martínez and Urriola 1994, 173). The only producers who managed to insert themselves successfully into the new global market conditions were large-scale producers of "new export crops" such as flowers and broccoli. However, they were a small minority even among the broader export sector, which, for the most part, also encountered problems with markets, international prices, and technology. In response to deteriorating conditions for agricultural production, many peasant farmers simply stopped producing for the market altogether and sought income from nonagricultural activities, particularly in the urban informal sector. Adjustment programs in Ecuador were thus pushing peasants out of the sphere of agricultural production altogether.

Fourth, as a result of SAPs, employment in the rural sector became increasingly precarious throughout the Andean region. Adjustment programs encouraged the adoption of labor-saving technologies on large estates in order to increase international competitiveness. As a consequence of the widespread shift toward the use of temporary and seasonal labor by large-scale producers, it became increasingly difficult to find stable employment in agriculture. This was reflected in a massive contraction in the overall demand for labor as well as in a concentration of remaining demand in peak harvest periods.

An exception to this dominant trend emerged in the new cut-flower and vegetable-export sectors that developed in traditional dairy-producing areas of highland Ecuador. In this case the new crops involved increased labor intensity along with a shift in the use of agricultural land and the penetration of nonagricultural capital into the rural sector. As in other parts of the Andes, the majority of temporary workers in Ecuador's cut-flower and vegetable-export sectors were women, a phenomenon that signaled the emergence of more flexible local labor markets adapted to the global market (Martínez 1993). In fact, a process of "double feminization" in agriculture emerged throughout the Andean region, as well as in the rest of Latin America; that is, women became increasingly engaged in both small-scale agricultural production and temporary salaried agricultural work (Kay 1995).

Fifth, adjustment programs created an increasingly semi-proletarianized rural population with decreasing connections to the land. As Kay explains, semi-proletarianization became the principal tendency among Latin American peasants as the majority began to derive their incomes from sources external to their plots of land (Kay 1995, 73). In Ecuador, data from 1990 reflected a rural social structure in which the majority of producers were in a very weak position to adapt to neoliberal economic reforms: 26.8 percent of households were made up of wage workers and poor peasants represented another 33.3 percent of households (Martínez 1995).

Finally, SAPs disarticulated many of the traditional peasant organizations in the region. During the "lost decade" of the 1980s, the peasant movement was seriously weakened as a consequence of the fragmentation of the rural labor force (Kay 1995). Nevertheless, other new types of organizations and movements emerged in response to the acute conditions of rural poverty—perhaps most important, the indigenous movement in Ecuador that attracted international attention through national uprisings in 1990, 1994, 1999, 2000, and 2001.[4]

THE VIABILITY OF THE PEASANT ECONOMY

The predominant analysis of the Latin American peasantry at the end of the twentieth century was highly contradictory. In spite of their poverty, peasant producers were also seen as having a very high organizational potential. In the most optimistic analyses, especially those of NGOs, this capacity for organization was presented as the key factor that would catapult the peasantry toward sustainable livelihoods in the twenty-first century. However, not only were many of the rural poor completely unorganized, but organization alone was not enough to provide a route out of poverty, as Korovkin makes clear in her analysis of the indigenous organizational "victories" in the province of Chimborazo (Chapter 7).

In addition to high levels of democratic and entrepreneurial organization (discussed below), at least four other elements are necessary for the peasant economy to become viable: (1) possession of sufficient land, water, and credit; (2) favorable macroeconomic policies; (3) reasonable access to markets that are not socially destructuring; and (4) sustainable external supports. I now turn to an examination of each of these factors.

Individual peasants have no control over the distribution of land, water, and credit or over macroeconomic policies, and they have little control over access to markets. Peasants do have greater control over organization and support from external agents. However, if access to productive resources and markets and a supportive macroeconomic policy context do not form part of the framework of agrarian policies, peasant organization and external support are unlikely to have much impact.

Access to Land, Water, and Credit

Problems of access to productive land and the need for agrarian reform were excluded from the new agrarian policies of the 1990s and replaced by strategies emphasizing rural land markets. The case for land markets, as argued by the World Bank in particular, is quite simple: If small-scale producers are more efficient than large-scale producers with respect to the volume of production per hectare, they should be able to obtain more land through the market. The Bank's expectations concerning redistribution through land markets, however, are based on two erroneous assumptions: The first is that large landholders are willing to cultivate their land more intensively so that they will need less of it; the second is that they are willing to sell their surplus land to peasants. The argument also fails to consider two other critical factors: First, control of land in the Andes is not only a source of wealth but also of social and political power; and second, in the current context, small-scale peasants cannot compete with other actors who are trying to purchase land. The solutions that land markets might provide to relieving land concentration thus exist only in the imaginations of neoliberal economists.

Rather than increasing access to land, the new agrarian laws have begun to destabilize indigenous communities through the elimination of regulations that once blocked the division and sale of communally owned lands.[5] In Ecuador, in response to the Agrarian Development Law and the resources made available by NGOs, many peasants shifted their demands from land redistribution to land titling. In fact, in the context of the new legal framework, land invasions stopped completely after the mid-1990s and calls for the expropriation of *haciendas* declined considerably (Chapter 6). At the same time, the subdivision of former communal lands increased, especially in the high altitude *páramo*, with at least three negative consequences: (1) the properties that entered the land market were primarily small parcels with the consequence that small landholdings became even smaller; (2) many of these properties passed from the collective control of communities to that of private individuals; and (3) ecologically sensitive *páramo* lands, which are not appropriate for agriculture, were divided and sold for use in agricultural production (FUNDAGRO 1996).

The control of water resources in the Andes was also rapidly shifting into private hands, and legal regulations were prepared throughout the region to accelerate this process. As the role of the state in water management declined, speculation over irrigated areas increased, driving up land prices and threatening to intensify land conflicts (FUNDAGRO 1996, 49). Moreover, the benefits that high-altitude indigenous communities had previously enjoyed as a result of their proximity to the sources of irrigation water deteriorated as water was privatized, user fees were increased, and other cost-recovery mechanisms were introduced to finance irrigation (Whitaker et al. 1996, 109–10). There is no doubt that state-managed irrigation systems in the Andes were inefficient and generally allowed irrigation water to be controlled by large property owners. However, the problems of publicly managed systems do not justify the potentially devastating social and ecological consequences that would result from the privatization of water (Bolens 1995). At the close of the 1990s, proposals involving the regulation of water supply by the state but the private delivery of irrigated water appeared to be one alternative to full-scale privatization (Dourejeanni 1993).

The Macroeconomic Policy Context for Rural Development

In the Andean countries neoliberal macroeconomic policies not only took precedence over agricultural development policies, but no policy measures were even implemented to confront the negative economic and social effects of adjustment in the countryside. The integrated rural development policies that were popular in the 1970s and 1980s were largely dismantled and continued to operate, in a much reduced form, only in Colombia and Ecuador. Moreover, those policies were focused almost exclusively on peasants considered to be economically viable or were simply designed as social welfare schemes. No policies were implemented to support small-scale peasant producers. Rather, emphasis was placed on macroeconomic and monetary policies that were expected to benefit the peasant sector, and policymakers simply bet on NGOs and other elements of civil society, accompanied by a policy of "select supervision" on the part of the state, to provide support for those peasants considered to be economically viable.

Socially "Destructuring" Market Access

Financial capital has always been scarce among small-scale peasants. Moreover, in the Andean countries, credit from state banks that was theoretically intended to support peasant producers almost always ended up in the hands of large-scale farmers. This phenomena was often cited by neoliberal advocates to support the privatization of state banks that offered preferential credit to rural producers. However, in Peru, the liquidation of the state-controlled Banco Agrario pushed market-oriented peasant producers even further toward informal sources of credit, which had lower "transaction costs" but also higher interest rates than credit offered by formal lenders (Alvarado 1994, 121). Similarly in Ecuador, the restructuring of the BNF into a commercial bank, with no special preference or lower interest rates for peasants, resulted in a reduction in the amount of credit available to peasant producers (see Younger et al. 1997).

The "real market," understood as a culturally and politically specific institution, has incorporated peasants in different ways (Hewitt de Alcántara 1993). Large sectors of peasant producers, and indigenous communities in particular, remained effectively outside the markets for agricultural products, simply because they were not "competitive." Gonzalez de Olarte, referring to one of the central problems facing Peruvian peasants, observed:

> The current macroeconomic and institutional context forces peasants to substantially raise their levels of productivity if they want to progress through agricultural activity. To become more efficient and to gain access to markets, peasants must incorporate new technologies, which in turn require new resources and knowledge. In the event that peasants are unable to access those resources and knowledge, their only alternative is isolation from the market or migration. (Gonzalez de Olarte 1988, 118)

Numerous studies, in Peru in particular, highlight the weak capacity of peasants to adopt new technologies in response to the challenges of higher productivity and competitiveness. In contrast to the rapid integration of global markets, technology in the peasant sector tends to change very slowly (Gonzalez de Olarte 1988). Without new technological inputs it is very difficult for small-scale peasant producers to become integrated into the market without extensive periods of migration, which have a highly "destructuring" impact on families and community (see below).

In Ecuador, at least, the romantic idea that peasants could opt out of market relations and develop self-sufficient production strategies as a response to adjustment programs has no empirical or historical basis. Most peasants and indigenous communities had no choice but to maintain the connections with the market. Moreover, in some areas of Ecuador production for the market increased, relative to production for self-consumption, as a result of adjustment programs.

By the 1990s the principal connection with the market for small-scale peasants occurred not through agricultural production but rather through urban migration and the sale of their labor. As indicated above, limited access to productive resources forced poor peasants to pursue livelihoods in activities outside of their farms and often beyond their home communities and even countries.[6] Research conducted in the areas of operation of PRONADER in Ecuador found that, in areas with predominantly indigenous populations, agricultural activities accounted for less than 40 percent of household incomes (Martínez and Barril 1995, 64). The connection between lack of access to critical productive resources and migration has been analyzed in numerous studies of migration as a "subsistence strategy" aimed at "re-peasantization," that is, saving money earned from wage labor to purchase agricultural land. However, in the predominantly indigenous areas of the Andes, little land remained available for purchase, while new agrarian laws blocked any collective political strategies aimed at acquiring it. Even more problematic was social decomposition of rural communities that began to occur as a result of increasing levels of labor migration. Not only was the principal labor force leaving rural communities, but as wage labor became the most important source of income, the logic of "exchange value" began to transform internal community practices and urban consumption patterns proliferated among the younger generations. There was a direct correlation between the marginal situation of households with only small plots of poor-quality land and the increasing diversification of socially destructuring income sources (de Janvry 1994).

Peasant and Indigenous Organization

Organization has become a central theme in debates about the viability of the peasant economy. Indeed, hope for the survival of the rural poor in the context of globalization is now almost always pinned on the apparent organizational potential of the peasant sector. However, most discussions of peasant organization fail to distinguish between traditional organizations that were created in response to state legal frameworks and exist only on paper, and the newer forms of organization that emerged in response to external financing and development programs in the 1980s. Ecuador, and especially its indigenous population, is frequently presented as a model of peasant organization, largely because of the sequence of massive indigenous uprisings that began in 1990. Indeed, the tremendous growth in the number of peasant and indigenous organizations, and especially of second-level peasant organizations (that is, federations of community organizations), led some researchers to challenge the view that the 1980s were a "lost decade" for development in the rural sectors. Those researchers articulated a vision of the 1980s as "the decade that was won" *(una decada ganada)* in the context of flourishing of peasant organizations (Bebbington et al. 1992). Donor agencies, NGOs, and IFIs also came to emphasize social organization as the key factor needed to make peasant production viable in the twenty-first century, a perspective that was reinforced by international debates about the importance of social capital—which came to be seen as one of the key strengths of Andean peasants.[7]

Unfortunately, those who highlighted the importance of peasant organization generally failed to consider the limited productive resources that peasants actually controlled. Moreover, enthusiasm for the indigenous movement also resulted in a generalized failure to examine carefully the entrepreneurial capacities of peasant and indigenous organizations. Systematic analysis of the type of organizations that are emerging and the question of whether or not they are capable of responding to the economic challenges of integrating into global markets and benefiting from the neoliberal macroeconomic policy context were generally left by the wayside.

A fundamental change is taking place in the world of Andean peasant organizations. Older traditional peasant organizations, such as community-level *cabildos* (elected councils) and microregional peasant federations, are in crisis. At the same time, however, new types of peasant corporations and businesses began to emerge in response to adjustment programs in connection with the promotional work of rural development NGOs (Chapter 8).

My own research on second-level peasant organizations in the majority of Ecuador's highland provinces revealed that many of them existed only on paper and that those actually functioning suffered from serious internal problems (Martínez 1997). Peasant organizations flourished in the 1980s in direct response to new sources of financing and development projects targeted specifically at indigenous communities. As those initiatives later began to dry up, many organizations became less active, often to the point of ceasing to function altogether. For example, only seventeen of seventy-one second-level peasant organizations examined in 1996 had any real capacity to formulate or carry out development projects. Moreover, of those seventeen, only three could be considered efficient and had clear future-oriented development strategies (Martínez 1997). By contrast, the vast majority of peasant organizations in highland Ecuador had little internal cohesion and little capacity to negotiate with external institutions and actors.

Significantly, the few organizations that could be characterized as efficient and internally cohesive bore little resemblance to traditional community-based peasant federations. Rather, their profile was much more similar to that of microenterprises. Moreover, although these new organizations had emerged as a consequence of external support, they tended to be more efficient than traditional organizations in responding to the demands of their members. The phenomenon of these new peasant organizations remains to be seriously examined, but their appearance certainly suggests that significant changes were taking place in rural organizations in the Andes.[8] These changes should be analyzed, not from the idealized theoretical perspectives of an assumed cooperative matrix of Andean social relations, popular in much of the academic literature, but from the perspective of the real accumulated experience and practices of the communities themselves.

Sustainable External Support for the Peasant Economy

The theme of external and sustainable support to peasant producers has two components. On the one hand, state support became increasingly limited and weak; on the other hand, support grew from NGOs. The declining role of the state was accompanied by flourishing hopes for the strengthening of civil society through community organizations and NGOs. These organizations became the new agents of much of the work previously carried out by the state, and many observers hoped that they would be more efficient agents of development than the state, capable of inducing a shift from production for self-consumption to production for the market (de Janvry 1994). However, there was little empirical evidence to support such optimism about the role of NGOs and civil society. Without evidence concerning their actual capacities, the simple growth in the number of peasant organizations provided no reason to be hopeful about the future of rural development. At least in Ecuador, which was often viewed as a model for other countries in the region, rural peasant organizations turned out to be much weaker than the euphoria surrounding them—as expressed in the notion of the "decade that was won"—had suggested.

At the end of the twentieth century there was still a long way to go to reactivate second-level peasant organizations, to understand better the problems of undemocratic administration that characterized many of them, and to support their embryonic business initiatives. Arguments that indigenous and peasant federations could form the basis of a more competitive model of rural development simply ignored hard realities. Rural civil society, even when supported by NGOs, simply was not able to fill the voids left by the state, as the case studies in this volume demonstrate.

NGOs represented the other great hope for confronting the problems of rural development within the framework of structural adjustment. However, there was little objective evidence available about their actual performance and capacities. Very few NGOs had conducted serious evaluations of their effectiveness in promoting rural development. Moreover, rather than basing rural development strategies on lessons learned from their own experiences, the vast majority of NGOs simply adapted to new development fashions and funding opportunities from the international development agencies. Even more problematic, NGOs frequently interpreted successful cases of community and local development as models that could be replicated without seriously examining their sustainability.[9]

NGOs in the Andean countries occupy ambiguous positions. Since they emerged in the 1970s, NGO interventions have not resulted in any sustainable solutions to the problems of either rural development or poor peasants. However, despite their widespread failures, NGOs were assigned a prominent place in the new "magic formula" for rural development that combined social organization with the "free market." NGO efforts were increasingly focused on strengthening peasant organizations as business enterprises and on searching for market niches that could make peasants economically viable in the context of the new economic model. NGOs, in short, were becoming highly functional to the interests of the IFIs and, as a result, received generous funding for their programs (see Chapter 8).

Sustainable NGO supports for the poorest peasants also began to disappear as the parameters of rural development were reshaped within the confines of the free market. As NGOs adapted to the new market-oriented development paradigm and abandoned their role as nonprofit organizations to become "organizations which sell specialized services" (Arcos Cabrera and Palomenque Vallejo 1997), poor peasants lost access to their support. This occurred for the simple reason that small-scale peasant production was not sustainable within the new market model and small-scale producers could not afford to pay for the costs of NGO services.

Many of the proposals for improving peasant livelihoods were based on organic agriculture as a technological alternative to the Green Revolution (Toledo 1995). NGOs were generally seen as the principal institutions that might encourage peasants to adopt this line of action, focused on agro-ecology, peasant organization, and specialty markets. However, these agro-ecological proposals almost always revolved around strategies for conservation and sustainable resource management that were feasible for only a minority of peasants with access to land and other resources. Without ignoring the theoretical importance of these ideas, which might provide solutions for peasants with sufficient productive resources, no similar proposals emerged for the majority of poor peasants who were dependent on small plots of land and highly diversified sources of income.

THE LIMITATIONS OF THE *NEW* RURAL DEVELOPMENT: THE CASE OF PRONADER

The rural development programs implemented in Ecuador over the 1980s and 1990s were repeatedly undermined by the absence of a macroeconomic framework favorable to small-scale rural producers. Neoliberal SAPs, the dismantling of state institutions, the "flexibilization" of labor, and trade and investment liberalization all worked against the development of the peasant economy.

Any rural development program aimed at reactivating peasant production requires a favorable macroeconomic policy context. As Echeverría argues, that policy context must both "allow small-scale agricultural production to be profitable and facilitate peasant access to productive resources and . . . promote non-agricultural rural development" (Echeverría 2000b, 4). In Ecuador, rural development programs did neither of these things. Rural development efforts were relegated to the realm of anti-poverty programs, and the state largely ceased to provide credit, marketing support, and technical assistance to the peasant sector. In this respect, it was no accident that Ecuador's Under-Secretariat for Rural Development was located in the Ministry of Social Welfare.

The National Rural Development Program (PRONADER) was the most recent state-administered rural development effort in Ecuador. It operated from 1990 to 2000 to support approximately twenty-three thousand peasant households in twelve rural areas, with US$112 million in funding, US$84 million of which came from a World Bank loan.[10] Unfortunately, PRONADER failed to address any of the economic problems that were created for poor peasants by Ecuador's macroeconomic and agricultural policy framework. As a result of its lack of understanding of the problems facing the peasant economy, a lack of vision in the design of its programs, and political interference, PRONADER generally failed to improve peasant livelihoods in project areas.

The analysis of PRONADER's impacts presented here is based on before and after surveys of a representative sample of program beneficiaries conducted by the author. Altogether, 1,572 families were interviewed in 1993 and 1,545 in 2000, with most of the latter being families that had been interviewed seven years earlier. In addition, in 2000, the research involved a review of the functioning of 180 organizations and interviews with personnel from 36 institutions that had collaborated with PRONADER. The reader should keep in mind that the program's twelve operating areas were chosen because peasants in those areas were considered potentially "viable" in the context of neoliberal adjustment. The program was not designed for the poor peasants who make up the majority of rural producers.

PRONADER's impact on the incomes of its intended beneficiaries was minimal. In fact, the average incomes of beneficiaries dropped from US$354 per annum in 1993 to US$337 in 2000, and only five of the twelve areas registered any increases in income. It is important to point out that three of those five areas—Daule, Tres Postes, and Playas de Higuerón—were located in the rice-growing region of the lower Guayas basin on the Pacific coast, an area where the size and quality of farms and the nature of production placed the producers at the top of the minority of "middle peasants" with good land, stable market access, and experience in adopting new technologies. To be effective, however, rural development programs need to give priority to the majority of poor peasants who rely on small plots of land and wage employment. In this respect, PRONADER's impacts in project areas in the highland region, where indigenous populations are concentrated and poverty is most acute, are revealing: Producers in the highland zones actually experienced a deterioration in economic conditions, and peasant incomes dropped by as much as 28 percent, even though the communities targeted by the programs were not among the poorest in the highland region.[11]

Analysis of PRONADER's initiatives also reveals that its development interventions had the greatest impact in areas that had previously experienced agrarian reform, as had the rice-growing areas in the lower Guayas basin. Where agrarian reforms had not been implemented, the impact of PRONADER's projects was much weaker. Similarly, its projects focused on agricultural production faced greater difficulties in increasing peasant incomes in areas where economic activities had by necessity become highly diversified and peasants had ceased to depend on agricultural production for most of their income, as is the case of the poorest areas in the highlands and in the coastal foothills.

Employment in PRONADER's areas of operation also declined between 1993 and 2000, from 87.1 percent to 76.4 percent of the economically active population. Moreover, underemployment in agriculture increased as the proportion of peasants engaged in agricultural activities rose in the face of declining nonagricultural employment opportunities.[12] The provision of credit for agricultural production by PRONADER and the crisis of urban employment in the construction and service industries were key elements that led many peasant households to focus their time on agricultural production. Because large-scale agribusinesses also failed to generate new employment opportunities,[13] small farms became a sort of employment refuge for members of peasant households who could not find employment in other sectors of the economy. Significantly, however, a higher degree of occupational diversification remained evident in the highland areas with poor access to land. Meanwhile, in the coastal areas with better resources and more advanced market agriculture, occupational diversification was much lower because peasants in that region could still earn basic livelihoods from agricultural production.

Land ownership in PRONADER's areas of operation also became more concentrated between 1993 and 2000.[14] The farms of peasants with less than fifteen hectares decreased in size between 1993 and 2000 as a result of economic pressures on peasants to sell their land and the division of properties through inheritance. By contrast, farms larger than twenty hectares increased in size, from an average of 31.1 to 39.8 hectares, a process of land concentration that was facilitated significantly by Ecuador's 1994 Law of Agricultural Development (see Lefeber's critique of the principles underlying this law in Chapter 4). The land titling programs established in accord with the 1994 law made considerable progress among peasants with small farms, but this did not translate into improved access to land for those peasants, as the proponents of land markets argue (World Bank 1995; Echeverría 2000a; Vogelgesang 2000; Jaramillo 2000).[15] Poor peasants, in fact, had great difficulty acquiring land that was supposed to become available through the market, and economic forces pressured many of them to sell their land to larger-scale farms.

PRONADER also failed to improve peasant access to technology, credit, and markets. These factors are all essential if peasant households are to increase their levels of production and productivity. However, the percentage of peasant households in PRONADER areas that received technical assistance actually dropped between 1993 and 2000, from 62.8 percent to 14.4 percent. Moreover, technical assistance was concentrated on the middle and wealthy peasants rather than on the majority with very small plots of land.[16] As noted above, the availability of technical assistance for peasant agriculture declined throughout Ecuador as a result of the withdrawal of state institutions that used to provide technical assistance for agricultural development (for example, the Ministry of Agriculture and Livestock) and the inadequacy of private sources of technical assistance.

Access to productive credit among peasants in PRONADER's areas of operation dropped from 32 percent in 1993 to 19.5 percent in 2000. Among the causes of this drop, it is important to highlight the national financial meltdown in 1999, which involved the bankruptcy of major banks and financial institutions and, in particular, the reorientation of the BNF, which was reorganized to become a traditional commercial bank with the elimination of its special preference for peasant producers. The proportion of credit provided to the peasant sector by the BNF in PRONADER areas plunged from 23.7 percent in 1993 to 9.3 percent in 2000. The lack of formal credit from the BNF was partly filled by new financial agents, such as savings-and-loan cooperatives, NGOs, and various churches. As well, a reactivation of informal credit from small-scale moneylenders and loans from family members accounted for 41.7 percent of all credit to peasants in PRONADER areas by the year 2000. However, the most common response to the 1999–2000 financial crisis among peasants was not to borrow money at all—which, although a prudent strategy for protecting their land, also resulted in lower levels of agricultural productivity and production.

The peasant economy in Ecuador remained very closely connected to the market. In PRONADER areas in 2000, 84 percent of production was directed toward the market, in contrast with only 16 percent for self-consumption. Significantly, 30 percent of peasant agricultural production for the market was processed in artisan enterprises that were set up in peasant households. This fact suggests a high potential for developing forward linkages from agricultural products. In PRONADER's areas of operation, such peasant processing activities had developed around two principal products, dairy goods and sugar cane. But those activities remained confined in family-based artisan businesses with low levels of technology and productivity, manufacturing low-quality goods for local markets. Unfortunately, and in spite of their potential importance for creating rural employment and generating income for peasants, PRONADER did not recognize the potential of these endogenous peasant initiatives and failed to provide supports that might have made them more productive.

One important advance in the new conception of rural development was the recognition that education and organization are essential for rural progress. De Janvry and Sadoulet (2000) argue that rural development in Latin America will only be possible if peasant access to secondary education increases dramatically. Secondary education is a prerequisite for peasants in order to develop their capacities to manage small businesses, improve marketing, produce higher-quality goods, and find nonagricultural employment, all of which require high levels of literacy, numeracy, and other skills. Although the percentage of the population with no education dropped in PRONADER's areas of operation, from 17.4 percent in 1993 to 15.2 percent in 2000, 67.1 percent of peasants still possessed only an elementary education, and illiteracy among women remained at 18 percent in 2000.[17] In general, levels of human-capital formation in PRONADER's areas of operation were low: in 2000, only 13.8 percent of the school-aged population had completed secondary school, and only 1.6 percent had tertiary education. These low levels of education represented a formidable obstacle to rural development efforts, because peasant businesses cannot be expected to survive and become competitive without a solid educational foundation. Moreover, in the prevailing context of economic crisis, the peasant population was not giving priority to the education of its children. Poverty induced a premature use of human resources with low levels of education in family-based farms and enterprises, as demonstrated by the extensive use of family labor in agricultural production.

PRONADER also failed to include efforts to strengthen peasant organizations in its rural development strategy. In its areas of operation, it worked only with those peasant organizations that demonstrated openness to the program, with little consideration for their capacities, legitimacy, or the size of their membership. Indeed, PRONADER's failure to screen carefully the peasant organizations with which it worked resulted in the formation of at least 137 ad hoc groups that were formed specifically to take advantage of PRONADER's programs but had few roots in local communities. Moreover, the training that PRONADER offered to peasant organizations was narrowly concentrated on agricultural activities, and, in light of the urgent needs of the peasants at the program sites, the number of training events offered between 1995 and 2000 (generally between one and three in each area) was entirely insufficient.

PRONADER's interventions had a similarly negligible effect on strengthening social capital in its areas of operation. Although the program took advantage of traditions of community labor in highland peasant communities to complete certain projects, it did almost nothing to strengthen social relations in those communities. Dependence on volunteer community labor has become a key component of rural development projects, but it was beginning to reach its limits. The unproven assumption that peasant organizations can provide such volunteer labor for local development projects on a permanent ongoing basis is being increasingly called into question. Moreover, not all rural areas have high levels of organization or traditions of community labor upon which to rely. PRONADER's failure to strengthen the peasant organizations in its project areas seriously limited the potential sustainability of its development efforts as local peasant organizations were generally left without the capacity to assume control over projects when PRONADER support ended.

Finally, it is important to point out that PRONADER failed to develop any kind of institutional synergy with the NGOs in its project areas that might have made possible a more coordinated and sustainable development effort. Among the most important causes for that lack of coordination were the changes in state policies that resulted from political interference and instability and the consequent frequent rotation of technical staff, as well as jealousy among NGOs. With regard to political interference, corruption was particularly pervasive in the appointment of project personnel who, in various cases, were given positions as a means of returning political favors, resulting not only in incompetent project staff but also in high rates of turnover.[18] In certain cases, moreover, PRONADER projects were manipulated by powerful local landowners who stood to benefit from increased agricultural land values that resulted from investments in irrigation in particular.

In sum, PRONADER's efforts to promote rural development addressed none of the principal problems facing the majority of peasants. Its failure to improve the livelihoods and living conditions of peasants in its specific areas of concentration was perhaps not surprising given its top-down approach, its failure to design policies for the majority of poor peasants, and its acceptance of the neoliberal macroeconomic policy framework. Indeed, it is difficult to imagine how a rural development program without improved access to agricultural land, credit, education and technical assistance, viable market strategies, and competent peasant organizations could have any positive impact on peasant production and livelihoods.

CONCLUSION

The situation of peasant and indigenous communities in the Andean countries, and in Ecuador in particular, has deteriorated significantly as a result of the SAPs implemented since the early 1980s. Putting a halt to that deterioration and making the peasant economy of the Andean region economically viable require a solution to the problem of poverty, which in turn depends on peasant access to those resources that are not being used at maximum efficiency by large-scale agriculture. However, the legal barriers that neoliberal policymakers have constructed to stop processes of agrarian reform and to consolidate land markets undermine the stability of the peasant economy. *Real* land markets—in the context of the poverty of the majority of peasants—have resulted in an increased concentration rather than a redistribution of agricultural land. As a result, without an immediate revision of agrarian laws and renewed state involvement in rural development efforts, most peasant producers will be marginalized no matter how efficient they are. It is also essential that the state make a major commitment to rural development initiatives that focus much more carefully on the needs and conditions of poor peasants and that are implemented through democratic processes. The state must also establish an overall macroeconomic framework that recognizes the economic value of the activities of poor peasant producers and must enable peasant organizations to participate in the design, administration, coordination, and regulation of rural development initiatives.

This chapter has criticized the neoliberal macroeconomic model for its adverse effects on small-scale agricultural producers. Nevertheless, recent proposals from institutions such as the FAO and the World Bank suggest that there may still be some hope for the peasant economy. The simple reason for their preoccupation with rural conditions is that the mass of impoverished peasants in unstable countries represents a threat to political stability that needs to be carefully contained. The FAO, for example, proposed "a reappraisal of the rural sector" and identified a need to develop strategies to protect food security (FAO 1995). The World Bank, for its part, recognized the need to make land more accessible to peasants, although still only through market mechanisms. The UNDP, in turn, has insisted that new strategies of agricultural development must be centered on small plots of land, the generation of employment, more efficient resource use, and an equitable distribution of resources (UNDP

1996, 86–105). There is thus a debate under way about creating at least the minimal conditions that would enable peasants to play a productive role in the context of structural adjustment. Strategies focused on reducing food insecurity, organic production for specialty export markets, and productive diversification throughout artisan activities and agricultural processes represent three politically and economically viable policy options that could help to promote the peasant economy and that already have some support from the development institutions mentioned above. While not solving all the problems of small-scale producers, initiatives in these areas would at least mitigate some of the worst impacts of SAPs as they have been implemented in Ecuador. One fact remains certain however: The opportunities for Andean peasants to use their knowledge, culture, and productive practices to build more equitable societies in the future will be much greater if development policies break away from the narrow focus on free markets and globalization.

Notes

[1] In the case of Ecuador, poverty affected 75.8 percent of the rural population in 1995, and 82 percent in 1998 (Larrea and Sánchez 2002, 12, table 5).

[2] As explained earlier, the Gini coefficient represents the degree of inequality in asset ownership, with 0.0 representing complete equality (all individuals owning equal assets) and 1.0 representing complete inequality (all assets owned by one individual).

[3] Indigenous leaders and organizations asserted that they won important concessions from the government and landlords (e.g., Pacari 1996). However, many analysts of the process who work with the peasant sector argue that those concessions were purely symbolic.

[4] "New" rural social movements also emerged in other Latin American countries with modes of organization and strategies that were very different from those that characterized the peasant organizations of the 1970s and 1980s. Prominent among these new movements were the MST in Brazil and the EZLN in Chiapas, Mexico.

[5] This process occurred in Mexico with the elimination of Article 27 from the Mexican Constitution in 1992; in Peru, with the approval of the Land Law 26.505, in 1995; and in Ecuador with the passage of the Agrarian Development Law in 1994.

[6] With regard to international migration, see, for example, Jokisch 2001.

[7] For more on this theme, see Putnam 1993; Bebbington et al. 1992; Arrobo Rodas and Prieto 1995; Flora 1995; Martínez 1997.

[8] The attention that has been given to the theme of *organization* needs to be questioned rigorously. Thus far, it has been much more closely connected to the apolitical deployment of the concept of social capital than to political and economic perspectives that question or challenge the status quo (see Chapter 1).

[9] In Ecuador, the case of the parish of Salinas in the central highland province of Bolívar has become a well-known model for NGO-led development. However,

few have investigated how much money was invested during the course of the 1980s and 1990s in this development effort, which ultimately benefited fewer than ten thousand people. Nor have they inquired into why the management and financing of development efforts in Salinas was not shifted from NGOs to peasant organizations. How much time will it take before the peasants in Salinas can manage their own enterprises? Finally, it is critical to recognize, as North does (Chapter 11), that the experience of Salinas is not replicable among poor peasant producers without access to land, other assets, credit, and a variety of services.

[10] PRONADER's areas of operation were, in the highland region, Espejo and Mira in the province of Carchi; Sierra Norte de Pichincha in Pichincha; Pangua and T.T.P. in Cotopaxi; Facundo Vela in Bolívar; Guano in Chimborazo; Santa Isabel in Azuay; in the Costa, Daule and Tres Postes in Guayas; Jipijapa and Paján in Manabí; Playas de Higuerón in Los Ríos.

[11] Between 1993 and 2000, the average income of beneficiaries in the Sierra Norte of Pichincha declined from $US203 to $US195, in Guano (Chimborazo) from $US360 to US$263, and in T.T.P. (Cotopaxi) from $US277 to $US202.

[12] The percentage of the economically active population in PRONADER's areas of operation engaged in agricultural activity rose from 53.6 percent in 1993 to 58.8 percent in 2000. Livestock production occupied 10 percent of the economically active population in 1993 and 14.5 percent in 2000. By contrast, non-agricultural activities declined from 19.5 percent of the economically active population in 1993 to 14.7 percent in 2000.

[13] The exception was the cut-flower industry of the northern central highlands, which employed between eleven and thirteen workers per hectare, more than any other agricultural product in the region. The majority of workers on cut-flower farms lived in nearby indigenous communities and represented a significant process of proletarianization in the provinces of Pichincha and Imbabura in particular (Mena 1999).

[14] At the national level 77.6 percent of farms smaller than five hectares controlled only 5.3 percent of land, while the 1.5 percent of farms over one hundred hectares controlled 50.5 percent of all land (Martínez 2000b).

[15] In 2000, 20 percent of farms still had no property title, down from 34.1 percent in 1993.

[16] Only 9 percent of peasants with one to two hectares and 15 percent of peasants with two to five hectares reported receiving any assistance, while 19.3 percent of peasants with five to ten hectares and 28.4 percent of peasants with ten to fifteen hectares received technical assistance from PRONADER.

[17] This problem was most severe in the highland areas with large indigenous populations, where female illiteracy is widespread.

[18] It is important to note that, especially during the presidency of Sixto Durán Ballén (1990–94), PRONADER became so politicized that its developmental goals were totally ignored, as was made evident by the appointment of incompetent political supporters of the president's party to technical positions in PRONADER. To provide a few examples, local area coordinators in the Sierra Norte de Pichincha site at various times included a hairdresser, a bullfighter, and an ice-cream store owner, all completely unqualified to lead rural development projects but politically well connected to the president's party machine. With regard to corruption, see Arcos Cabrera 2001.

Chapter 6

Rural Land Conflicts
and Human Rights Violations
in Ecuador

LIISA L. NORTH, WADE A. KIT, AND ROBERT B. KOEP

During the last two decades of the twentieth century Ecuador appeared
an island of peace in the midst of the violence that engulfed her neighbors to the south and the north. The egregious violence of the Shining
Path guerrilla movement and the military dominated Peru's politics during the late 1980s and early 1990s, while an immensely destructive civil
war, combined with drug violence, continued into the new century in
Colombia. By contrast, the indigenous uprisings or *levantamientos* that
punctuated Ecuador's politics during the 1990s were distinguished by
their largely peaceful character and negotiated outcomes. A closer examination of events, however, reveals that Ecuador was not immune to
persistent human rights abuses and violence on the part of public security forces and private armed groups in the employ of the powerful.

The Quito-based and church-linked Ecumenical Commission for
Human Rights (CEDHU), which has compiled reports and evidence on
human rights abuses in Ecuador since the early 1980s, received information on 389 deaths at the hands of the police, the military, and privately
employed gangs of armed thugs that occurred during the fourteen years
extending from January 1985 to November 1998. In addition, the reports compiled by the commission documented cases of arbitrary arrest,
denial of access to a lawyer, physical abuse, and torture that occurred
throughout the three governments that completed their terms of office
during that period: the right wing León Febres Cordero presidency
(1984–88), the social democratic administration of Rodrigo Borja (1988–
92), and the conservative government of Sixto Durán Ballén (1992–96).
Although the frequency of abuses was lower under Borja, the data suggest that by the end of the Febres Cordero presidency, rights violations

on the part of the state had become institutionalized.[1] Indeed, according to a highly respected human rights leader, "torture became routine" during Febres Cordero's years in office; however, his "most fatal legacy" was "the establishment of a carefully structured repressive apparatus" that, for lack of political power or political will, was not dismantled under his successor, Borja. Indeed, four new police units were created in the name of national security during Febres Cordero's years in office. Moreover, members of these units worked as private guards alongside retired police and military officers, who were contracted frequently by the security firms that began to proliferate in Ecuador in the 1980s, both in its urban areas and in the countryside. Thus public security institutions became linked to private security enterprises, and some of these provided legal cover for the operations of private armed groups.

The proliferation of both state and private security agencies and the overall patterns of human rights abuses, whose perpetrators enjoyed impunity, reflected the fragility and corruption of the country's judicial system following the transition from military rule to elected civilian government in 1980. They formed part of the political-juridical context within which abuses related to land conflicts between peasants and large-estate owners took place. Since this volume is concerned with the possibilities of promoting grassroots-based rural development, it is on the rights violations associated with those conflicts that this chapter focuses. In Ecuador, as elsewhere in Latin America, conflict over land has arisen largely from the failure of agrarian reforms to transform highly inequitable structures of rural asset and power distribution. At the beginning of the twenty-first century, the exercise of repressive public and private violence against peasants and agricultural workers still constituted a principal means of sustaining those structures, holding back the advance of democratization and development (e.g., Kay 2001b; Plant 1999, 101–2).

The data for the analysis of land conflict related abuses are drawn, first of all, from CEDHU's registry of rural land-conflict reports (DCTR), and secondarily from reports and statistics presented in its bi-monthly publication, *Derechos del Pueblo* (DDP). Since the commission maintains records only on cases that have been brought to its attention by persons and organizations that have sought its assistance, the data do not capture the full extent of land conflicts and related rights violations. Moreover, since CEDHU's only office is located in Quito, the capital city in the northern highlands, its coverage of abuses in areas distant from the capital—the southern regions of the country in general—is particularly deficient. Nevertheless, the commission's data open a window on the dimensions and patterns of human rights violations in the Ecuadorian countryside and allow us to understand better the obstacles that lie in the path of rural social and political organization and economic advance.

Below, we first provide a brief description of the context of failed agrarian reform in which violence and abuses take place in Latin America in general and Ecuador specifically. We then turn to an analysis of the CEDHU data to identify types of conflicts and the trends in their frequency in Ecuador's three principal regions—the coast, the highlands, and the Amazonian rain-forest area. This is followed by a brief analysis of the peaks and troughs in conflict frequency and rights abuses in relation to state policies and initiatives taken by NGOs, with special reference to the debt-for-land swap program carried out by the FEPP. Many of the arguments presented here should be considered heuristic. The data base available to us is revealing, but it presents only a part of the picture.

THE RURAL CONTEXT

Despite agrarian reforms in the 1960s and 1970s, at 61 percent, "the proportion of the rural population whose income and consumption fell below nationally defined poverty lines was higher in Latin America and the Caribbean than in any other developing region" (Plant 1999, 89). As a consequence of such deprivation, which dates back to the region's conquest and colonization, waves of peasant rebellion and harsh repression have characterized its history (Wolf 1969; Burns 1980).[2] Furthermore, a leading scholar of Latin American rural society argues that the last two decades of the twentieth century witnessed an unprecedented escalation of violence that was directed "to prevent the empowerment of the subaltern classes" (Kay 2001b, 741). He refers especially to the tens of thousands of peasants who died in civil wars in Nicaragua, El Salvador, Guatemala, Peru, and Colombia, as well as to the reaction of the Mexican government to the Zapatista rebellion in Chiapas. However, countries with less well-known but persistent violence against agricultural workers and peasants included Brazil, where the MST continued to struggle for agrarian reform; Bolivia, where coca-leaf cultivators clashed with state security forces; and Ecuador, where indigenous peasants, beginning in 1990, organized a series of nearly nationwide uprisings against the state's agrarian and structural adjustment programs.

Almost all over the hemisphere, human rights violations tended to be systematic in, but certainly not limited to, areas of large-estate agriculture, where the personal security forces of great landlords—in collusion with the police and armed forces—had historically maintained arbitrary systems of privately enforced "law and order." Violations were also more prevalent and severe in indigenous and black regions, which include much of the Ecuadorian countryside as well as small highland towns where mestizos in the 1990s became threatened by—and lashed out against—indigenous cultural revitalization and social organization (Muyulema Calle 1997; León 2001, 53–54).

Although agrarian reforms were pursued in Ecuador and most other Latin American countries during the 1960s and 1970s, with the prominent exception of Cuba, the power of the old landlord classes was not broken. In addition to maintaining their grip on the most productive land, large-estate owners were often able to diversify into commercial, financial, and industrial activities and to form partnerships with foreign capital, effectively maintaining their influence over national policymaking in general and agricultural policies specifically. Such processes of portfolio diversification and fusion among different sectors of capital have been documented in studies of various Latin American countries (e.g., Zeitlin and Ratcliff 1988; Baloyra 1983; Paige 1997), including works on Ecuador (Hansen 1971; Brownrigg 1972; Conaghan 1988). Even in countries where comprehensive reforms were undertaken (for example, Peru from 1969 to 1975), the institutional arrangements imposed on the reformed sectors were inappropriate and/or the mix of support policies required to make them viable were not forthcoming (Korovkin 1990; Thorp and Bertram 1978, 301–20). Moreover, reform was often followed by counter-reforms of varying intensities (Kay 2001b).

In Ecuador, far-from-comprehensive agrarian reforms were pursued, along with ISI policies, by military governments. The first reform law, in 1964, was decreed in the midst of the country's banana export boom (1950s-60s), and the second, in 1973, in the midst of the petroleum boom (1972–82). Despite the export-boom resources available to the governments of the times, little land was distributed, and policy strongly favored the modernization of large-scale commercial and export sectors controlled by elite groups. In fact, rather than redistribution, government policy favored colonization of the Amazonian region as a way to relieve pressure for land in the highlands and parts of the coast.

Agriculture for domestic consumption, for the most part in the hands of peasant producers, actually suffered from import "desubstitution" during the height of ISI from 1975 to 1982 (Vos 1987, 31). In general, agriculture, where employment could have been generated at low cost, was held back by a "lack of basic rural infrastructure and its unequal distribution in favour of the large producers" while peasant cultivators suffered from worsening terms of trade, "reinforced by state price and subsidy policies" (Vos 1987, 96; see also Vos 1988; Griffin 1983). In 1978, per capita subsidies to urban sectors were almost eleven times those available to rural sectors, and in the countryside the modern capitalist producers received almost eight times more support than peasant cultivators (Larrea 1992, 157).

While they basked in government support programs, the country's civilian elites effectively sabotaged the implementation of the rather modest goals of the reform laws decreed by military governments (North 1985, 433–43). Consequently, they had paltry redistributive impacts and only in some areas of the country (Larrea 1992, 112). According to the

World Bank, the very unequal distribution of land was not altered: In 1994, "1.6% of farms in the Sierra occup[ied] 42.9% of land; in the Costa 3.9% of farms command[ed] 55.1% of the land" (World Bank 1995, 32). Further, the Bank found that "regardless of which measure of poverty we use, there is a clear relationship between the degree or extent of poverty and the household's per capita land holdings" (World Bank 1995, 33).

At the same time that peasants and agricultural workers were denied the land promised in the reform laws, the mechanization of agriculture on the coast and a turn to dairy farming by estate owners in the highlands reduced employment opportunities and provoked increasing temporary and permanent migrations to urban areas (PNUD 1999, 39). Meanwhile, despite the very high growth rates of the urban industrial and commercial sectors during 1974–82, due to their capital intensity, the proportion of wage workers in the urban economically active population also fell, from 67.2 to 65.7 percent (PNUD 1999, 39).

Overall, despite state programs that ensured some important social advances, economic policy choices in the 1970s promoted asset concentration rather than redistribution. Elite sectors, with direct access to the centers of policymaking, obtained the lion's share from both ISI promotion and agricultural modernization programs financed, first, by the petroleum boom and, later, by foreign indebtedness. When the petroleum boom broke and the economy entered into crisis in the early 1980s, many migrants lost their non-farm jobs and were forced to return to their rural communities, where lack of land began to breed increased militancy and land conflicts (Chapter 7). During the following years, as SAPs were pursued, improvements in social welfare were also arrested and even reversed (see, e.g., SIISE 2001).

In this context land conflicts began to increase, and a large proportion of the indigenous populations of the highland and Amazonian regions, led by the CONAIE, founded in 1986, was mobilized into nearly nationwide uprisings against government policies in 1990, 1994, 1997, 2000, and then again in 2001. Access to land featured prominently among the demands of the first two of these uprisings in particular (Chiriboga 2001; García 2001; León 2001). In 1990, CONAIE called for the resolution of dozens of land conflicts,[3] and indigenous people engaged in "recoveries" of land that they considered to have been stolen from them. There were forty such land takeovers in the two northern highland provinces of Imbabura and Pichincha alone (Selverston-Sher 2001, 58–59, citing Moreno and Figueroa 1992). The 1994 uprising was directed primarily against the original text of the Agrarian Development Law, which, among other things, proposed the privatization of water sources and the elimination of communal land ownership (Pacari 1996).

Below, we first review the data on land conflicts and human rights violations available in CEDHU's archives. We then briefly explore the reasons for the dips and troughs in these phenomena.

LAND CONFLICTS AND HUMAN RIGHTS VIOLATIONS: PATTERNS AND CASES

CEDHU's DCTR contains information on conflicts brought to its attention from July 1983 onward. On the basis of data available in that registry, as well as other sources, Alain Dubly and Alicia Granda identified and analyzed 217 *serious rural conflicts* that occurred in the seven-year period extending from July 1983 through June 1990 (96 percent were about land and 4 percent about the control of infrastructure, such as water). Their analysis included only those conflicts that involved peasant communities or other grassroots-based rural organizations or, in their words, "violent agrarian conflicts" in which "popular groups" were protagonists (Dubly and Granda 1991, 10, 12). Their study chronicles violent evictions involving the destruction of crops and houses, land invasions that indigenous villagers considered recoveries of stolen properties, and homicides fueled by the peasants' struggle for land and the estate owners' opposition to agrarian reform. Ecuador's provincial and local police forces, the armed gangs or private armies of landlords, and (less frequently) the country's armed forces battled with peasant and rural worker organizations throughout the 1980s.

Such battles continued into the next decade, and it is on the frequency and types of conflicts in the 1990s that we focus here, comparing them with those of the 1980s. The DCTR contains information on 317 land conflicts that took place during the eleven years extending from August 1990 through August 2001. These 317 reported incidents, however, are not strictly comparable to the conflicts analyzed by Dubly and Granda for two reasons: first, some of the DCTR incidents did not involve organized popular groups, and second, quite a few of them were episodes in a single ongoing conflict. Consequently, to maintain comparability with the Dubly and Granda study and to consider only those cases that clearly affected the possibilities of promoting grassroots-based rural development, we excluded 118 DCTR incidents from our analysis, even though just about all, in one way or another, reflected abuses of power on the part of local elites as well as the weaknesses of the country's judicial institutions.[4] A further thirty-nine incidents were identified as additional episodes of previously registered conflicts and hence were not counted as distinct cases.

The criteria that we employed for selecting cases from the DCTR—criteria that are consistent with Dubly and Granda's work—are twofold. First, we considered as *significant* only those reported incidents that involved more than ten individuals. Disputes between individual peasants, individual estate owners, or family members were excluded from Table 6.1. Second we included only conflicts that were clearly rural, excluding those that took place in peri-urban areas that involved clashes for con-

trol over undeveloped land that pitted urban real-estate interests, specu-
lators, and municipal authorities against squatters and residents' associations (e.g., DCTR 6064, March 19, 1993). The process of elimination
left us with a total of 199 *serious incidents* during the eleven years extending from August 1990 through August 2001. However, when we combined separate incidents related to a single ongoing conflict, we were left
with a total of 160 *serious cases* for that period, that is, fewer than the 217
serious cases identified by Dubly and Granda for the seven-year period
of the 1980s. Table 6.1 also shows that the number of serious conflict
incidents reported in the 1990s fell steadily until 1995 and then remained
at low levels up to mid-2001.

Another problem remains with regard to the comparison of 1990s
trends with those of the 1980s. In addition to the CEDHU registry, Dubly
and Granda used other sources, including newspaper reports and data
from various archives. Consequently, the 1990s cases presented here
underreport the actual frequency of conflict. In this respect it must be
emphasized that even Dubly and Granda were not able to identify all
cases of conflict during their chosen period of analysis. Nevertheless, the
DCTR data we analyze here, we believe, do reflect principal trends: in
short, a peak in conflict at the end of the 1980s and the early 1990s,
followed by a steady decline, particularly in the indigenous highland areas. Most important, whatever the limitations of the data may be, the
CEDHU registry tells a story that is not well known and that should be
told. Below, we will first review the frequency of *serious incidents* in the
three principal regions of Ecuador: the coast, the highlands, and the
Amazonian rain-forest area (the *ongoing serious cases* of conflict do not
lend themselves to annual presentation because they stretch over a number of years). We then provide descriptions of several specific conflicts in
each of these regions.

Serious Conflict Incidents by Region

Ecuador's three regions represent distinctive socioeconomic, cultural,
institutional, and political spaces. The highlands are characterized by
the presence of a large indigenous population that was historically subject to servile social relations on large estates oriented toward production for the domestic market. Agriculture in the coastal region (Costa),
by contrast, has been export oriented. The region was largely settled by
highlanders who migrated to work on cacao and banana estates—the
export-boom crops of the turn of the twentieth century and of the post–
World War II period respectively. The Amazonian region, traditionally
populated by nomadic indigenous groups, was colonized by commercial
estate owners, land-hungry peasants from the highlands and coast, and
transnational petroleum corporations from the early 1970s onward, when

oil exports from that region became Ecuador's principal foreign-exchange earner.

Land conflicts in both the highlands and the Amazon were permeated by indigenous claims and ethnic tensions. In the latter region, on some occasions local indigenous populations clashed with poor peasant colonizers who had been encouraged to move there from other areas of the country (see, e.g., Selverston-Scher 2001, 32–35); on other occasions, they joined forces with the colonizers in claims against foreign petroleum companies and large commercial growers. By contrast, in the Costa, disputes over land tended to take the form of class conflict between large-estate owners on the one hand, and peasant cultivators and agricultural laborers on the other.

Turning to the data presented in Table 6.1, *incidents* related to serious conflicts reported to CEDHU declined in number from the highs of forty-two in the last five months of 1990 and fifty in 1991 to lows of only three in 1995 and 2000. The coastal provinces accounted for 115 (or 58 percent) of the total number of 199 conflicts. The province of Guayas, the historic seat of the country's agro-export oligarchy, registered nearly as many serious incidents of rural violence as all the highland provinces combined. Seven out of the country's twenty-one provinces accounted for 82 percent of the violence: Guayas, Esmeraldas, and Los Ríos on the north and central coast; Pichincha, Imbabura, and Cotopaxi in the north and central highlands; and Napo in the central Amazonian region.

Clearly, the southern provinces of all three regions appear to be under-represented in the CEDHU DCTR. As noted earlier, those provinces are relatively distant from Quito. However, an additional factor was at work in parts of the central and southern highlands. The progressive bishop and church agencies that functioned in Riobamba, the capital of Chimborazo province, were recipients of reports and the mediators of conflicts in their areas of influence. In this highly indigenous and notoriously conflictive province treated by Korovkin (Chapter 7) and Bretón (Chapter 8), Bishop Proaño, an aggressive advocate of indigenous rights from the 1960s to the early 1990s, created a strong and activist pro-peasant culture among representatives of the Catholic church.

Despite the gaps in our data, an examination of the geographical distribution of the cases underscores continuities in rural human rights abuses. The comparatively high frequency of reported conflict in the Costa during the 1990s reflects a trend identified by Dubly and Granda for the 1980s. In the 217 conflicts they analyzed, they found that 120 (55 percent) occurred in the Costa provinces (Dubly and Granda 1991, 15–16, 56–114). Similarly, during the period from 1990 to 2001, Guayas, Esmeraldas, and Los Ríos maintained the highest frequencies of rural conflict: fifty-three (27 percent), twenty-five (13 percent), and twenty-three (12 percent) of the total number of incidents respectively. Moreover, Dubly

Table 6.1 CEDHU-Reported Incidents of Serious Rural Conflict by Year and Province

	1990*	1991	1992	1993	1994	1995	1996	1997	1998	1999	2000	2001*	Total	%
Costa														
Esmeraldas	3	5	3	1	2		1	1		4	3	2	25	13
Manabí					2								2	1
Los Ríos	5	5	3	1			3	2	1	2		1	23	12
Guayas	10	15	7	7	3	1	4	3	1	1		1	53	27
El Oro	1	5	1		2	1	2						12	6
Total Costa	19	30	14	9	9	2	10	6	2	7	3	4	115	58
Sierra														
Carchi		1		1									2	1
Imbabura	6	2	7		1								16	8
Pichincha	2	3	2	3	1	1	2		1				15	9
Cotopaxi	4	4	3	2	1		1						15	8
Tungurahua			1										1	
Bolívar	5												5	3
Chimborazo	1	3											4	2

* 1990, August–December only; 2001, January–August only.

Source: CEDHU, Registry of Denuncias de Conflicto de Tierra Rural.

	1990*	1991	1992	1993	1994	1995	1996	1997	1998	1999	2000	2001*	Total	%
Sierra, con't														
Cañar	1						1						2	1
Azuay														
Loja									1				1	
Total Sierra	19	13	13	6	3	1	4		2				61	31
Amazonia														
Napo	3	8	1		2			3					17	9
Sucumbíos		1			1		1						3	1
Pastaza				1									1	
Morona Santiago	1	1											2	1
Zamora Chinchipe														
Total Amazonia	4	10	1	1	3		1	3	4	7	3		23	11
Grand Total	42	53	28	16	15	3	15	9	4	7	3	4	199	100

and Granda found the highest levels of land conflict related violence—including destruction of property and deaths—in the Costa (Dubly and Granda 1991, 204). Below, we provide a few examples of this type of violence during the 1990s in the Costa and the highland regions (a discussion of Amazonian cases is included in North, Kitt, and Koep 2003).

Stories of Conflict

To begin with the Costa, historically, the region's landowners have deployed gangs of armed thugs *(grupos de matones)* to suppress peasant and agricultural workers' organizations, and the activities of those gangs have often been supported by local police and civilian authorities. The 1980s and 1990s were no exception.[5] Indeed, throughout those two decades the landed elites of Guayas and Los Ríos resorted to strong-armed extralegal tactics to intimidate peasants from claiming unoccupied or under-utilized lands, from initiating legal proceedings to acquire title, or from invading estates.

For example, in the canton of Babahoyo in the province of Los Ríos, the families of Pedro Cedeño Bajaña, Augusto Guerrero, and Julio Ronquillo frequently resorted to violence to repress peasant activism. Their modus operandi included threats, paralegal evictions, illegal arrests, and even murder (Dubly and Granda 1991, 65–67, 71–72). The Banda Armada Cedeño became particularly notorious for its tactics of intimidation and violence. In November 1996, for example, Banda thugs occupied rice-growing lands belonging to the cooperative Esperanza de los Beldacos in the canton of Montalvo in Los Ríos. Even though the cooperative had acquired the ex-*hacienda* twenty years earlier, with the recognition of the IERAC, Gabriel Cedeño and a group of armed civilians invaded the property, expelled thirty families, assaulted the inhabitants, destroyed their homes and their crops, and robbed them of their produce (DCTR 8649, November 8, 1996).

Two months later the Escobar family, landholders in Babahoyo, contracted the Cedeños' services to eliminate the leadership of a group of thirty rice producers organized into the Cooperativa Guarel. Given the success of the Cedeños' earlier efforts to amass property by evicting peasants, the Escobars also decided to intimidate cooperative members and take over their lands (DCTR 8802, January 22, 1997). Altogether, fourteen assassinations were attributed to the head of the Cedeño family, who remained at liberty, supported by the local police and civil authorities in addition to his armed thugs, until his death from natural causes. The Banda, however, did not dissolve with his death; it continued to operate at the beginning of the twenty-first century under the leadership of his sons.

To turn to yet another case, in the canton of El Empalme in Guayas, a foreign landholder and his Ecuadorian wife contracted armed groups to defend their abandoned or under-utilized estate against a peasant organization. In 1994, 250 landless peasant families, who had formed the Asociación Agrícola Campo Verde, presented a claim to the lands to Congress and the Minister of the Interior. In January 1996 the absentee landowners hired armed thugs to terrorize the association members and dislodge them from the disputed land. On January 22, when hostilities escalated, sympathetic peasant cooperatives and associations sent representatives to offer their support and solidarity to the members of Campo Verde. Upon their arrival they found that sixty thugs hired by the landowners had murdered one association leader, destroyed houses and fields, and set ablaze the community school, the church, and forty homes (DCTR 8054, January 22, 1996; DCTR 8055, January 22, 1996). Four days later the landowners succeeded in dispatching local police to arrest eight Campo Verde members (DCTR 8072, January 26, 1996).

A more recent case from Esmeraldas displays patterns of violence and abuse similar to those found in Guayas and Los Ríos. The antagonists in this instance were the forestry company BOTROSA S.A. and a local association of agricultural workers known as Ecuador Libre. Problems began in 1998 when the agency set up by the 1994 Agrarian Development Law, INDA, awarded BOTROSA control over 3,123 hectares from the El Pambilar estate in the canton of Quininde. The circumstances surrounding this award were subsequently brought into question since the principal shareholder in BOTROSA was at the time of the award acting Minister of Commerce, Industry, and Fisheries and due to the fact that the land in question was thought by some to form part of a "Patrimonial Forest of the State" and hence entitled to special protection from the activities of forestry companies. In fact, the case eventually led to the resignation of the INDA head and to criminal charges against him due to the "irregularities" surrounding the ruling (DCTR 11288, April 3, 2000; DDP 119, October 2000, 7).

As might be expected, however, it was the members of Ecuador Libre who had to bear the full brunt of the INDA head's misdeeds. Once control over the land passed to BOTROSA, the *campesinos* who had owned and worked it for many years effectively became "invaders" in the eyes of the state. In June 1999 the Minister of the Environment asked the army to place at BOTROSA's disposal all units in the sector and to offer full support to the private guards of the company in the task of evicting the "invaders." With the full weight of state power and resources behind it, BOTROSA began a campaign of intimidation and violence against the *campesinos*, using armed thugs, private security guards, and at times its own employees. Homes were burned, crops were destroyed, animals were killed, death threats were issued, and families were constantly harassed and restricted in their movements in the area (DCTR 10863, September 29, 1999; DCTR 11722, October 24, 2000; DDP 109, February 1999, 7; DDP 119, October 2000, 7; DDP 120, December 2000, 11).

Similar acts of intimidation, abuse, and violence occurred in the highlands, where estate owners' private armed forces evicted indigenous peasants intent on "recovering" their "stolen" lands, threatened their families, and periodically murdered peasant association leaders in order to stifle organization. In the canton of Otavalo in the largely indigenous highland province of Imbabura, a long-smoldering dispute between the La Clemencia estate and the Comuna Huaycopungo ignited in violence in 1991. The conflict stretched back to 1757 when the Spanish Crown had issued a land title of twenty-six *caballerías* (1,677 hectares) to the *caciques* (headmen) and indigenous inhabitants of the villages of Caluquí and Gualacata in Otavalo. However, over the next two centuries non-Indians had gained access to much of the communities' land. Meanwhile, the descendants of most of the original title holders, more than eight hundred families, were living in "extreme poverty," "with little land, insufficient even to build their houses." In 1985 they initiated legal proceedings with IERAC to reclaim their ancestral land (*DDP* 62, April 1991, 12). Their petition succeeded, and in May 1990 they took possession of a tract of land they called the Comuna Huaycopungo—a total of 220 hectares expropriated from La Clemencia estate by IERAC order (DDP 62, April 1991, 12; Dubly and Granda 1991, 90).

However, the story did not end there. From the outset, neighboring large landholders had looked on with apprehension as the members of the Pre-Asociación Agrícola Huaycopungo petitioned IERAC. Violent confrontations began to erupt between *campesinos* and forces allied with the estate owners. In 1989–90, dozens of indigenous community members were beaten, at least seven were detained by the police, residents' houses were burned, and some of their livestock disappeared mysteriously (Dubly and Granda 1991, 90). When these tactics failed to dislodge the community members, the owners of La Clemencia hired *paramilitares negros* (black paramilitaries) from the neighboring province of Esmeraldas, playing on and exacerbating the mutual distrust and fear between Ecuador's coastal black and highland indigenous peoples. In March 1991 witnesses identified a gang of such thugs who shot and killed one of the most vocal defenders of the Comuna Huaycopungo and a leader of the FICI (Korovkin 2000). Despite the condemnations of peasant and indigenous leaders and human rights advocates, police released the accused gunmen after only eighteen months of incarceration. For CEDHU, all this corroborated "the impunity of the paramilitary bands and the [Borja] government's lack of political will to resolve the agrarian conflicts that are causing grave violations of human rights" (DDP 62, April 1991, 12). By November 1992, when the Durán Ballén government was in power, the owners of La Clemencia had once again reverted to the long-tested tactics of harassment and intimidation (DDP 72, November 1992, 7).

In another highland province with a large proportion of indigenous people, Cotopaxi, landholder-community violence erupted in the canton of Pujilí, where twelve property owners refused to recognize the 1825 land title of five indigenous communities. In March 1991 a landowner and his armed gang fired on community members while they tried to reclaim their lands. During the skirmish, one community member was killed and four others were injured (DDP 66, November 1991, 6; DCTR 4466, May 13, 1991; DCTR 4743, September 25, 1991).Then, in January 1992, landowners robbed cattle, and three community members died as a result of shots fired by gunmen (DCTR 4969, January 23, 1992).

With regard to the Amazonian region, suffice it to note that Indian community organizations, mestizo colonists, large-estate owners, the Ecuadorian armed forces, local officials, and foreign oil companies clashed as they sought to maintain control over land and other resources. In comparison to other regions, however, the conflicts in the Amazonian provinces were far more likely to involve the participation of Ecuadorian military or local state officials as the perpetrators of human rights abuses (DCTR 9297, May 20, 1997).

These cases demonstrate the absence of the rule of law in much of the Ecuadorian countryside, collusion between private interests and state authorities, the unwillingness of the large landlord class to accept agrarian reform, and repression of peasant organizations carried out by local agents, all acts that seldom received publicity in the elite-controlled national media. The degree of elite penetration of the state achieved its most concrete expression when the resident *político*, the army officer, the police chief, and the local judge all lined up to do the bidding of the large-estate owner or resource-extraction corporation that was battling against poor peasant farmers. The profound asymmetry of asset and power distribution that characterizes most rural areas of Ecuador was manifested in the impunity that landlords enjoyed while engaging in often brutal suppression of peasants and their organizations.

In sum, the stories of violence tell us that where large estates prevailed in Ecuador, the possibilities of peasant organization and the emergence of civic activism—what the World Bank calls social capital—that could underpin local development and democratization were severely restricted.

INTERPRETING THE DECLINE IN AGRARIAN CONFLICT-RELATED HUMAN RIGHTS VIOLATIONS IN THE 1990s

To explain the decline in violent land conflicts, especially in the highlands—keeping in mind that the CEDHU registry data are far from comprehensive—we here draw attention briefly to programs sponsored by both Catholic and evangelical churches along with church-linked NGOs, especially the FEPP; certain national government policies; and other factors, including the employment opportunities created by the rapid growth of the cut-flower export industry and increasing amounts of remittances sent to just about all parts of the country by Ecuadorians who had migrated to the United States, Spain, and elsewhere. All of these phenomena, taken together and in different ways, alleviated tensions in the countryside and contributed to the decline in the number of land-conflict related human rights violations after the peak from 1990 to 1992, during and immediately following the first indigenous uprising.

Church and NGO Programs

In an effort to further rural development and defuse land conflict, in 1970 the church created the FEPP to provide economic, legal, and moral support to indigenous, Afro-Ecuadorian, and poor mestizo peasant organizations and assist them in acquiring access to land through nonconfrontational methods (Navarro, Vallejo, and Villaverde 1996). Between 1977 and 1990, FEPP provided credit to sixty-five communities in one coastal, one Amazonian, and eight highland provinces, playing a particularly active role in Chimborazo (see Chapters 7 and 8). By 1999 FEPP had eleven regional offices (in addition to its central office in Quito) that provided credit for land purchases and agricultural extension and other services to peasant communities, primarily in the highlands.

With the accumulation of tension and increasing numbers of land conflicts during the 1980s, in 1988–89 FEPP and the CEE completed negotiations with the Borja government and foreign banks to exchange a part of Ecuador's foreign debt in order to establish a rotating credit program that would permit peasant organizations to purchase land. Significantly, an agreement was signed in October 1990, just a few months after the first of the indigenous uprisings that paralyzed the country during that decade took place (Zamosc 1994; Pacari 1996).

Over the next five years, 153 peasant communities and over 5,700 families benefited from the FEPP-administered debt-for-land exchange (North, Kit, and Koep 2003). By the time the program drew to its end, 9,235 families (or about 50,000–60,000 persons) had obtained land. Credit was concentrated in highland areas where rural violence and land conflict were, for the most part, inextricably linked to indigenous claims for ancestral lands. Indeed, four highland provinces—Imbabura, Chimborazo, Cotopaxi, and Bolívar—accounted for 75 percent of the funds disbursed by FEPP during the first phase of the program. Interviews with FEPP personnel in Quito and Riobamba, in combination with the Dubly and Granda and CEDHU data, allow us to conclude that the program succeeded in reducing conflict in the rural highlands in particular.

FEPP disbursed very little credit in the Costa, where it had only two offices, in the provinces of Manabí and Esmeraldas. The acquisitions in Manabí and Esmeraldas were negligible, and no lands at all were purchased with the FEPP's credit program in the provinces of Guayas, Los Ríos, and El Oro, where FEPP had never established a presence (Navarro, Vallejo, and Villaverde 1996, 39–67). Significantly, violence remained at higher levels in the Costa than in the highlands throughout the 1990s.

However, it was not only FEPP that provided alternatives for highland peasants and especially for indigenous communities. As both Korovkin and Bretón point out (Chapters 7 and 8), evangelical churches and many NGOs financed growing numbers of local projects and provided an increasing variety of services to rural communities in indigenous areas.

State Policies

While the FEPP was executing the debt-for-land swap, transformations in the political and economic structure of opportunities affected the peasants' propensity to demand land and invade estates. First of all, it is possible that members of *campesino* organizations and rural cooperatives expected the social democratic Borja government (1988–92) to respond favorably to their demands for land and social justice. Therefore, the spike in violence and abuse in the countryside during his presidency may have indicated, in part, a reaction to increased peasant militancy on the part of estate owners, local officials, and police forces, and (to a much lesser extent) the Ecuadorian armed forces. Moreover, Borja also reduced the amount of conflict that would be experienced in subsequent years: he approved the FEPP-administered debt-for-land swap program and settled two major disputes over indigenous ancestral lands in the Amazonian provinces of Pastaza and Napo.

After Borja left the presidency in mid-1992, rural violence diminished, in part as a consequence of the FEPP program and other factors discussed below. In addition, however, rural popular organizations would have registered the shift in policy represented by the Durán Ballén administration (1992–96) and, as a consequence, would have been persuaded to follow less aggressive paths. The knowledge that the government would respond with force to peasants' confrontational tactics to claim land on large estates may have reduced peasant militancy and, in turn, lessened estate owners' fears of government expropriation and peasant land invasions. Moreover, Durán Ballén's government brought agrarian reform to an end through the 1994 Law of Agrarian Development. Although an indigenous uprising against the original text of that law resulted in some modifications, among other things it established harsh penalties in cases of "illegal" occupation or invasion of titled lands. For peasants and landless rural laborers, the message of the new law was clear: The period of moderate state-sanctioned agrarian reform was officially over (Navarro, Vallejo, and Villaverde 1996, 33–38).[6]

However, the governments of Durán Ballén and those that followed him did not rely entirely on restrictive legislation and repression. They also followed the time-honored tactics of sponsoring divisions within indigenous and peasant movements and creating mechanisms of cooptation in the form of two programs in particular: CODENPE and PRODEPINE. Both provided jobs for indigenous and black leaders and project funding for their rural constituencies. PRODEPINE was particularly well funded, with about US$40 million from the World Bank (Arcos Cabrera 2001, 54–55), and it was administered by indigenous organizations, with minimal government involvement (Carroll and Bebbington 2000). At the same time, in 1990, the Ecuadorian armed forces began to pursue civic action programs of various types in the countryside and especially in those areas in which the indigenous uprisings had received most support (see, e.g., Selverston-Scher 2001, 113).

Other Conflict-Reducing Factors

While the FEPP assisted with land purchases, and the government, armed forces, and World Bank responded with new programs, employment opportunities in the cut-flower export industry of the northern and central highlands increased spectacularly: from 3,569 relatively well-paying direct jobs in 1990 to 49,881 in 1999 (Korovkin 2003, 5; Krupa 2001, 7). At the same time, remittances from the exterior became the second most important source of foreign currency by mid-2001 (*The Economist* Intelligence Unit 2001), as up to a million Ecuadorians—10 percent of the economically active population—left the country during the second half of the 1990s (Acosta 2002; Barragan and Velasquez 2000, A3).

The provinces that manifested low levels of land conflict in both periods under consideration here were variously characterized by high receipts of remittances from the early 1980s onward (the provinces of Azuay and Cañar); the presence of middling-sized commercial peasant producers who enjoyed access to good quality land (the provinces of El Oro and Carchi) (Larrea et al. 1987; Larrea et al. 1996); and/or the historical presence of highly productive small properties (*minifundios*), which had facilitated rural diversification processes akin to those described by North in the canton of Pelileo (Chapter 11) (in most of Tungurahua and parts of Azuay and Cañar).

The conjunction of factors that led to decline in land conflicts during the second half of the 1990s, however, was beginning to unravel at the turn of the century as dollarization led to an overvalued currency that began to hurt seriously peasant agricultural and artisan production as well as peasant employment opportunities, in the case of the flower-export industry. Meanwhile, the limits to migration may have been reached, especially in light of restrictive measures adopted by the United States and European countries following the September 11, 2001, destruction of the World Trade Center. Moreover, the fundamental problems of inequity in the distribution of land were not resolved by the programs described above; the structures that gave rise to the rural conflicts discussed here remained firmly entrenched and, overall, land concentration was on the rise (Chapter 5).

Notes

[1] For a more detailed discussion of the rights violations discussed in this chapter, see North, Kit, and Koep 2003.

[2] The exception is, of course, Costa Rica, where small-scale producers were prominent in the coffee-export sector. Costa Rica is also the most successful democracy in the hemisphere (see Winson 1989; Colburn 1993; Paige 1997). The implementation of SAPs, however, began to erode its democratic system during the period from 1980 to 2000 (Seligson 2002).

[3] According to Zamosc, there were seventy-two land conflicts between peasants and *hacienda* owners in the highlands alone (Zamosc 1993, 289). Bretón (Chapter 8) refers to eight hundred conflicts. However, that number includes conflicts between peasants and between peasant communities in addition to conflicts between peasants and estate owners.

[4] To provide just one example of the types of conflicts that were excluded, in 1994 two elderly sisters sought CEDHU's assistance to defend themselves against a lawyer who allegedly had tricked them into transferring title to their farm to him (DCTR 7178, September 22, 1994).

[5] For a detailed analysis of land conflicts in the province of Guayas during the 1960s, see Uggen 1975. For analyses of agrarian conflict and truncated agrarian reform in rice and banana production areas in the Costa, see Redclift 1978 and Striffler 2002. Human Rights Watch 2002 reports on current human rights violations on banana plantations (Human Rights Watch 2002).

[6] Another explanation for the decline in land conflict during Durán Ballén's presidency may be related to repression. The number of arbitrary arrests during a three-year period of his administration climbed up to 925 from 488 during an equivalent period of Borja's term in office. The question is: Were detentions and abuses designed to decapitate the leadership of peasant and other popular organizations in order to deter collective action?

Part III

CASE STUDIES FROM THE ECUADORIAN HIGHLANDS

ର ର ର

Chapter 7

Agrarian Capitalism and Communal Institutional Spaces

Chimborazo After the Land Reform

TANYA KOROVKIN

In the 1980s and early 1990s Ecuador witnessed the rise of a powerful indigenous movement. At the national level this movement was represented by the CONAIE, which included Andean peasant communities, largely Quichua and Spanish-speaking, along with native communities of the Amazon and coastal regions. In 1990 the CONAIE organized a nationwide indigenous uprising that proved to be especially strong in the Andean region. Hundreds of thousands of indigenous peasants blocked the roads and took over government buildings in provincial capitals and towns. Their demands were focused mostly on land but also on the improvement of rural infrastructure and the recognition of indigenous cultural rights. Over the following decade the CONAIE also made clear its opposition to structural adjustment, forming an alliance with other social movements that challenged the national policy shift toward economic neoliberalism.

The political agenda of the Andean community movement raises questions about the nature of indigenous peasant struggles. Early studies saw peasant resistance to the expansion of commercial *haciendas* as a major cause of rural political mobilization. Rural conflicts in this view were generally identified with peasant land struggles (Wolf 1969; Landsberger 1969). In the 1960s and 1970s, however, the Latin American countryside underwent state-sponsored capitalist modernization, in many cases accompanied by land-reform legislation. By and large the sprawling,

---

This chapter is a revised and updated version of Korovkin 1997.

semi-feudal *haciendas* were replaced by medium-sized capitalist farms producing food and agro-industrial crops for the domestic market. After the transition to economic neoliberalism, this trend was reinforced by the growth of nontraditional agricultural exports, such as winter fruit, vegetables, and cut flowers. The result was a rapid process of socioeconomic differentiation among the peasantry. While a few peasant producers were able to develop into successful commercial farmers, often with the help of state-sponsored rural development programs, the vast majority was transformed into a pool of cheap temporary labor for capitalist agriculture and urban economies (de Janvry, Sadoulet, and Young 1989; Llambi 1990; Kay 1995; Thrupp 1994; Carter, Bradford, and Mesbah 1996). This led scholars working in the dependency and world-economy perspective to suggest that the impoverished and semi-proletarianized peasantry had become "functional" to global capitalism (de Janvry 1982; Wallerstein 1979).

Although the socioeconomic implications of the capitalist modernization of agriculture have been widely discussed, its effect on rural political struggles has received less scholarly attention. Moreover, the exiting studies point in different directions. Influenced by the Marxist analysis of agrarian capitalism, Paige argued that the transformation of the Latin American countryside resulted in a gradual disappearance of land conflicts, which in his view were increasingly replaced by labor conflicts involving agricultural workers and conflicts around prices and credit with small commercial farmers as their protagonists (Paige 1975, 1985). The historical evidence, however, casts doubt on Paige's conclusion. Instead of withering away with the semi-feudal *haciendas*, land conflicts persisted into the 1980s and 1990s. Thus, access to land continued as one of the major demands of peasant organizations in Brazil, Colombia, Mexico, and Peru, in addition to Ecuador (Paré 1990; Grzybowski 1990; Zamosc 1989; Montoya 1989).

The decades of state economic intervention did, however, take a toll on peasants' capacity for autonomous political action. A pioneering study conducted by Powell in Venezuela revealed a tendency toward the growth of clientelism in relations between the state and peasant organizations (Powell 1970). Subsequently, this line of analysis was developed by Galli (1981) and Grindle (1986), who argued that land reform and integrated rural development programs in Latin America were often used by governments as instruments of social and political control. One should not, however, underestimate the peasant potential for autonomous political action. In fact, such action was frequently fueled by state intervention. For example, Peru's land reform was questioned by both peasant communities excluded from the process of land redistribution and peasant beneficiaries unhappy with the bureaucratic structure of state-sponsored cooperatives (Korovkin 1990).

Significantly, the struggle for land and the questioning of state controls seem to be especially prominent in rural areas with predominantly indigenous populations. The CONAIE in Ecuador, the Katarista movement in Bolivia, and the Consejo Regional Indígena del Cauca in Colombia are some of the indigenous organizations that have been able to mobilize the indigenous peasantry under a largely ethnic political banner. Indeed, the 1980s and 1990s in Latin America were characterized by the unprecedented growth of indigenous movements (Van Cott 1994). Increasingly, it was national and regional indigenous federations that championed the indigenous peasant demand for land previously voiced by class-based peasant organizations. Peasant and agrarian studies, however, stand in an uneasy relationship with ethnic studies. Following the tradition established by Wolf's early writings on indigenous corporate communities, it has frequently been assumed that the indigenous identity will largely disappear with the development of the market economy as ethnic conflicts become subsumed by class (peasant or proletarian) struggles. More recent findings, however, question this assumption. It has been argued that what looks on the surface like peasant collective action is often grounded in ethnic values that provide it with both culturally defined goals (for example, access to land seen as territory) and institutional means (for example, communal organization with indigenous roots) (Rasnake 1988; Riviera Cusicanqui 1990; Ströbele-Gregor 1994).

This chapter will not address ethnic issues in Ecuador, a topic that has been discussed in a number of studies (Almeida et al. 1993; Moreno Yañez and Figueroa 1992; León 1994; Korovkin 1998; Selverston-Scher 2001). Nor will it deal with indigenous peasant struggles against economic neoliberalism. I limit myself here to an analysis of the social and political implications of the state-sponsored capitalist modernization in the Ecuadorian countryside. The focus will be on Chimborazo, an impoverished Andean province with the largest proportion of Quichua-speaking population in the country and with a remarkably high level of indigenous peasant activism. Special attention will be paid to the policies of land reform and rural development conducted by the national government over the period from the mid-1960s to the early 1990s. I argue that these policies unleashed a series of conflicts, ranging from the centuries-old struggle for land to a relatively new quest for the control of the rural infrastructure. These conflicts gave rise to an indigenous peasant movement and resulted in the emergence of communal institutional spaces on the margins of agrarian capitalism. Unable to reverse dominant economic trends (as discussed in Chapter 4), Chimborazo's communities, with their long historical record of social—as opposed to physical—capital formation, formed the basis of a new rural civil society, a necessary—although insufficient—precondition for meaningful rural development.

THE RISE OF THE INDIGENOUS
PEASANT COMMUNITY MOVEMENT

From the seventeenth century on, Chimborazo's countryside was dominated by the commercial *hacienda* system, geared toward the domestic market and based on relations of service tenure. This system started to crack in the 1940s and 1950s in the course of the post–World War II economic boom that resulted from export expansion in the coastal region. The export boom accelerated urbanization and increased the urban demand for food, which triggered the capitalist modernization of the Andean *hacienda*, including its increased reliance on wage labor. At the same time, export expansion increased the scope of peasant migration, which eroded the power base of the *hacienda* owners. However, the most explicit challenge to Chimborazo's *hacienda* came from the *huasipunguero* political mobilization. This was led by the FEI, organized in 1944 by the Communist Party. Inspired by the Marxist analysis of agrarian capitalism, FEI leaders saw the objective of the *huasipungueros'* struggles in the replacement of the service tenure with wage relations, which in turn would allow the transformation of the supposedly disunited and submissive indigenous peasantry into a militant agricultural proletariat. With this vision and objective in mind, the FEI encouraged the organization of *hacienda* unions, which became involved in a struggle for the payment of wages in accordance with the existing labor legislation.

Even though the union demands invariably focused on wages, in many cases what was actually at stake was the *hacienda* land. According to Sylva, *hacienda* owners were generally not able to pay wages because of the prevailing low agricultural productivity, nor were the peasants really interested in cash payments (Sylva 1986). What they wanted was land. To some extent, this was due to the fact that even though many peasants received part of their family income in wages, they continued to rely on access to land for their subsistence. In this sense the *huasipunguero* struggle against the *haciendas* can be considered a peasant struggle despite its proclaimed proletarian goals. At the same time, however, it can be seen as an ethnic struggle. Land, for the indigenous peasantry, was not only an economic asset but also a territory on which they could reconstruct their social practices and cultural identity.

Chimoborazo peasants largely lost their economic struggles. The 1964 land reform abolished service tenure and granted former *huasipungueros* property rights to their small plots of land. It also created the IERAC to implement the land-redistribution policy. The actual transfer of land from the *hacienda* sector to peasant communities, however, was insignificant. In the seven years following the land reform, only 3 percent of Chimborazo's land was allocated by IERAC to small landowners. At the same time, peasants lost access to the *hacienda* pastures and other resources (water, firewood) to which they had been entitled as *huasipun-gueros*.

Although the 1964 land reform was an economic defeat for the majority of the indigenous peasantry, it was a clear victory in political-institutional terms. The collapse of the semi-feudal *hacienda* order was followed by a rapid growth of indigenous community organization. After 1964 an increasing number of the now freehold communities in Chimborazo took advantage of the 1937 Law of Communes—something that the *hacienda*-bound *huasipungueros* had been unable to do.[1] In only seven years, from 1964 to 1970, more than 100 Chimborazo communities legalized their status as communes, as compared with 156 over the previous quarter century.

To some extent this organizational explosion demonstrated the extraordinary vitality of the indigenous communal tradition, rooted in the precolonial past as well as in the colonial and the *hacienda* experiences. However, the importance of traditional values and institutions in Chimborazo's community movements should not be overestimated. It was a renewed tradition—a tradition reinforced by political expediency and blending old social patterns with new influences and aspirations. These influences and aspirations were reflected in the rise of a new generation of indigenous leaders—young people with a secondary or higher education and a good understanding of provincial and national politics. They replaced the older generation of indigenous leaders who were generally appointed by *hacienda* owners in concert with Catholic priests and local representatives of the central government (Lentz 1987).

The younger community leaders were more willing to look for external allies who could offer legal, economic, or political support to their communities. In the 1960s and 1970s these allies came mostly from the ranks of Chimborazo's Catholic church. Under the leadership of Monsignor Leonidas Proaño, Archbishop of Riobamba, the progressive members of the Catholic clergy proclaimed their "preferential option for the poor" and became increasingly involved in promoting indigenous culture. The progressive church emphasized the importance of land reform and the need for indigenous peasant organization. It provided local communities with legal advice in their struggles against the *haciendas* and helped them achieve official recognition as communes. Moreover, Chimborazo's clergy supported the organization of provincial and regional indigenous federations—the MICH and the ECUARUNARI—that became active members of CONAIE.

These developments underscore the importance of the progressive Catholic church as a catalyst in the rise of Chimborazo's indigenous community movement. By the late-1970s it had largely replaced the Communist Party as the main ally of the indigenous peasantry. The FEI leadership underestimated the organizational potential of indigenous communities, giving preference to the organization of the *hacienda* unions (and, later, agricultural production cooperatives), whose political and economic objectives were not always acceptable—or even sufficiently clear—to the communal peasantry. By contrast, the progressive Catholic church, willing to accommodate Christian and indigenous values and institutions, gave its wholehearted support to the existing communal forms of organization. This cultural and political flexibility accounts for its remarkable influence within Chimborazo's indigenous peasant movement.

Considerable as it was, the influence of the Catholic church did not go unchallenged. In the canton of Colta and other parts of the province the Catholic church was questioned by Protestant missionaries who organized a federation of indigenous Protestant churches, the AIECH. Like many Catholic priests, Protestant missionaries became heavily involved in social work with indigenous peasant communities. The Protestants, however, put more emphasis on individual and family economic achievement. Moreover, in an attempt to promote savings and eliminate alcoholism they banned communal religious festivals, which they associated with excessive drinking and unproductive spending. They also minimized the importance of indigenous struggles for land, insisting that thrift and hard work were the only legitimate ways to economic security.[2]

In the following years, however, the Protestant missionaries' teachings were significantly modified by their indigenous followers, whose number skyrocketed at the expense of the Catholic parishes. Not only had the Protestant churches actively promoted Quichua as a means of religious communication, but they also had incorporated indigenous believers into the clergy, something that Chimborazo's Catholic church had failed to do on a large scale. Indigenous Protestant pastors and deacons tried, in turn, to reconcile the largely foreign religious ideas with their own communal values and practices. As a result, in some areas (for example, Cacha) the indigenous Protestant clergy played an important role in the development of local communal organizations, side by side with the Catholic community leaders. Many Protestant communities took part in the 1990 indigenous uprising despite strong criticism from the provincial leadership of the AIECH.

Both the political involvement and the organizational heterogeneity of Chimborazo's peasantry increased as a result of the growing influence of the new political left. Most influential was the MPD, a broad-based electoral front that emerged from a Maoist splinter of the pro-Moscow Communist Party. In Chimborazo, the MPD-led UCAE gained support in both indigenous and mestizo areas. Along with the heavily Catholic and Protestant communities, the MPD-influenced communities took part in the 1990 uprising, even though the MPD national leadership did not support this initiative.

The decline of the FEI, the growth of the progressive Catholic and Protestant influences, and the presence of a new political left in indigenous and mestizo communities all point to the complexities of Andean indigenous politics. Ethnicity, class, religion, and ideology intertwine, producing political-institutional outcomes not easily understood when any of these factors is considered in isolation from the others. The common denominator in this increasingly complex political game was, however, the growing strength of the indigenous community movements. The 1964 land reform is generally viewed as a defeat for Ecuador's indigenous peasantry because it had to settle for an exceedingly limited form of land redistribution (Barsky 1984a; Velasco 1979; Guerrero 1983). This view, however, should be qualified in the light of later events. The communities lost the game in terms of access to land, but they won an impressive victory in political and institutional terms. Limited as it was in economic terms, the 1964 land reform was followed by an opening of the local political arena and the growth of a province-wide community movement. These contradictory outcomes resulted in the emergence of autonomous institutional spaces in the dominant context of agrarian capitalism.

THE INDIGENOUS PEASANT COMMUNITIES' QUEST FOR LAND

The decline of the semi-feudal *hacienda* order was accelerated by an increase in state economic intervention. In the 1960s the IERAC had a relatively low profile, dedicating itself mostly to colonization projects in the Amazon region. The situation changed under the reformist government of General Guillermo Rodríguez Lara (1972–76) and his military successors (1976–79), whose terms coincided with the oil boom. Influenced by UNECLAC's developmentalist ideology, the Rodríguez Lara government used the swelling oil revenues to give a new impetus to the land redistribution program. In 1973 it passed new and more radical land reform legislation designed to promote the capitalist modernization of agriculture by eliminating economically inefficient estates. By law, *hacienda* owners had to have at least 80 percent of their land used in accordance with specific technical standards. Under-utilized land was subject to expropriation. According to article 30, section 9, of the law, the state could expropriate land in areas of high demographic pressure regardless of its economic efficiency and/or type of labor relations. This article, however, was seldom applied by IERAC officials. Between 1974 and 1983 it was used, nationwide, only ten times, as compared to the hundreds of expropriation cases based on *haciendas'* economic inefficiency (Martínez 1985, 31).

Chimborazo Province was at the top of the IERAC's priorities, as most of its land was controlled by *haciendas* and the local indigenous peasant movement was highly mobilized. After the two rounds of land reform, Chimborazo was cited as one of the three provinces with the highest rates of land redistribution (Zevallos 1989; Chiriboga 1988). According to the Central Bank, between 1964 and 1988 the IERAC reallocated 19.3 percent of the total amount of provincial land—more than twice the national average of only 9 percent (Banco Central del Ecuador 1988, 92). Even so, in 1989 farms under five hectares (83 percent of all farms in the province) controlled only 15 percent of the province's land (Ministry of Agriculture and Livestock, cited in *Ecofuturo* 1990, 70). This situation was not much different from that in 1954, when farms under five hectares accounted for 87 percent of agricultural units in the province and controlled 17 percent of provincial land (INEC 1954). Still worse, less than half of the land reallocated by the IERAC fell into the category of farmland; the rest was unsuitable for either agricultural or pastoral activities (Banco Central del Ecuador 1988, 89). Unfortunately, there are no official figures on the proportion of Chimborazo's farmland affected by the land reform. According to an unofficial 1989 survey, conducted by *Ecofuturo*, only 20.1 percent of the land transferred to Chimborazo's peasants could be used as cropland or natural pastures. The rest was unproductive land and steep hillside covered with forest, unsuitable for any kind of farming (*Ecofuturo* 1990, 78).

The most notable consequence of the 1973 land reform was the conversion of the remaining *haciendas* from traditional food crops (wheat, barley, potatoes) to livestock production (beef and dairy products). The expansion of livestock production in Chimborazo followed political logic as well as economic logic. The growth of the cities of Guayaquil and Riobamba over the previous decades had increased the urban demand for beef and dairy products. At the same time, the continual land claims by peasant communities made the *hacienda* owners look for ways of reducing their dependence on local labor and improving agricultural productivity, or at least creating the impression of such an improvement in the eyes of IERAC officials. Livestock production suited both purposes admirably, which is why in the wake of the land reform it was increasingly practiced by large- and medium-sized farmers.

The expansion of dairy farming in the Ecuadorian Andes is generally seen as part of the process of capitalist modernization that involves a technological upgrading of agricultural production (Barrill 1980; Barsky and Cosse 1981). In Chimborazo, however, the expansion of dairy farming can be better understood as capitalist reorganization without any significant technological change or productivity gains. It involved an increased use of wage labor and a certain amount of capital investment in livestock, infrastructure, and pasture management. This investment, though, was kept to a minimum and was evident in the persistently low productivity of Chimborazo's dairy sector. In other words, instead of embarking on a full-fledged process of capitalist modernization, most large- and medium-sized farmers simply replaced low-productivity food crops with low-productivity livestock.

While the productivity gains in this truncated version of agrarian capitalism were minimal or nil, the implications for rural employment were devastating: livestock production requires much less labor than do food crops. The problem of labor displacement was aggravated by the fact that most dairy farms and cattle ranches were located in areas of high demographic pressure. As a result, so-called peasant families in Chimborazo became increasingly dependent on income from urban labor, which required regular periods of temporary migration of at least one family member (usually males). The migrants generally were hired as unskilled workers in construction projects, markets, dockyards, or, to a smaller extent, as temporary laborers in the capitalist agricultural sector (MAG 1983). According to Haney and Haney the proportion of farm income in total peasant family income in Chimborazo's non-reform sector was 62 percent in the central part and only 46 percent in the south of the province (Haney and Haney 1989, 85).

Even though near-landless communities can be better described as communities of migrants in terms of their economic condition, this term does not necessarily reflect their members' self-perception. Stubbornly, many of them continue to identify themselves as peasants, even when the size of their family plot is a small fraction of a hectare. The incongruity between the objective condition of community members and their self-identification may have several explanations. Some may actually have owned land outside their communities (this may have been the case for some relatively prosperous traders). Others may have been using this self-identification as a device for luring the Ministry of Agriculture and Livestock and/or other institutions into supporting whatever small-scale farming activities still existed in the area. Many others, however, were probably calling themselves peasants simply because they did not want to give up their peasant identity—or rather, because their wanderings in search of income could not provide them with an alternative "modern" identity.

The persistence of peasant identity is closely related to the adoption of a "re-peasantization" strategy by most of Chimborazo's migratory workers. Carrasco's study of urban migrants from the community of Puesetus indicates that only those who had been able to find a stable, relatively well-paying job (approximately one-tenth of the respondents) opted for permanent urban residence. The remaining nine-tenths—unskilled laborers and street vendors, for the most part—still had their life projects tied to land. By reducing their living expenses below subsistence levels, 83 percent of the migrants interviewed had succeeded in saving part of their income. These savings were intended to be used for the purchase of land (Carrasco 1990, 180–81).

Another manifestation of peasant resistance to proletarianization (and "informalization") is the persistence of land conflicts and the steadily growing number of communes after the transition to capitalist agriculture—

and well after the official closure of the land reform period. The late 1970s and early 1980s witnessed the end of both the oil bonanza and political reformism. Pressed by the international financial institutions, Ecuador's government started moving in the direction of economic neoliberalism. The 1979 Law of Agricultural Promotion emphasized the need for increasing agricultural production, bringing to an end the previous policy of land redistribution. At the same time, peasants' non-farm incomes dropped as a result of the deterioration of real minimum wages and urban employment rates brought about by the end of Ecuador's petroleum boom and the beginning of the debt crisis.[3] These developments changed the frequency of land conflicts in Chimborazo. The number of land claims reached its peak in the late 1970s and early 1980s, after which they showed a certain tendency to decline. The number of new communes, however, continued to increase steadily all through the 1980s and 1990s.

At the same time, the character of the land conflicts changed considerably. In the 1970s most land claims were directed against the vestiges of the semi-feudal *hacienda* sector. By the turn of the decade, capitalist agriculture had spread throughout the province. Most of the marginal land was transferred to peasants. The remaining *hacienda* land was largely occupied by low-productivity dairy farms and cattle ranches, which hired a small staff of permanent workers. Many of these were strangers to the area because, after the beginning of the land reform, the *hacienda* owners had tried to avoid any dealings with the local communities for fear of losing their land. This meant that in the 1980s most of those who filed land claims to the IERAC had no labor relations with the *hacienda*. In other words, they were claiming land not because they were subject to economic exploitation by the landowners but because they were marginalized by capitalist agriculture. Moreover, because of the national economic crisis that followed the end of the oil boom, it was getting more and more difficult for rural migrants to find jobs in the construction sector or on coastal plantations. Thus, whereas in the 1970s the peasant struggle for land had developed largely as a struggle against the remnants of pre-capitalist relations, in the 1980s and 1990s it was increasingly a struggle against marginalization in the context of the capitalist economy.

In both cases the indigenous peasants generally expressed their interest in buying land instead of filing a land claim with the IERAC, but in the 1980s and 1990s it was harder for them to make private deals with the capitalist farmers than it had been with the traditional *hacienda* owners. In the 1970s the availability of low-productivity, low-priced land in the *hacienda* sector had facilitated such arrangements. In the 1980s and early 1990s—although landowners, exhausted by constant confrontations with peasants, were often willing to sell the remaining *hacienda* land—its price was often far beyond the reach of peasant farmers. To obtain credit for the purchase of land, many communities turned to the FEPP, one of Ecuador's most important rural development NGOs (Chapter 8). While the presence of NGOs was increasing in Chimborazo's countryside, the IERAC was rapidly losing its ability to serve as an institutional mediator in land conflicts. Bogged down by bureaucratic inertia, chronically under-funded, and with its decisions in favor of peasants increasingly overturned by an appeals courts staffed by representatives of the local power groups, the IERAC led a shadowy existence—a stepchild in the country's increasingly neoliberal economic order. In the 1980s and early 1990s, most of the land claims in Chimborazo came under the 1973 clause that dealt with demographic pressure, so that their settlement in favor of peasants would have contradicted the emphasis on production implied in the 1979 Law of Agricultural Promotion. Moreover, it would have required an infusion of new government funds, since the expropriation of presumably efficient capitalist farms involved substantial reimbursement to their owners. In the face of these obstacles, IERAC officials found it easier to take the side of the capitalist farmers, declaring their properties, when claimed by peasants, exempt from the land reform.

In 1994, in a political climate of economic restructuring and cuts in government spending, the IERAC was dissolved and its functions were assigned to the INDA. INDA's staff and budget were only a small fraction of the IERAC's.[4] It dedicated itself mostly to the legalization of individual land titles rather than to land redistribution. INDA's emphasis on individual property rights was consistent with the 1994 Law of Agricultural Development. Creating legal incentives for entrepreneurial development in the private sector, the law also permitted the subdivision and sale of communally owned lands (Gobierno del Ecuador 2001).

The closing of private and institutional channels for land redistribution was complemented by the creation of a legal framework for police action against the communities. The 1973 land reform had been followed by a wave of violence against peasant communities that laid claim to *hacienda* land. The violence, however, came mostly from the landlords and their mercenaries, with the local police either turning a blind eye or intervening on their behalf in a sporadic and spontaneous fashion. Typically, the armed gangs hired by the *hacienda* owners would burn peasants' houses, kill their livestock, and issue threats against community leaders. There were also occasional armed police raids, involving acts of physical aggression and arbitrary detentions. Similar cases of violence were registered throughout the 1980s and with more frequency after the 1990 indigenous *levantamiento* or uprising. In addition, the 1979 Law of Agricultural Promotion put the habitual collaboration of the landowners and the police on a legal footing. The law was directed against land seizures. These were generally peaceful in character and were used by communities as a bargaining tool in their negotiations with landlords and the IERAC. In effect, the most common form of land seizure was letting community livestock graze on the *hacienda* land without the consent of its owner. The 1979 law classified these actions as delinquent acts whose perpetrators could be subject to criminal prosecution. It also disqualified communities involved in land seizures from government assistance.

To sum up, the land reform put an end to pre-capitalist relations in Chimborazo's countryside, while at the same time transferring huge tracts of unproductive or marginally productive land to indigenous peasant communities. After this, the redistributive process came to a halt, giving way to a new emphasis on entrepreneurial agricultural development and individual property rights. Blocked in their quest for high-productivity land, Chimborazo's peasant communities were nevertheless able to increase their territorial base, a base upon which they could build communal organizations. This, along with the gradual closing of national institutional channels of land redistribution, explains the increased importance of rural development projects as a target of peasant communal struggles.

RURAL DEVELOPMENT: CLIENTELISM OR A STRUGGLE FOR POWER?

Unwilling to pursue a policy of land redistribution after the capitalist transformation of the *hacienda*, the national government proclaimed its commitment to the strategy of rural development in the communal sector. Formulated by the World Bank as a "technical" and "uncontroversial" alternative to the conflict-ridden land-reform policies, this strategy was designed to upgrade and commercialize peasant agriculture by improving rural infrastructure and services. One of the most widely publicized instruments of rural development in Ecuador was the FODERUMA. Created in 1978 under the umbrella of the Banco Central del Ecuador (Central Bank of Ecuador), FODERUMA was supposed to channel financial assistance to the most impoverished sectors of the peasantry. From the very start, however, its ability to deal with the problem of rural poverty was undercut by its limited funding. The under-funding was aggravated by the problem of bureaucratic management and the difficulty of reaching target groups. This difficulty manifested itself in underspending: Between 1978 and 1985 FODERUMA spent less than half of the available funds (Banco Central del Ecuador 1985, 25). Ironically, this reduced even further the meager amount of financial assistance directed to the impoverished peasantry.

The limited scope of FODERUMA activities raised discontent not only among the communities that had been denied its assistance but also among those which obtained it; it was generally seen as inadequate by community members. A similar situation could be seen in the case of communities involved in integrated rural development projects (DRIs). Since these projects were much larger than FODERUMA's, the government's counterparts were not individual communities but federations of communities. In fact, there is generally agreement that the implementation of these projects served as a catalyst for the formation of inter-community federations. Although at first glance these hasty organizational efforts looked like an exercise in clientelist politics, the reality often was more complex.

In 1985 the integrated rural development program included twenty-two projects with a total cost of 13,193 million sucres (approximately US$105 million)—almost ten times FODERUMA's budget (Jordán Bucheli 1988, 240, 251). It still seemed a drop in the bucket of national credit, but it was a relatively large drop. The program was designed to alleviate rural poverty through technical and financial assistance to peasant agriculture in combination with investment in physical and social infrastructure (roads, irrigation canals, drinking water systems, school, child care centers, and so forth). Like FODERUMA, the integrated rural development program rapidly became a target for peasant discontent. One of the main reasons was cultural and political: While program officials extolled the virtues of peasant participation, in practice they frequently shied away from a meaningful dialogue with indigenous peasant organizations. FODERUMA officials avoided working with highly politicized peasant organizations and sought instead to develop clientelist ties with organizations that could be manipulated by the state agency. Such strategies created an appearance of peasant participation while at the same time weakening autonomous indigenous and peasant federations.

Government officials' apprehension with regard to autonomous federations contrasted with the supportive attitude of local NGOs. FEPP, for example, made a consistent effort to promote communities' political activism as part of their participation in rural development projects. Apart from its impressive program of land transfers, FEPP offered support for rural development and community training with an eye on strengthening inter-community organization (Chapter 8). Rural development, however, remained a key issue in the case of both governmental and nongovernmental organizations. It was also moving to the top of the Chimborazo communities' political agenda. Indeed, along with the persistent demand for land, demands for control of infrastructure grew in number and came to form part of the indigenous peasant consciousness—a new community consciousness.

CONCLUSION

Chimborazo's community mobilization of the 1980s reached its peak during the 1990 nationwide indigenous uprising called by the CONAIE and supported by the UCAE. Its success in terms of grassroots participation came as a surprise not only to urban dwellers but also to many indigenous and peasant leaders, who had not expected such a massive turnout. According to some estimates, between 150,000 and 200,000 people (roughly 70 percent of Chimborazo's rural population) participated in the uprising. It lasted seven days, during which the communities blocked the roads leading to the provincial capital, cutting off its food supplies. After one of the indigenous protesters was killed by the police, the communities staged a march on Riobamba with the participation, according to indigenous leaders, of 60,000 people (20,000, according to the local press). Twenty-five military and police personnel were captured and later set free by community members, but generally speaking the uprising was peaceful. Fundamentally, it was a political statement, a demonstration of communal strength designed to press the national government into a political dialogue.

It is generally agreed that the 1990 uprising made Ecuador's government more willing to negotiate with the indigenous organizations. At the national level it resulted in several rounds of talks between the CONAIE and government representatives. In Chimborazo it led to a series of meetings between the provincial federations and the IERAC designed to decide the outcome of persisting land conflicts. These meetings were followed by others—with the Rural Electrification Corporation, the Potable Water and Sanitation Institute, and the National Institute of Hydraulic Resources (in charge of the irrigation projects). The question remains whether these as well as numerous subsequent negotiations were conducted by the government in good faith. Despite the long rounds of discussions, little progress was made with regard to either land redistribution or community projects.

To conclude, the preceding analysis casts doubt on the characterization of the indigenous peasant sector as "functional" to global capitalism. To be sure, Chimborazo's indigenous peasantry supplied coastal plantations and cities with abundant cheap labor, subsidizing the growth of the capitalist economy. At the same time, however, it clearly proved "dysfunctional" to capitalist development in political and institutional terms. Organized into communities and inter-communal federations, Chimborazo's indigenous peasants challenged the post-reform capitalist order based on the collaboration of private agricultural enterprise and the state. It should be emphasized that they did this not where they were subject to wage relations but at home in the rural Andes, where they were increasingly marginalized by the capitalist reorganization of agriculture.

Not surprisingly, the Ecuadorian government's controversial attempts at land reform did not solve this problem. Neither did its rural development policies, which spurred the growth of patron-client relations between communities and the state. The tendency toward clientelism, however, was curbed by at least two factors. To begin with, the state did not always have the resources to maintain its clientelist structures. The government's commitment to rural development programs was insignificant from the start. Moreover, it diminished over time. Established during the period of the oil boom, the state-sponsored rural development projects started to fade into oblivion with the 1980s economic recession, followed by a policy shift in the direction of economic neoliberalism. As a result, the expectations that these projects had created among indigenous peasant communities could not easily be met by the government development agencies. This failure caused a considerable amount of community discontent—a discontent that can be properly understood only in the context of an unprecedented growth of the communal organizations born out of the indigenous and peasant struggle for land during the land-reform period. The wellsprings of this discontent were related to the indigenous tradition of regulating the use of local resources within the communal territory, resources that in the 1980s and early 1990s included not only land but also state-provided infrastructure and services. Thus, while government rural development policies created a tendency toward clientelism, they also spurred community struggles for the control of rural development. These struggles were a continuation of the earlier land conflicts. Both formed part of the communities' quest for power and resources. Both widened alternative institutional spaces on the margins of agrarian capitalism, signaling the emergence of an indigenous and rural civil society (Korovkin 2001). In socioeconomic terms, the redistributive outcomes of these struggles were admittedly modest. In political terms, however, the growth of the communal organization should be seen as a prerequisite for local democracy (Chapter 9).

As the twentieth century drew to a close, indigenous and peasant demands for rural development continued to grow, intertwining with the struggle against structural adjustment. At the same time, the national government modified its rural development strategies in accordance with the now predominant neoliberal ideology. The state-administered FODERUMA and DRIs were allowed to slip into neglect. They were replaced by what Segarra described as a new welfare network that involved state agencies, local NGOs, and international development actors (Segarra 1997, 490–91). This network crystallized around the FISE. Created in 1993 as an initiative of the World Bank and placed under the direct control of the presidency, the FISE was supposed to mitigate the negative impacts of structural adjustment on the rural and urban poor. In 2000 the FISE administered approximately one thousand small-scale development projects (Ministerio del Frente Social 2000). Unable to provide a meaningful solution to the problem of poverty, these projects contributed to the growth of local NGOs, which in many cases played an important role in project design and implementation. While NGOs cannot be seen as genuine representatives of local community interests, there is little doubt that many of them have been able to form close, albeit often controversial, ties with communal organizations (Chapter 8). The new welfare network also increased spaces for indigenous peoples' participation. In the mid-1990s the national government created the PRODEPINE and the CODENPE. Funded largely by international agencies, but managed by indigenous leaders and intellectuals, these institutions were designed to promote development in impoverished, mostly rural areas populated by indigenous and black communities. These and other initiatives were followed by the nomination of a prominent indigenous intellectual as the Minister of Social Welfare—still another interesting move in the complex game of conflict and cooptation. The social and political outcomes of these developments—taking place in the conflict-ridden context of economic neoliberalism, administrative decentralization, and political democracy—require a closer analysis that takes us beyond the scope of this chapter.

Notes

[1] The 1937 Law of Communes granted the registered communities an official status as "communes," legally sanctioning their control over communal territory and promising state support for communal development. It also established elected community councils *(cabildos)* as the highest authority within communal boundaries.

[2] For further discussion of the role of Protestant churches in Ecuador, see Muratorio 1980; Padilla 1989.

[3] From 1980 to 1990 real minimum wages in Ecuador fell by more than 300 percent. In 1986 urban unemployment reached 10.7 percent, as compared with 5.7 percent in 1980 (FLACSO-IICA 1994, tables 1.2.7 and 4.2.1).

[4] In 1993 the IERAC had a staff of 2,200. By contrast, in 1998 INDA counted only 320 employees (Navas 1998, 192).

Chapter 8

The Contradictions
of Rural Development NGOs

The Trajectory of the FEPP in Chimborazo

Víctor Bretón Solo de Zaldívar

During the late 1960s and the early 1970s, in the context of peasant mobilizations for land reform, the traditionally conservative Catholic church in the province of Chimborazo became actively engaged in helping highland peasants to resolve land conflicts. The willingness of the church in Chimborazo to play this role followed its embracing of liberation theology under the leadership of Monsignor Leónidas Proaño ("Bishop of the Indians").[1] In that progressive ideological climate, lay and religious groups created a number of NGOs to support peasant and indigenous demands and mobilizations. Most prominent among those early NGOs were the CESA, the CEAS, and the FEPP. The FEPP, founded in 1970 by Monsignor Cándido Rada, is one of the most important NGOs working in rural development in Ecuador, both with regard to the resources it has invested and the nature and breadth of its interventions. This chapter analyzes the changes in the FEPP's ideological orientation and development policies and its gradual accommodation to neoliberal precepts of rural development over the course of the period from 1981 to 2000. It does so through an evaluation of programs undertaken to support peasant livelihoods by the FEPP's regional office in Riobamba, the capital of Chimborazo province.

THE FEPP AND THE CRISIS OF RURAL DEVELOPMENT

In a recent work Manuel Chiriboga and others identified five key stages in the FEPP's thirty-year history (Chiriboga et al. 1999). In its founding

This chapter is drawn from a larger work, Bretón 2001.

period, from 1970 to 1975, the FEPP established itself as a lending agency that specialized in providing credit to small-scale peasants, but it operated primarily through other institutions, especially CESA and the local dioceses of the church. In a second transitional phase, from 1976 to 1980, the FEPP enhanced its institutional autonomy but continued to act almost exclusively as a credit fund. A third and longer period, from 1980 to 1989, was characterized by continued support to the peasant movement, with priority given to strengthening second-level organizations (OSGs), which united groups of community-based peasant organizations and operated at the parish and municipal levels. In a fourth stage, from 1990 to 1994, following the 1990 indigenous uprising *(levantamiento)* and in the context of increasing levels of rural violence associated with land conflicts, the FEPP implemented a highly controversial program to convert part of Ecuador's foreign debt into credit for peasant land purchases and established a rotating credit fund to facilitate continued access to land in peasant communities (see also Chapter 6). Finally, in a fifth phase that began in 1995, the FEPP shifted its emphasis to market-oriented strategies, such as small-scale agricultural processing and marketing initiatives, and administrative support to peasant enterprises (Chiriboga et al. 1999). Each of these phases corresponded with a particular period in Ecuador's recent political-economic history and thus represented the FEPP's specific responses to the changing circumstances and demands created by that larger context.

Over the three decades that followed its establishment, the FEPP became one of the most important NGOs in Ecuador. In 1997, Arcos Carera and Palomeque Vallejo (1997) identified only fifteen NGOs with budgets of over one million dollars in the country. In that same year the FEPP's budget reached over ten million dollars, and its activities benefited almost forty thousand poor rural families, that is, 8.57 percent of all poor rural families and 4.03 percent of all peasant households in Ecuador (Chiriboga et al. 1999, 8). Moreover, by 1998 the FEPP operated in 19 of Ecuador's 22 provinces, in 77 of its 175 rural cantons, and in 182 of its 772 rural and semi-urban parishes, and it worked directly with 1,042 peasant organizations (FEPP 1999a, 12). In 1998 the FEPP had 282 employees and received NGO and state resources from Ecuador and abroad in addition to revenues generated by its own work. Between 1987 and 1999 the FEPP received financial support from seventy-nine different organizations in thirteen countries, and it collaborated with four major multilateral agencies and two programs of the European Union (Chiriboga et al. 1999, 221–22). The FEPP's activities and decision-making processes were increasingly decentralized in the 1980s, and by 2000 it had ten regional offices, which operated with considerable autonomy from the central office in Quito.

An in-depth analysis of the trajectory of the FEPP's regional office in Riobamba offers a window to reflect on the ways in which macroeconomic and macro-political changes in Ecuador shaped the FEPP's operations at the micro level.[2] In light of the particular intensity of struggles over land redistribution and the liquidation of the feudal social relations of *hacienda*-based agricultural production, the province of Chimborazo provides a revealing case of the structural transformations experienced by rural Andean societies over the last thirty years (see Sylva 1986; Haney and Haney 1989, 1990; Carrasco 1991, 1997; and Chapter 7 herein). Chimborazo is also notable for having the highest proportion of indigenous population of any province in Ecuador (Zamosc 1995), as well as the highest indices of poverty and indigence in the country's highlands (Larrea et al. 1996; ODEPLAN 1999). The high rates of poverty in the province are particularly troubling and in need of careful analysis because they have persisted in spite of both ambitious rural development efforts and the presence of very large numbers of local and regional grassroots-based organizations. External development agencies have been active in Chimborazo since the rural development initiatives of the Andean Mission of the United Nations in the 1950s and 1960s. At the end of the twentieth century, Chimborazo had the highest concentration of NGOs of any province in Ecuador.[3] Moreover, the province was widely perceived as a model of indigenous organizational capacity because of its high numbers of community and second-level organizations (see, for example, Bebbington 1999; Bebbington et al. 1992; Bebbington and Perrault 1999).

FEPP RIOBAMBA, 1981–1987: FROM AGRARIAN REFORM TO INTEGRATED RURAL DEVELOPMENT

In response to a 1980 evaluation of its first ten years of work, the FEPP began to decentralize its activities in order to become more responsive to local conditions. As part of that effort, the FEPP established an office in Riobamba in 1981 to support peasant groups in the central highland region, which until then had been served from the central office in Quito. The Riobamba office began its work with four basic objectives: (1) to increase the effectiveness of support to peasant groups; (2) to improve credit, training, and technical assistance services; (3) to continuously evaluate the progress of its projects; and (4) to deepen its understanding of rural development in Chimborazo in order to better plan future interventions (FEPP 1987, 32).

The FEPP opened its Riobamba office in June 1981 with one employee. In 1987 office staff numbered a still-modest six employees. From 1983 on, the regional office worked with seven OSGs (five in Chimborazo, one in Tungurahua, and one in Bolívar). Its objective was to promote the formation of "provincial peasant organizations where none existed and to strengthen those that already existed," so that "these organizations would lead the process of development and social transformation in accordance with their needs and interests" (FEPP 1987, 33).

Unfortunately, in 1987 the technical staff of the FEPP's Riobamba office recognized that they had made little progress toward these goals during their first six years of operation. The principal problem encountered by the FEPP was that its efforts to promote strong second-level peasant organizations were regularly undermined by other external actors, particularly the state, which sought to weaken peasant organizational capacity by promoting a proliferation of small and unaffiliated community-based organizations (FEPP 1987, 35).

The directors of the Riobamba office concluded that their efforts during the first six years had "highly positive results" in very few cases, specifically in projects designed to support peasant land purchases (eight in total), to promote livestock production (fifteen in total), and to process marketable products (three in total). These projects resulted in the generation of significantly increased peasant incomes, the prompt repayment of loans, community labor, and the strengthening of peasant organizations. In only a few cases did the FEPP identify clearly negative impacts from its projects, such as the improper use of resources, recurrent financial losses, or the disintegration of peasant organizations. The most common results of projects sponsored by the regional office were considered positive but limited in impact as a result of difficulties that emerged from production, organization, the limited importance of the specific activity being supported, and insufficient amounts of support from the FEPP (FEPP 1987, 36–37).

The strategic focus of the FEPP's initiatives during the 1980s, and the degrees of success or failure, must be understood in the general context of the agrarian policies that emerged over the course of that decade. The 1980s were crisis years marked by a significant decline in peasant incomes, a shift away from the paradigm of agrarian reform to the new strategy of "integrated rural development," which represented an abandonment of all pretenses to pursue the structural changes in land ownership patterns that were initiated in the 1960s and 1970s, and finally the introduction of neoliberal SAPs. It was also during this period that many international development agencies began to emphasize the strengthening of peasant organizations, especially OSGs. Many of those organizations had been established in the context of peasant mobilization to gain access to land, and it was now hoped that, by helping them to consolidate, they would become actors capable of carrying out rural development projects. Indeed, this was the logic underlying the FEPP's work.

THE FEPP RIOBAMBA, 1988–1995:
TARGETED SUPPORT FOR EFFICIENT PEASANT PRODUCTION

During the period from 1988 to 1995 the FEPP's Riobamba office continued with its strategy of working to strengthen the capacities of peasant organizations to promote local development. Within that general strategy, the FEPP identified ten specific objectives:

1. To support popular education activities that would *raise the levels of political consciousness and organization of peasant groups.*
2. To promote and strengthen *second-level organizations* by providing services, financing social promoters, and providing training for organization members in literacy, administration, accounting, production, and marketing.
3. *To support base organizations,* giving priority to those with the largest numbers of members, and which emphasize community-oriented projects and combine efforts with other base organizations.
4. To promote democratic meeting spaces within the Riobamba office.
5. *To provide sufficient credit to base and second-level organizations for the development of productive projects.*
6. To provide landless peasants with credit to purchase land.
7. To support the protection and recovery of natural resources (land, water, forests, etc.) through credit, small grants, training, and technical assistance.
8. To promote and support initiatives to diversify and improve small-scale production.
9. To promote productive activities which will increase self-sufficiency and decrease dependence on external markets.
10. To provide technical training to raise levels of production and productivity, and to enable peasant organizations to maintain proper accounting procedures. (FEPP 1987, 8)

The privileged social subjects of the FEPP's strategy were peasants who possessed some means of production (land, agricultural tools, and so forth). The FEPP had found that it was this peasant category that had the greatest capacity for social organization and engagement in agrarian struggles. In addition to this group of "middle peasants," who were able to reproduce themselves through small-scale agriculture, the FEPP also directed its efforts toward a second category: poor peasants with some resources but not enough to reproduce themselves through agriculture and who were therefore forced to sell their labor to survive. The FEPP's decision to focus on these two categories of peasants—

and not, for example, to work with landless peasants—was based on the conviction that it was these groups that could take greatest advantage of the services that it was able to offer (FEPP 1987, 9).

The medium-term (six-year) objective of the FEPP's new strategy was that "peasants themselves would become the key agents of development through their local organizations" (FEPP 1996b, 16–17). To that end the FEPP emphasized the strengthening of peasant organizations and educational and training activities oriented toward economic development. Work in its first two zones of concentration, the parishes of Cacha and Cumandá, in the cantons of Riobamba and Cumandá, respectively, extended from 1988 to 1995. It was divided into two successive three-year phases and a one-year bridge period in each location. Financing for the work in the two parishes came from COTESU, which also enabled the Riobamba office to expand its technical staff to eleven.

The residents of the parish of Cacha, located close to Riobamba, belonged in the category of poor peasants. They were for the most part indigenous peasants who—since their landholdings were very small, eroded, and unirrigated—were unable to reproduce themselves through agriculture and were forced to migrate to cities in search of work.[4] In these circumstances, and in an effort to reduce migration rates and improve local living conditions, the FEPP sought to create new local employment opportunities and to diversify production through technical training and financing for productive projects channeled through the existing OSG, the UNOCIC (FEPP 1987, 39).[5] In the end the principal achievement of the FEPP's work in Cacha was a potable water system. In addition, efforts to strengthen the OSG and to help establish beekeeping and various artisan enterprises also supported local development and the diversification of income sources (FEPP 1996b, 16).[6]

In contrast to Cacha, the parish of Cumandá is located at a considerable distance from Riobamba in the western, subtropical part of Chimborazo, and its population is a heterogeneous mix of migrants from both the coastal and highland areas.[7] The FEPP's diagnosis of peasant agriculture in the parish emphasized the need to rationalize and diversify agricultural production, to strengthen local organizations through socio-educational initiatives, and to support the creation of an OSG through which to channel assistance (FEPP 1987, 39). With these goals in mind, the FEPP offered a credit program for production for both the market and self-consumption, and it implemented an agro-ecology program to promote alternatives to the excessive use of chemical fertilizers and pesticides.

Beyond the parishes of Cacha and Cumandá, the FEPP worked in the rural parishes of Pallatanga, in the canton of the same name, and Cebadas, in the canton of Guamote. In its work with OSGs, the FEPP emphasized the importance of providing both credit for productive activities and grants for training in order to help peasant organizations administer their resources more effectively. The FEPP would deliver services directly to individual peasant families only on the explicit request of an OSG (FEPP 1987, 40).

In line with these principles, the FEPP devised various types of support for OSGs, including: training courses and scholarships, market research, accounting assistance, rotating credit funds for productive initiatives, credit for producing and marketing artisan goods, the acquisition of storage and retail space for marketing artisan goods, infrastructure works, training and funding for peasant extension workers, support for publications and educational material, support for conducting evaluations and programming, and assistance in presenting project plans to community organizations. With the clear understanding that the FEPP could not initiate all of these activities with every peasant organization, and that support to organizations would be reviewed annually (FEPP 1987, 68), the regional office chose to work with eight OSGs and OTGs (third-level organizations) representing 181 base organizations in Chimborazo and Tungurahua.[8]

Evaluation of the First Phase of the FEPP's Riobamba Program, 1988–1991

A 1991 report commissioned by the FEPP recommended that the office concentrate its efforts in a maximum of two zones and three OSGs, and that it carefully terminate its activities in other locations and with unaffiliated peasant groups. The report concluded that the dispersion of activities by the Riobamba office limited its effectiveness and prevented it from achieving more solid results. It warned of dangers and problems emerging from the large number and heterogeneous nature of the Riobamba office's project sites, which made it not only humanly impossible to respond adequately to each situation (with the limited number of staff members) but also expensive and time consuming to travel to multiple sites. In the final analysis these recommendations were based on two key strategic issues: (1) a concern to find ways to promote the peaceful resolution of land conflicts in Chimborazo; and (2) the realization that the FEPP projects were most successful in the zones where they were most highly concentrated (Crespo and Bischof, 1991, ii).

What is most remarkable about the credit policies that were implemented during the first phase of the Riobamba program (1988–1991) is the significant amount of credit destined for land purchases. Of all the credit provided by the FEPP, 34 percent was used for land purchases, making it the single most important type of credit.[9] During this period, the Riobamba office made available approximately one hundred million sucres (approximately US$60,000 in 1991) in loans to seventeen base organizations (representing four hundred members), enabling them collectively to purchase thirteen hundred hectares of land (Crespo and Bischof 1991, 31).

The preferred recipients of the FEPP credit were base organizations committed to the collective ownership and management of the newly purchased land. The authors of the above-mentioned report highlighted seven positive aspects of this initiative that are worth emphasizing: (1) credit was actually invested in the uses indicated by beneficiaries; (2) the processing of loan requests was careful but also timely; (3) loans were well supervised; (4) the percentage of unpaid loans was low (only 4.5 percent); (5) loans for fixed capital had a direct impact on the capitalization of peasant communities; (6) loans were made almost entirely to collective repayment groups; and (7) the return to borrowing groups of a percentage of interest payments for use in training activities and to capitalize community savings and loan funds had positive impacts on organizational strengthening (Crespo and Bischof 1991, 28–29).

The FEPP's credit program for peasants between 1988 and 1990 also had various negative results. Most prominent among them was the excessive use of credit for subsistence-oriented production and for activities with low profit levels (such as vermiculture). This led to both the development of economically unviable activities and the expectation on the part of peasants of easy access to inexpensive credit from the FEPP. The loans made by the Riobamba office were also heavily subsidized. For example, for livestock purchases the FEPP offered loans at interest rates of 15 percent (1988) and 24 percent (1990), while the interest rates charged by the state-affiliated FODERUMA and the BNF were 38 percent and 39 percent respectively, and those of commercial banks were 54 percent. Such high levels of subsidization quickly created serious problems, including the reduction of the real value of the credit fund managed by the FEPP's Riobamba office,[10] the projection of the FEPP's image as a "donor" rather than lender, the growth of peasant dependence on the FEPP's low-interest credit, and the undermining of community-based savings-and-loan cooperatives, which had to charge real interest rates in order to avoid decapitalization (Crespo and Bischof 1991, 31).

The FEPP's Riobamba office subsequently decided to concentrate its credit on two organizations that it recognized as mature in terms of their age, experience, and levels of political consciousness: Jatun Ayllu in Guamote and the UCASAJ (FEPP 1987, 40).[11] In both cases the goal of strengthening the OSG through the self-management of credit for productive projects was only partially fulfilled. The experience of UCASAJ was clearly positive: Credit for livestock was administered with high levels of self-management and loan recovery, and the OSG provided veterinary training to base members with the portion of interest payments returned to the organization by the FEPP (Crespo and Bischof 1991, 23; Camacho 1991, 24). However, Jatun Ayllu's experience was much more problematic: Credit management was poor, and problems emerged from the use of the credit by the OSG; record keeping on the status of loans was also very poor, largely as a result of inadequate monitoring by the FEPP and the failure to provide training in accounting (Crespo and Bischof 1991, 23–24).

Adjustments to the Riobamba Program After 1992

In response to the evaluation of its first phase (1988 to 1991), the FEPP's Riobamba office chose to concentrate its activities from 1992 to 1995 on the parishes of Cacha and Cumandá, deepening support for the types of projects that had been most successful during the previous three years. The FEPP also saw this period as an "exit phase" and accordingly emphasized social and technical training aimed at self-management and the search for alternative sources of support. The credit policy of the Riobamba office was directed at gradually eliminating subsidies by raising interest rates to the level of the BNF, with the exception of loans for agro-ecology and environmental improvement, which continued to be subsidized (FEPP 1992, n.p.).

The external evaluators of this phase of the program highlighted the importance of the agreements established with Jatun Ayllu for community-based veterinary and accounting trainers despite the fact that those trainers could not work beyond their home communities due to a lack of funds to pay them (FEPP 1995, 34). The evaluators described the relations between the FEPP and UCASAJ as "punctual and oriented toward the recovery of outstanding loans" (FEPP 1995, 34). In tune with the new orientations of donors and IFIs, the 1995 evaluation concluded by urging the Riobamba office to make its development strategies more market oriented (FEPP 1995, 51).

THE FEPP'S CREDIT FUND
FOR PEASANT LAND PURCHASES, 1990–1995

Credit support for land purchases was a component of the FEPP strategies from its establishment in 1970. It first responded to requests for credit in Chimborazo in 1977 and continued to provide such support throughout the 1980s.[12] However, in the period between 1990 and 1995 the establishment of a rotating credit fund made the provision of land-purchase loans to peasants the FEPP's most important initiative. This process began in 1990, when the CEE negotiated the purchase of US$28 million dollars of foreign debt in what has been termed a debt-for-land swap. The CEE then proposed that the FEPP administer part of this package to finance a rotating credit fund to strengthen its lending program for peasant land purchases.[13] As a result, the FEPP directors argued, "the debt was transformed into land for indigenous and Afro-Ecuadorian peasants" by providing credit for land purchases and supporting the titling and legalization of land that peasants already possessed (Navarro, Vallejo, and Villaverde 1996, 59).

Understandably, this initiative generated a great deal of criticism. The FEPP was accused of legitimating Ecuador's foreign debt and of undermining the position of those who were lobbying for debt relief. The FEPP was also criticized for undertaking an initiative that had little impact on the total amount of debt still owed, but that increased the price of the debt in secondary markets, gave foreign donors a reason to decrease assistance, and partially relieved the state of its obligation to promote the welfare of its citizens (Navarro, Vallejo, and Villaverde 1996, 59). Well aware of these criticisms, the FEPP nevertheless placed priority on another problem: rising levels of rural violence associated with land conflicts (Chapter 6).

Because of the limited structural changes that resulted from the 1973 Agrarian Reform Law, the struggle for agricultural land was still a central cause of rural conflict in Ecuador at the beginning of the 1990s. According to data from the CONAIE, in 1992 there were conflicts over land in almost eight hundred rural communities. These ongoing conflicts helped to explain the agrarian roots of Ecuador's spectacular 1990 indigenous uprising *(levantamiento)* (Martínez 1992, 74). The FEPP's strategy from 1990 to 1995 was thus motivated by a concern to resolve these land conflicts and to reduce the associated levels of violence. The FEPP also recognized that agricultural land was a necessary but insufficient condition for peasant reproduction and survival. Accordingly, it supported an ambitious mix of activities, provided services to improve peasant production and productivity, negotiated with public and private institutions to improve rural infrastructure, facilitated the transfer of environmentally appropriate technology, helped to create new rural employment opportunities, and attempted to establish local financial markets capable of capturing surplus capital at the community level and channeling it back into local investment and services (Tonello 1995, 112–13).

The debt-swap program sought to alleviate the worst land conflicts through land purchases negotiated with property owners. Among Afro-Ecuadorian groups on the Pacific coast and indigenous groups in the Amazon basin the program focused on establishing legal title to land that was already occupied; in the highland region it focused primarily on land purchases by peasant communities. The program thus generated benefits for all the actors involved—large landowners, peasants, and the state. For the large landowners, the FEPP's program created the opportunity to sell conflict-ridden properties at good prices and to invest in other, more dynamic sectors of the economy (Navarro, Vallejo, and Villaverde 1996, 72). The program helped peasant producers who had not been able to acquire and/or gain legal title to land as a result of their lack of resources and the lack of state support. And finally, the program helped the state by creating an escape valve for reducing the tensions generated by the still unresolved struggles over rural land.[14]

In order to benefit from the program, base organizations had to belong to an OSG; in no case did the FEPP make loans available to individuals. It helped to negotiate purchase prices with landowners and then made credit available at interest rates between 8 and 18 percent, with ten year repayment periods (extendable to twelve years) and with the purchased land as collateral for loans. OSGs were also required to contribute at least 10 percent of the purchase price of land in cash, although some exceptions were made. While demanding these guarantees, the FEPP did not lose sight of its principal objective, which was the financial viability and strengthening of the OSGs (Navarro, Vallejo, and Villaverde 1996, 92–93).

The Design of the Land Credit Program in Chimborazo

Between April 1990 and June 1995 the FEPP implemented what effectively represented an agrarian reform sponsored and administered by a private agency. As the data in Table 8.1 reveal, during that period the FEPP made credit available to 199 peasant organizations, enabling them to purchase a total of 382,324.9 hectares of land for the benefit of 7,894 families (Navarro, Vallejo, and Villaverde 1996, 274). An examination of the distribution of land credit by province during the 1990 to 1995 period also highlights the exceptional concentration of credit in Chimborazo, where the demand from peasant organizations for credit for land purchases was highest, especially in the southern parts of the province, primarily because of the unfinished nature of agrarian reform (Navarro, Vallejo, and Villaverde 1996, 152). Chimborazo also represented the

Table 8.1 The FEPP Land Purchase and Land Titling Programs (1977–1996)

Time Period	Beneficiaries		Hectares of Land Acquired
	Number of Organizations	Number of Families	
1977–1990	65	1,700	2,205.3
1990 (April)–1995 (May)	199	7,894	382,324.9
1995 (July)–1996 (June)	43	1,341	24,831.8
Total	397	10, 935	409,362.0

Source: Navarro, Vallejo, and Villaverde 1996, 274.

largest proportion of organizations and families to receive credit (33.3 percent and 33.2 percent respectively). Moreover, the actual area of land purchased in Chimborazo represented 58.9 percent of all land purchases supported by the FEPP in the highland region.[15]

The OSGs played a controversial role in the land credit program in Chimborazo. The credit agreements specified that the FEPP would transfer 5 percent of the interest payments from base organizations back to their respective OSGs to provide training, technical assistance, and administrative support. However, with certain exceptions the base groups received little support from their OSGs, either for resolving organizational problems or for matters related to training, technical support, administration, and the recovery and monitoring of credit. Feeling abandoned, many peasants developed attitudes of indifference and even hostility toward their respective OSGs (Navarro, Vallejo, and Villaverde 1996, 174). Even more problematic, however, many OSGs came to see the 5 percent interest transfer as a right and refused to accept the conditions placed upon it by the FEPP (Navarro, Vallejo, and Villaverde 1996, 175).

The Division and Privatization of Collectively Purchased Land

In spite of the FEPP's insistence on the importance of communal organization, much of the land purchased collectively by peasant organizations was divided and privatized, often even before loans had been repaid. A prime example of this phenomenon occurred in the community of Pachamama Chico, in Tixán. As Navarro, Vallejo, and Villaverde recounted:

> For the first three years, community members worked the land collectively with considerable success. Collective production not only enabled them to make loan repayments but also to produce for their own consumption and to re-invest in production. They collectively purchased a tractor, a truck, a weight scale, and a threshing machine. By the fourth year, however, pressure from the directors of the OSG, the intensity of the work, and the small size of dividends from communal labor led to burnout and de-motivation. Community members decided to repay the remainder of the loan to the FEPP individually, so that they could divide the communal property into individual titles. Following the division of the land, they decided to sell all of the collectively purchased machinery. (Navarro, Vallejo, and Villaverde 1996, 210)

An even more dramatic case of collectively purchased land being privatized and divided occurred among six peasant associations in Guamote, which had purchased 350 hectares of land, 200 of which were irrigated and very fertile. An external evaluation of the division of collective land by the six associations in Guamote found that none of the FEPP's goals had been achieved three years after the land purchase. Earnings from the new land did not satisfy basic needs, and as a result the project actually contributed to increased rates of migration (Grundmann 1995, ix).

The land acquired by the six indigenous associations had previously belonged to *haciendas* and was used very productively for dairy-cattle production. Having witnessed that productivity, the new peasant owners of the land expected that they would be able to generate significant incomes. Indeed, the peasants anticipated repayment of their loan from the FEPP in only seven years. The FEPP, for its part, also thought that access to these new lands would lead to a decline in migration as a result of rising agricultural incomes. On the basis of those perceptions, the six peasant associations signed a contract with the FEPP that, in addition to specifying rapid repayment, required that the land be collectively owned and managed. The FEPP believed that this provision would help to strengthen indigenous communal traditions and slow down the growing economic differentiation between peasant families (Grundmann 1995, 117–18). Unfortunately, the experience of the following four years (1991 to 1995) disappointed all of the hopes for the new land and resulted in privatization and division of the land among the members of the six associations.

What happened in Guamote? The external evaluation contracted by the FEPP identified a series of variables that led to the breakdown of the communitarian initiative stimulated by land credit from the FEPP. First, in order to repay the loan from the FEPP, members of the associations were obliged to engage in a wide range of activities, including work on their own plots of land, work on the collective land, and paid work—often in distant cities. This *triple workload* was one of the principal reasons for the poor functioning of the six peasant associations, as collective work required high levels of organization and planning and left little time for work on other individual tasks (Grundmann 1995, ix). A second problem was the lack of experience in managing production for the market, reflected in the lack of long-term business planning (Grundmann 1995, x). Third, the lack of management experience was further complicated by the indigenous system of rotating the leadership positions of community associations, which often left insufficient time for learning and acquiring experience (Grundmann 1995, 118). Fourth, a cumbersome community-based decision-making process slowed the making of important management and production decisions. As a result of these difficulties, technical-productive problems were not resolved, economic losses increased, and members of the associations became discouraged (Grundmann 1995, 118). Productive problems and the lack of knowledge about market dynamics eventually contributed to the overall failure of the initiative.

On top of all these problems came the weight of loan repayments. Aggravated by the failure to maintain the rates of productivity and profitability of the previous landowners, the repayments left very little money either for reinvestment in the land or for distribution among the members. As a result, migration from the zone actually increased. Moreover, the degradation of individual peasant plots in high-altitude zones created pressure to exploit the new fertile and irrigated ex-*hacienda* land (Grundmann 1995, 120). With the failure of the project, the six associations chose to divide the communal land into individual plots, which pleased those members with no land of their own (young people in particular).

Lessons from the Land Credit Program

It is important to highlight certain elements of the land credit program that illustrate broader changes in the strategic orientation of the FEPP's Riobamba office after 1996. Beyond the moral and ethical questions surrounding the debt-for-land swap, the decision to engage in this type of project reflected the FEPP's adaptation to the new rules of the game in the neoliberal economic model. Clearly, the program was implemented with the goal of eliminating a part of the social debt generated by neoliberal policies themselves. However, the acquisition and administration of a portion of the foreign debt also implied the FEPP's condoning of one of the most basic mechanisms of domination sustaining the current global economic order.

The land credit program was also particularly important from the perspective of social peace. It is essential to remember that the program developed in the context of rising levels of ethnic conflict and rural violence and the emergence of an indigenous movement with a considerable capacity to mobilize its members (Almeida et al. 1993; Selverston-Scher 2001). The FEPP was particularly concerned that rising levels of conflict over rural land would lead to unacceptably high levels of violence with inevitably devastating results for the human rights and lives of indigenous and peasant populations. At least in the case of the indigenous peasant organizations of Chimborazo, the FEPP land credit program did have a direct impact on the resolution of land conflicts and the liquidation of what remained of the *hacienda* regime, as well as at least a temporary decline in rural violence in the highland region.

However, an analysis of that process also reveals a shift in the leadership of indigenous peasant organizations away from political strategies rooted in struggles for agrarian reform to a much more technical approach focused on the management of rural development projects. This new generation of leaders downplayed the combative spirit that characterized the indigenous peasant movement in the 1960s and 1970s in order to increase its capacity to negotiate with aid agencies and NGOs, thereby attracting resources and development projects to their organizations at the cost of implicitly renouncing any criticism of the structural causes of rural poverty and exclusion. The FEPP's land credit project was thus perfectly functional for a state undergoing structural adjustment and abandoning its obligations in the areas of social policy and development promotion.

At the same time it is important to emphasize the FEPP's continued emphasis on strengthening the organizational capacity of the indigenous population. By making loans to OSGs, the rotating credit fund became an important mechanism for consolidating the administrative and developmental capacities of many OSGs, some of which became truly representative and effectively managed for the first time as a result of the FEPP's initiatives. The FEPP's reimbursement of 5 percent of the interest payments made by their respective base organizations played a key role in strengthening many OSGs. Unfortunately, it also created numerous tensions and conflicts.

We cannot close this section without discussing the ambivalent results of the FEPP's efforts to promote the collective management of land and other development resources. By the 1990s growing numbers of indigenous peasants in the Ecuadorian highlands were dismantling collective forms of land and resource management in favor of individual forms of agriculture. The implications of this growing individualism in areas like Guamote and Tixán forced the FEPP to make important changes in the strategic direction of its projects after 1996.

In the late 1980s Martínez provided evidence that agrarian reform, the commercialization of the peasant economy, demographic forces, and increasing pressure to exploit ecologically fragile lands were leading to an unstoppable process of dismantling the communal management of the *páramos* (Martínez 1987). In the context of the decline in communal practices, the FEPP's emphasis on collective work was condemned to an uncertain fate, as much because of the dynamics of the highland peasant economy as because of the FEPP's limited resources to counter such a trend. As a result of its growing awareness of a decline in collective resource management, the FEPP's Riobamba office made a significant shift after 1996 toward market-oriented strategies.

THE FEPP RIOBAMBA, 1996–2000: SUPPORT FOR ORGANIZED PEASANT PRODUCERS IN THE ERA OF NEOLIBERALISM

From 1996 to 2000 the FEPP's Riobamba office implemented a second program: the Project for Agriculture, Livestock, Small-Scale Agro-Industry, and Rational Use of Land Acquired by Peasant Organizations in Guamote and Tixán. In response to the recommendations made in the final evaluation of its first program and as a consequence of lessons learned from the land credit program, the FEPP's Riobamba office made Guamote and Tixán priority zones for its work. In the project area in Guamote, the FEPP worked with peasant organizations with abundant potential resources (land and irrigation) and with a productive infrastructure already in place. Within this framework the FEPP began to promote commercial agriculture and livestock production. The peasant communities with which the FEPP worked in Tixán, however, had fewer options, particularly because of the lack of irrigation. In Tixán, the FEPP focused its efforts on the introduction of new and more profitable crops and the creation of small agricultural processing and marketing centers. The FEPP also decided to continue operating in other already established zones of concentration in Chunchi, Lincto-Pungalá, and San Juan.

The specific lines of action for the Riobamba office's second program included training technically competent and socially committed field staff; implementing profitable and ecologically sustainable development projects; creating new lines of credit for peasant production and marketing; establishing small infrastructure works; and generating occupational alternatives for youths unable to find agricultural employment. With these projects, the FEPP hoped to demonstrate both to project beneficiaries and to the general public that land transferred to small-scale peasant farmers could be "managed rationally, produce food needed in the cities, help peasants to stay in their communities with decent levels of well-being, and promote social peace" (FEPP 1996a, 54).

In order to realize such ambitious objectives, the FEPP recognized the importance of good planning and analysis (FEPP 1996a, 53). Through a process of critical self-analysis, the FEPP identified eight crucial obstacles to project viability: support to unprofitable projects; the dilution of efforts among too many projects; paternalism; underestimating peasant capacities; fostering the dependence of peasant groups on the FEPP support; promoting inappropriate forms of organization and management; excessive flexibility regarding peasant failures to comply with loan agreements; and working with other development institutions with different methodologies and priorities. Finally, in contrast with its past practices, the FEPP recognized for the first time the importance of strengthening the gender focus of its projects, especially in the context of high rates of male migration in Chimborazo (FEPP 1996a, 46).

Successes and Failures of the FEPP's 1996–2000 Program

The first external evaluation of the Agriculture, Livestock and Agro-Industrial Development Project, conducted in 1999, saw the new strategic direction of the FEPP's Riobamba office as a great improvement. Indeed, representatives of the IICO, one of the FEPP's major financial supporters, were encouraged by what they considered to be the FEPP's more realistic approach to understanding and promoting rural development:

> Increased attention to the importance of markets, the need to link agricultural production with processing and marketing, and the importance of finding an equilibrium between individual and collective initiatives are some of the most important concepts that have been incorporated into the FEPP's vision. (FEPP 1999b, 4)

The 1999 evaluation identified three important achievements of the project. The first success was an increase in peasant production of beef and dairy products in zones appropriate for that activity. The second accomplishment was the improved functioning and efficiency of irrigation systems. An important factor contributing to that improvement was the requirement that beneficiaries of the FEPP irrigation projects contribute financial resources as well as labor, resulting in contributions from peasants often in excess of 50 percent of irrigation project costs. The FEPP's third major achievement in this project was the promotion of value-added agricultural processing enterprises, which resulted in the establishment of two small cheese factories, a meat-processing plant, a sausage-making plant, a blackberry jam operation, and six greenhouses for tomatoes. As a negative result of the project, the evaluation called attention to the FEPP's total failure to conduct market studies before initiating new activities (FEPP 1999b, 12). The evaluation also criticized the absence, despite much rhetoric to the contrary, of any genuine gender perspective in the FEPP's daily operations (FEPP 1999b, 10–12).

The general objective of the FEPP Riobamba's second program was to support the development of the peasant associations that had acquired land through the land credit program. To that end it implemented projects to promote the rehabilitation of irrigation systems, microenterprise development, the creation of processing and marketing centers, the diversification of agricultural production and increases in agricultural productivity, the training of peasants in agricultural and livestock production, the promotion of soil conservation, genetic improvements in livestock, access to credit and the creation of savings and credit cooperatives, and literacy training.

However, as in its first program, the division of collectively purchased land by peasant producers created a significant obstacle to the realization of the FEPP's objective, as its efforts often ended up being directed toward individual peasant families rather than peasant cooperatives or communities (Stumpf 1999, 8). By 1999, only a few of the communities that had purchased land with credit from the FEPP continued to administer and cultivate the land collectively. The division of land meant that individual properties were often smaller than half a hectare, which made dairy production difficult and forced producers to focus on vegetable production, which lacks the price stability of dairy production and also requires specific production knowledge that most peasants lack. Marketing, the rational use of farm machinery, the wholesale purchase of inputs, and the delivery of training programs also became much more difficult after land was divided. Despite these challenges to the effectiveness of its interventions, the FEPP did not withhold services from peasants who divided their land but rather sought to adapt its strategies to these new circumstances (Stumpf 1999, 43).

NGOS, RURAL DEVELOPMENT
AND STRUCTURAL ADJUSTMENT: FINAL CONSIDERATIONS

It is important to return to the observation made at the beginning of this chapter that the evolution of development strategies promoted by the FEPP's Riobamba office between 1981 and 2001 represented an adaptation to different phases of state agrarian policy in Ecuador. More specifically, there were critical connections between the negative social implications of neoliberal SAPs and the proliferation and strengthening of NGOs, like the FEPP, which worked in rural areas (see Petras 2000; Sogge 1998). Indeed, the current model of development cooperation, largely based on the efforts of NGOs, is a critical counterpart to neoliberal social policy in many Latin American countries. By taking over responsibility for rural development from state agencies (Sogge and Zadek 1998; Bebbington 1997b), NGOs are rapidly becoming "functional" to neoliberal economic policy.

NGOs are certainly not new to the Andes. In Ecuador the largest NGOs, with the FEPP foremost among them, have been active since the 1970s. What is new, however, is the massive proliferation of these organizations since the beginning of the 1980s. As Jorge León pointed out, 72.5 percent of the NGOs established in Ecuador between 1900 and 1994 were created after 1981, that is, following the implementation of SAPs after 1982 (León 1998).[16] There is thus an almost direct correlation between the withdrawal of the state from the sphere of rural development and the increase in the numbers of NGOs, which have tried to soften the social impacts of that withdrawal. From this perspective NGOs represent an accommodation with SAPs.

The rapid and radical change in the macroeconomic context that followed the debt crisis also left older NGOs with little choice but to go through an often traumatic process of redefining their priorities, methods, and roles in development. The FEPP's Riobamba office went through exactly this process. The FEPP itself began operating in 1970 as an organization that actively supported the peaceful resolution of peasant demands for agrarian reform. Two decades later, however, it had largely accepted the basic neoliberal prescriptions for rural development: the formation of microenterprises, business training for indigenous peasants, the consolidation of viable and competitive businesses, and so on. These changes came about slowly. During the 1980s, under the influence of integrated rural development programs, the FEPP decided to concentrate its work in specific zones in order to strengthen peasant organizations, which was considered a critical condition for social change. After 1990, however, the FEPP progressively adapted to dominant neoliberal perspectives on development, first through the financing of the land credit program with the purchase of part of Ecuador's foreign debt and subsequently by shifting its focus away from peasant organization to an explicit emphasis on productive projects to support peasant reproduction in the context of an increasingly globalized rural economy.

This process of accommodation with neoliberalism occurred in spite of the ethical beliefs of staff working for the FEPP and other NGOs. It has generally been the external donor agencies (typically based in Europe and North America) that have imposed the themes, time lines, and approaches to development that NGOs working in the Andes have had to follow. Through the funding conditions of donor agencies, older NGOs were forced to rethink and revise their relationships with the state, the market, and their beneficiaries, often resulting in a genuine crisis in terms of institutional identity, legitimacy, and survival (see Chiriboga 1995; Bebbington 1997a and 1997b; Bebbington and Thiele 1993).

The medium and long-term viability of the types of rural development initiatives in which the FEPP is engaged also needs to be questioned. What future can the FEPP's efforts have in the context of profoundly *anti*-peasant state agrarian and agricultural policies? Is it even realistic to expect peasant agriculture to be economically viable in contexts such as Chimborazo—characterized by increasingly high levels of migration and of nonagricultural activity—without at least incorporating those activities into a new, broader understanding of rural development? Has the time not come for all of the actors involved in rural development—NGOs, popular organizations, foreign donors—to reflect on the role that states need to play to guarantee a place for small producers within regional and national markets? Or to put the question differently: Does it make any sense to continue working with peasants if the rules of the game do not change?

Paradoxically, the NGO development paradigm, of which the FEPP is a part, is not, in fact, a paradigm at all, but rather a kind of anti-paradigm. There are as many different models of rural development in peasant communities in the Andes as there are NGOs. Indeed, in Ecuador it is common to find numerous different development agencies simultaneously working in the same rural communities.[17] In addition to the resulting juxtaposition of so many small bureaucratic-administrative structures, which should raise questions about efficiency, this phenomenon also has resulted in the implementation of projects with opposing goals and methods in the same communities. It is not difficult to find, for example, communities in which some NGOs are promoting agro-ecology while others are simultaneously promoting Green Revolution technologies. The heterogeneity of interests and methodologies among NGOs has often blocked efforts to promote inter-institutional coopera-tion, while at the same time provoking a fierce competition among NGOs for donor resources, which are vastly insufficient in relation to the enor-mous needs of rural communities.

The consequence of the fragmentation of the development apparatus is the fragmentation of the theoretical perspectives underlying develop-ment interventions. Development projects themselves have become the only real end of NGO initiatives, entailing a whole variety of problems, including the lack of coordination among projects, the shrinking of the state apparatus and the privatization of responsibility for rural develop-ment, and increasing competition among NGOs for donor funding. As a result of the multiple understandings of development, and the varying short, medium, and long-term interests of both donors and NGOs, de-velopment projects and initiatives of all kinds are now scattered through-out the rural Andes. In the absence of any holistic and integrated under-standing of social reality, the image that emerges is one of "a mirror broken into a thousand pieces, each one reflecting its own dislocated image of development" (Paniagua 1992, 209). Sadly, the FEPP, although important, is but one of the many broken shards that compose the pic-ture of rural development in the era of globalization.

Notes

[1] It is important to remember that until this time the Catholic church was the single largest landowner in Ecuador.

[2] Although the FEPP's Riobamba office also works with peasant organiza-tions in the provinces of Tungurahua and Bolívar, the focus here is on its work in Chimborazo.

[3] Although there is no detailed census of NGOs in Ecuador, this conclusion is evident from the data collected by the Fundación Alternativa in Quito, which has the best statistics on NGO activities in Ecuador (see Bretón 2001).

[4] The FEPP's efforts in Cacha involved eighteen hundred families directly and another four hundred indirectly; altogether these families owned twenty-three hundred hectares of land.

[5] UNOCIC later became FECAIPAC. The OSG was first created in 1981 with fourteen member communities and eventually grew to incorporate twenty-three communities.

[6] The strengthening of the OSG also resulted from the support of numerous other development institutions working in Cacha. It is not an accident that a relatively strong organization such as the FECAIPAC developed in a parish where there were twenty-nine public and private development agencies working at the end of 1989.

[7] The Cumandá project involved directly 184 peasant families, who belonged to nine different peasant organizations.

[8] OTGs represent groups of OSGs, generally at the provincial level.

[9] FEPP credit for other activities was made available in the following proportions: agriculture (26 percent), livestock (25 percent), artisan production (5 percent), marketing (4 percent), reforestation (4 percent), infrastructure (2 percent) (Crespo and Bischof 1991, 27).

[10] For example, a 340 million sucres (US$309,000) fund initiated by the FEPP and COTESU in 1988 had shrunk by 41 percent to 201 million sucres (US$183,000) by 1990.

[11] Jatun Ayllu represented nine base organizations and nine hundred families and had worked with the FEPP since the creation of the first rotating credit fund in 1985. Jatun Ayllu received six loans worth a total of thirty-two million sucres to create a rotating credit fund and to make small grants to base organizations for infrastructure development (primarily electrification). UCASAJ included eighteen base organizations representing 440 families, and had a relationship with the FEPP dating back to 1987, when it received its first loan. UCASAJ received two loans worth a total of US$50,000, destined primarily for livestock purchases.

[12] The FEPP chose to provide credit for land purchases in spite of concerns that it was taking on what should have been a state responsibility, with the consequent danger of demobilizing peasants demanding fulfillment of their legal rights. The FEPP concluded that it would make credit available to peasants only when they had exhausted all legal means available for forcing the state to respond to their demands (Navarro, Vallejo, and Villaverde 1996, 43). Between 1977 and 1990 the FEPP provided seventy-six loans to sixty-five peasant organizations, benefiting seventeen hundred families, who purchased 2205.3 hectares of land (Navarro, Vallejo, and Villaverde 1996, 274).

[13] Six million dollars were transferred to the FEPP for the rotating credit fund with another US$4 million dollars for projects to support productive activities on the newly acquired land.

[14] The FEPP's efforts to support peasant land purchases in the 1990s vastly exceeded those of the Ecuadorian state. With approximately US$3 million, the FEPP provided credit for 199 cases of land purchase, land titling, and land legalization in fifteen provinces of the country, while the state (during the presidency of Sixto Durán Ballén) managed to resolve only five or six cases with the equivalent of roughly US$2.7 million (Navarro, Vallejo, and Villaverde 1996, 78).

[15] The quality of the land made available for purchase was generally very poor, often only high altitude *páramo*, which is ecologically sensitive and inappropriate for any agricultural purposes other than sheep grazing. Also problematic was the size of the properties purchased, which varied from community to community. The average size of land plots purchased with the FEPP credit was slightly over four hectares (Stumpf 1999, 44), insufficient to support a family.

[16] Arcos Cabrera and Palomeque Vallejo raise this figure to 80 percent (1997, 25–26).

[17] For example, in the relatively small zone comprised of Guamote and Tixán, CESA counted thirty-five private and public agencies between 1985 and 1996 (CESA 1997, 86). Even more extreme is the case of the rural parish of San Juan (near Riobamba), where sixty NGOs operated over an even shorter time period (Bebbington et al. 1992, 194).

Chapter 9

Municipal Democratization and Rural Development in Highland Ecuador

John D. Cameron

Over the course of the 1980s and 1990s local indigenous-peasant organizations in Ecuador became increasingly engaged in municipal politics as a means of asserting greater control over rural infrastructure and processes of local development. In the 1990s indigenous mayors and municipal councilors closely linked to indigenous-peasant organizations were elected for the first time in history in over thirty of Ecuador's 215 municipalities (see Beck and Mijeski 2001). Marking a radical departure from the clientelism, corruption, and weak administrative capacity that had long characterized rural municipal politics in Ecuador, some of those indigenous-led rural municipalities created new institutions for participatory decision-making, actively promoted local social and economic development, and, for the first time, effectively extended local citizenship rights to long-excluded indigenous and peasant populations. Indeed, the most remarkable cases of municipal democratization in Ecuador emerged from this group of rural municipalities.[1]

At the same time the potential importance of municipal governments in Ecuador and throughout Latin America is quickly increasing in the context of the decentralization of public services to local levels of government, actively promoted by IFIs and development agencies as part of a broader package of "second-generation reforms" (see Burki and Perry 1998; World Bank 1997 and 2000). Proponents of decentralization, who span the entire ideological spectrum, argue that transferring decision-making power to levels of government that are "closer to the people" can strengthen democracy, administrative efficiency, and opportunities for economic development. Local governments, they argue, can—in theory—respond more adeptly to the needs and concerns of local populations. In rural settings municipal governments are also seen as institutions that might play a central role in confronting the lack of citizen participation, local knowledge, and local coordination that have contributed to the failure of many rural development efforts.

However, efforts to put the theoretical benefits of decentralization into practice face considerable obstacles in the context of the extremely unequal socioeconomic power relations and clientelist political culture that prevail at both the local and national levels in Ecuador and other Latin American countries. Two key questions thus emerge for processes of decentralization and democratization in rural municipalities. First, under what conditions can rural municipal governments become more democratic and more effective as agents of local development? Second, are those conditions in place or might they be created with certain policy instruments such that the benefits of decentralization might be realized in large numbers of municipal governments?

In an effort to answer these questions, this chapter examines processes of municipal democratization in the three rural municipalities in Ecuador that, in 1999, had been most widely recognized for their efforts to promote citizen participation and local development: Guamote (Chimborazo province), Cotacachi (Imbabura province), and Bolívar (Carchi province).[2] Ironically, by 2000 it was clear that the participatory and developmental initiatives in the municipality of Bolívar had broken down. That municipality thus became an important case for examining the failure of efforts to democratize local government.

Research conducted in the three municipalities between 1999 and 2002 found that participatory municipal governments with the capacity to regulate local development processes emerged only where four factors were present: (1) a relatively equitable distribution of agricultural land; (2) strong local indigenous-peasant organizations; (3) high levels of external technical and financial support; and (4) economic marginality.[3] It must be emphasized that the first three factors are highly exceptional; that is, they are not widely present in rural municipalities in Ecuador or any other Latin American states. The fourth factor, economic marginality, reflected a balance of socioeconomic power favorable to municipal democratization but ironically also undermined possibilities for local social and economic development. As a result, decentralization in Ecuador is unlikely to be accompanied by either a deepening of municipal democracy or by inclusive forms of economic and social development unless the Ecuadorian state and IFIs make serious changes to the prevailing agrarian and macroeconomic policy agendas.

Section 1 proposes a working methodology for studying municipal governments in rural Latin America. Section 2 analyzes the efforts to implement participatory decision-making processes in the three municipalities. The conclusion examines the central factors that contributed to the relative successes and failures of the three participatory initiatives.

THE SOCIAL ORIGINS OF MUNICIPAL DEMOCRACY:
A METHODOLOGY FOR STUDYING
RURAL MUNICIPAL GOVERNANCE

In the context of decentralization processes, local governments in Latin America are emerging from years of neglect in studies of both democratization and economic development (Fox 1994; Nickson 1995; Reilly 1995; Tendler 1997). However, studies of municipal politics in Latin America have focused overwhelmingly on large urban centers to the widespread exclusion of rural municipalities, despite the disproportionate concentration of poverty in rural areas and the potentially important role that they might play in coordinating rural development efforts to ensure that they respond to local needs. Moreover, from a methodological perspective, the analysis of citizen participation in local governments in Latin America has emphasized the institutional design of participatory mechanisms and the particular strategies pursued by municipal authorities as the key variables to explain the success and failure of efforts to promote citizen involvement (Abers 2000; Tendler 1997; Winn and Ferro-Clerico 1997).

While the particular form of municipal institutions is clearly an important force shaping citizen participation in Latin America (and the widespread lack thereof), the development of those institutions can be fully understood only in the context of the economic, political, and social forces within which they are created and operate. An understanding of the political opportunities for making rural municipal governments more democratic, therefore, demands an analysis of broader conditions, such as the distribution of productive assets and levels of popular organization at the local level.

Building on the comparative historical method and "relative class power" approach to democratization proposed by Moore (1966) and further developed by Rueschemeyer, Stephens, and Stephens (1992), this chapter proposes an approach to the study of rural municipal politics based on an analysis of local-level socioeconomic and political power relations. The relative class power approach seeks to explain the political trajectories of nation-states by analyzing: the distribution of productive assets and the corresponding balance of socioeconomic power among different classes and class coalitions, the centrality of political organization to the power of subordinate groups and classes, the impact of international and transnational power relations on the local balance of class power, the institutional structure and relative autonomy of the state, and the ways in which the political actions of elites are shaped by their perception of the threats posed to their interests by subordinate groups and classes (Rueschemeyer, Stephens, and Stephens 1992).

While this approach has been used primarily to explain the political trajectories of states at the national level, the cases examined in this chapter suggest that an analysis of similar factors is equally useful for understanding the political trajectories of local states, that is, municipal governments. To explain different patterns of municipal governance in rural settings, I adapt the relative class power approach to the local level, focusing attention on the local distribution of productive assets (primarily agricultural land) and the corresponding balance of socioeconomic power, the organizational strength of local indigenous and peasant populations relative to other local power holders, the availability of external technical and financial support, the appropriate design of participatory and developmental institutions, and the responses of local elites to municipal regulatory efforts. Within this framework the chapter also considers the ways in which local class power relations are mediated by ethnicity, with a particular focus on the ways in which ethnic tensions exacerbate unequal class power relations as well as processes of class differentiation within local indigenous populations. The chapter also highlights the connections between relative lack of socioeconomic and cultural power of women at the local level and the failure of rural municipal governments to include them in local decision-making.

Although socioeconomic power relations are highly unequal and democratic institutions perform very poorly at the national level in Ecuador (Conaghan 1996; Cueva 1982; Larrea and North 1997), there is considerable diversity in the distribution of socioeconomic power and the performance of political institutions at the local level. A clear example, and indeed partial cause of this diversity is the varied impact of Ecuador's 1973 Agrarian Reform Law. While the reform had little impact on land-tenure patterns and power relations in overall national terms, in certain locales the legal reforms and subsequent political struggles to implement the law had a significant effect on the distribution of land and political power.[4] Similarly, historical processes in certain areas of Ecuador, such as the rural parishes of Pelileo and Salinas analyzed by North in Chapters 10 and 11 herein, the rural parish of Tisaleo studied by Forster (1989, 1990), and the province of El Oro examined by Larrea (1992), led to changes in the highly uneven balance of socioeconomic power that prevails in most of the country and to subsequent processes of somewhat more equitable economic and social development. An understanding of the diversity of local power relations is thus critical to any analysis of the political opportunities for local development and democratization, and thus also the success of decentralization.

CITIZEN PARTICIPATION IN RURAL MUNICIPAL GOVERNMENTS

At the beginning of the twenty-first century, in spite of incipient decentralization initiatives and internationally funded programs to strengthen municipal administration, municipal governance in Ecuador was still widely characterized by clientelism, corruption, elite domination, and weak administrative capacity (Barrera 1999; Nickson 1995; Ojeda Segovia 2000; Rosales 1999; Torres 1999). Elected municipal leaders jealously protected their discretionary power over municipal budgets in order to maintain political clienteles, and resisted pressures to improve citizen participation, accountability, and efficiency. Moreover, poorly trained and underpaid municipal staff generally lacked both the motivation and the capacity to improve citizen involvement in municipal governance, and the pressures for change from rural civil society were still relatively weak. The developmental role of rural municipal governments remained limited to small, unplanned works in the relatively privileged town centers of rural cantons, where rural populations and socioeconomic power were most heavily concentrated. By contrast, residents living outside of the town centers of rural municipalities were broadly excluded from the sphere of attention of municipal officials. Rural indigenous populations, in particular, continued to suffer from systemic neglect and racist abuse in many municipalities.

The three cases of rural municipal government examined in this chapter were chosen because, in the late 1990s, they appeared to represent important contrasts to the widespread pattern of municipal governance just described. All three municipalities were broadly recognized in NGO and academic communities as well as the press in Ecuador as exemplary cases of citizen participation in municipal decision-making, although, as mentioned above, it quickly became clear that participatory and developmental initiatives in Bolívar were in crisis.

As the data presented in Table 9.1 make clear, the populations of the three cantons were all overwhelmingly rural and faced high levels of poverty. The indigenous population of the three cantons varied from 97 percent in Guamote, to 50 percent in Cotacachi to zero in Bolívar, the significance of which is discussed in the next section, "Making Sense of Participatory and Developmental Municipal Governments."

Guamote: Municipal Democratization in the Context of Land Reform

Over the course of the 1990s the municipal government of Guamote underwent a remarkable transformation that involved the election of indigenous mayors and councilors for the first time in the canton's history and the creation of new institutions for participatory decision-making and local social and economic development. To understand that process, it is necessary to examine the much broader and more gradual transition of economic and social power from a tiny white-mestizo elite to the indigenous-peasant majority of the canton that began in the 1970s.

Table 9.1 Demographic and Municipal Indicators for Guamote, Cotacachi, and Bolívar

Demographic indicators	Guamote	Cotacachi	Bolívar	Ecuador
1990 population	28,058	33,240	15,157	9.6 million
1990 rural population	89.19%	81.8%	68.3%	41.8%
% of rural population in predominantly indigenous areas[a]	100%	54.04%	0.0%	n/a
Surface area	1,223 km²	1,809 km²	360.85 km²	284,000 km²
Poverty	89.25%	84.15%	79.68%	58.4%
Indigence	68.26%	56.21%	36.67%	21.4%
Poverty ranking in 1999 (x/214; 214=poorest)	210	192	168	n/a
Infant mortality (x/1,000 live births)	122.63	74.95	64.1	53.2
Illiteracy (males over 15)	33.1%	2.1%	9.2%	9.5%
Illiteracy (females over 15)	54.3%	37.3%	15%	13.8%
Land tenure:				
Agricultural units > 100 hectares affected by agrarian reform[b]	54.37%	3.49%	14.25%	9%[c]
Economy:				
Agricultural workers in economically active population	83.7%	57.5%	78.2%	31.0%
Manufacturing workers in economically active population	1.7%	16.5%	3%	15.9%
Municipal administration:[d]				
Number of municipal employees (1999)	52	70	46	n/a
1998 budget (in 1998 US dollars)	$1,091,049	$1,521,860	$862,025	n/a

[a] Zamosc 1995, 80; [b] Zamosc 1995, 82–83; [c] Banco Central del Ecuador 1988, 92; [d] data on the municipal administrations is from the financial records of each municipality.

Source: Unless otherwise noted, data is from ODEPLAN 1999, the most up-to-date source of comparable canton-level demographic statistics in Ecuador (based on the 1990 census).

In the decade following Ecuador's 1973 Agrarian Reform Law, Guamote experienced a process of land and power redistribution more far-reaching than any other canton in Ecuador. In 1974 six *haciendas* still controlled 72 percent of all land in Guamote (INEC 1974), the most unequal distribution in any canton in the country (CIDA 1965). Peasant mobilization for land in the canton had become increasingly radical in the early 1970s, first under the influence of the FEI—affiliated with the Communist Party—and later under the leadership of the progressive Catholic church. In response to this pressure, and in the context of the particularly backward agricultural practices and low productivity of the canton's *haciendas* and the poor quality of local soils, the Ecuadorian state made Guamote a specific focus of the 1973 Agrarian Reform Law (Sylva 1986). By 1980 all of the large *haciendas* in Guamote had been broken up, and more than 50 percent of the canton's land had passed into the hands of peasants (Gangotena et al. 1980, 15). After 1980 almost all of the remaining land in the canton passed into peasant hands through land sales.[5]

Local power relations changed only slowly following the land reform process. Until the mid-1970s, economic, political, and social power in Guamote was completely dominated by local estate owners, who operated with the acquiescence of municipal officials and local priests (Sylva 1986). After Guamote's *haciendas* were broken up, the town-based mestizo middle class took over political power in the canton. However, two parallel processes helped to shift local power gradually toward the indigenous majority. The first process was demographic. After the land reforms there was an exodus of mestizo landowners and merchants from Guamote, which resulted in a significant relative increase in the indigenous and rural population of the canton (Carrasco 1997, 21–24). The second process was organizational. Peasant struggles for land in Guamote involved widespread community and parish-level organizing, which not only increased the relative political power of the local indigenous-peasant population but also helped to make Guamote an important focus of development initiatives in Ecuador following the land reform. Although the developmental impact of those interventions has been highly questioned (see Chapter 8), they nonetheless helped to consolidate the intracommunity federations, known in Ecuador as second-level organizations (OSGs), which would eventually play the lead role in transforming municipal politics.

As the organizational capacity of the OSGs in Guamote developed, they became increasingly engaged in municipal politics in the canton. Guamote's OSGs nominated the first indigenous candidate for a position on the municipal council in 1980. By 1992 they had ended the mestizo domination of the council by electing the canton's first indigenous mayor. By 1996 candidates nominated by Guamote's OSGs occupied all of the positions on the municipal council, a situation that continued after the 2000 elections. It was under the leadership of OSG-affiliated indigenous mayors and councilors that the municipality of Guamote became one of the most participatory and developmentally oriented local governments in Ecuador.

The most important participatory initiative of Guamote's municipal government was the creation of the Indigenous and Popular Parliament, the first institution of its kind in the country. The parliament was created in 1997 to give a stronger voice and decision-making power to the elected presidents of the *cabildos* (councils) that formally represented each of the 121 legally recognized rural communities in the canton. Its central functions included overseeing the work of the mayor and municipal council and holding them accountable, allocating the municipal budget, debating municipal investments and projects, and nominating the authorities appointed by the central state in the canton as well as the candidates in municipal elections. Between 1997 and 2002, the parliament met an average of five times a year.[6] Indigenous peasant leaders, including Guamote's mayors, insisted that the parliament was the highest instance of political representation in the canton and that the mayor and municipal council had the *moral* although not the *legal* obligation to implement its resolutions.

Marking a clear shift in authority over local development interventions in Guamote, the parliament asserted its authority to regulate and coordinate the work of NGOs and other external development actors in the canton, including central state agencies and the Ecuadorian army. Because the work of outside actors had never been regulated in Guamote, development efforts in the canton had generally failed to respond to local priorities, had privileged some communities while completely neglecting others, and had operated in a paternalistic and often authoritarian manner. With its strong moral authority, the parliament confronted these problems by insisting that external development actors operate under its direction in accordance with locally determined development priorities and in coordination with local communities and OSGs.

The parliament became an important mechanism for bringing external development interventions in line with an endogenous development agenda, a process called for by many critics of traditional approaches of development (Escobar 1995; Scott 1998). However, it is important to emphasize that the power of the parliament remained limited to regulating the direct provision of development aid from outside actors. The parliament had no influence over national and global macroeconomic policies, the priorities of development agencies, or what kinds of assistance external actors actually offered. Moreover, the willingness of the parliament's members to reject external support that did not respond to local priorities tended to diminish in almost direct proportion to the monetary value of the assistance offered. The performance of the parliament was also undermined by very passive participation by its members, extremely low representation of women, and a tiny operating budget.

The developmental initiatives of Guamote's municipal government were initially channeled through the Local Development Committee, created in 1997 with a major grant from the IAF. Composed of the presidents of twelve of Guamote's OSGs and members of the municipal council, the committee was intended to serve as a mechanism for the joint management of community-based business enterprises. By 1998 the committee operated six projects: a reforestation initiative, a trout hatchery, a composting facility, a grain-processing center, a training/meeting center, and a cultural revival project. However, the inappropriate institutional design of the committee, largely imposed by the IAF, seriously restricted its capacity to fulfill its intended role. The OSGs had little interest in giving up their autonomy to manage their own projects and placed little value on the committee. As a result, by 2002 the coordinating functions of the committee had largely ceased to function, and the projects that had been initiated in 1998 were simply managed by technical staff with little involvement on the part of the OSGs, which operated their own projects in isolation from one another and from the Local Development Committee.

That indigenous leaders in Guamote quickly came to appreciate the importance of designing local institutions in accord with local capacities and needs was reflected in the process of creating a series of "development roundtables" to implement the initiatives called for in the canton's development plan. Some of the external actors that expected to be involved in the roundtables advocated for an institutional design in which both local and external actors would be represented. However, recognizing that the relative lack of formal education of the local members of the roundtables would result in domination of discussions by outside actors, Guamote's indigenous leaders, with the support of certain NGOs, insisted on a model in which only local actors would be formally represented and external agents would be invited to participate in certain meetings as consultants.

Just as important as the specific institutions created by Guamote's municipal government were the open lines of communication established with the indigenous-peasant residents of the canton's rural communities. Guamote's indigenous mayors went to great lengths to make themselves accessible to their constituents and to work cooperatively with community leaders and OSGs to implement public works and development programs. Municipal offices also became much more welcoming to indigenous peasants, who for the first time were treated by municipal leaders as local citizens. Once a site of discrimination and abuse, where indigenous petitioners were made to wait endlessly for routine paperwork and where "gifts" were required to receive public attention, the municipal building became a focal point of local indigenous organizing. By 1999 indigenous residents breezed in and out of municipal offices as comfortably as if they were visiting their own OSGs.

Cotacachi: Municipal Democratization Without Land Reform

In contrast to Guamote, agrarian reform laws had almost no impact on the distribution of land in Cotacachi. In 1991 farms over fifty hectares and *haciendas* (which together represented only 18.6 percent of agricultural units) still controlled 90 percent of all land in the canton (CAAP 1991, 49). Moreover, by the mid-1990s, seven of those *haciendas* had become highly modernized producers of cut flowers and fresh vegetables for export. Surprisingly, given the context of highly unequal property control, the municipality of Cotacachi emerged in the late 1990s as a leader of participatory governance in Ecuador. In recognition of the high levels of democratization and citizen participation in its municipal government, Cotacachi was selected as the Latin American recipient of UNESCO's 2002 Cities for Peace Prize and won the UN-Habitat sponsored Dubai International Prize in 2000 for "best practices in the democratization of municipal management for equitable and sustainable development" (UN-Habitat and Municipality of Dubai 2000).

Cotacachi's experience with participatory local government began in August 1996 with the election of a well-educated and politically talented indigenous leader, Auki Tituaña, as mayor. His election victory followed the election of indigenous leaders as municipal councilors in every municipal election after 1980. Those councilors had been nominated and supported by the local OSG, the UNORCAC, which had focused attention on capturing municipal power shortly after its creation in the late 1970s. Support from the UNORCAC, which mobilized indigenous voters from the canton's forty-three rural highland communities, was essential for the election of the indigenous mayor in 1996 and his reelection in 2000, although it must be emphasized that that support was far from automatic.

Cotacachi's principal mechanism for participatory decision-making was the annual Canton Assembly, first organized under Tituaña's leadership in 1996 to bring together representatives of local organizations in order to devise strategies for promoting local development. The assemblies quickly grew in the number of participants—from under two hundred in 1996 to over six hundred in 2001—the number of social sectors represented, and the "quality" of the participation itself. At the first assembly, in 1996, there were almost no representatives from Cotacachi's mostly mestizo town center, and the municipal government was almost completely dependent on NGO assistance for the organization of the event. By the fourth assembly, in 1999, the urban sector was well represented through a Neighborhood Federation and neighborhood-level organizations—created through municipal leadership—while municipal employees had taken over almost all of the organizational logistics of the assembly. Regarding the quality of participation, observers of the first assembly recalled that residents had come primarily to ask for public works for their communities; by the fourth assembly, however, it was clear that they had come prepared to debate issues related to the canton's development and were behaving as agents rather than as objects of local development efforts. By 2001 the assembly had acquired significant institutional autonomy from other local actors and had its own offices, budget, and a permanent staff of seven. At the same time, however, the role of the assembly in the local development process remained heavily dependent on the political will of the mayor and on financial support from NGOs.

Following resolutions of the assemblies in 1996, 1997, 1998, and 1999, the municipality created a series of permanent inter-sectoral committees that drew together representatives from a wide cross-section of Cotacachi's social sectors to pursue solutions to the particular problems facing the canton in the areas of health, education, agricultural, artisan production, tourism, and the environment. By 1999 the municipality had decentralized significant planning and management responsibilities to these inter-sectoral committees, a sharp contrast to the majority of municipal governments in Ecuador, which remained highly centralized and autocratic in their administrative practices. Moreover, by 2002 the municipality had not only significantly increased the proportion of its budget dedicated to rural communities but had also shifted much of the control over its budget away from the municipal council to a participatory budgeting process based on the model established in the Brazilian city of Porto Alegre (see Abers 2000).[7]

In addition to establishing new participatory and developmental institutions, the municipality of Cotacachi also actively promoted the formation of citizen organizations in the canton, such as neighborhood organizations and a neighborhood federation in the town center and an OSG in the isolated western lowland region of the canton. The municipality also made active efforts to promote the leadership capacities of children and youth and to incorporate them formally into municipal governance.

Understanding both the successes and limitations of the participatory and developmental initiatives in Cotacachi requires an examination of socioeconomic power relations in the canton and an analysis of the responses of the town-based middle-class mestizos and the *hacienda* owners to those initiatives. Significantly, the large landowners did not resist or make any notable attempts to frustrate the changes in municipal governance in Cotacachi. Nor, however, were they willing to participate in the process or be taxed or regulated in any way by the municipality. They tolerated the participatory process because they were powerful enough to operate beyond its reach. *Hacienda* owners did not produce for the local market, in many cases did not live in the canton, and were generally not interested in local politics. Rather, their outlook was oriented toward national and global markets and policies. Although they did not stand in the way of the municipality's participatory initiatives, local landowning elites in Cotacachi placed clear limits on the jurisdiction of the municipal government and forcefully resisted municipal efforts to regulate their operations.

In contrast to relations with large-scale landowners, the indigenous mayor managed to cultivate considerable support from the town-based mestizo middle class in the canton. Ironically, however, much of the legitimacy and respect that Tituaña won from the town-based mestizos did not result from the opening of participatory spaces or the promotion of local organization and leadership development. Rather, it was the municipality's impressive record in completing public-works projects—electrification, street lighting, sewage, potable water, road improvements, sports fields—that gave legitimacy to the participatory process and to Tituaña's presence as an indigenous mayor. The financial capacity to complete such public-works projects within the constraints of Cotacachi's small budget resulted primarily from the very significant financial and technical support that the municipality brokered from NGOs and donor agencies—support that is unlikely to be sustained over time and that is not broadly replicable.[8]

Under Mayor Tituaña's leadership, the municipal development strategy in Cotacachi was not limited to working through local institutions. It also included social mobilization and protest aimed at macroeconomic policymaking. Following Tituaña's election in 1996, the municipality consistently gave both moral and logistical support to nationwide indigenous protests for macro-level policy changes. Indigenous mayors in Guamote similarly convoked massive protest actions, including road blockades of the Pan-American highway during nationwide uprisings against macroeconomic policies that threatened opportunities for local development. While the indigenous mayors of Guamote and Cotacachi focused their political energy on formal politics and institutionalized participation at the local level, they did not ignore political strategies of protest aimed at bringing about the broader macroeconomic policy changes needed to make local development possible.

Bolívar: Failed Efforts to Democratize Municipal Governance

Local residents in the canton of Bolívar were excited and optimistic when they elected Fabián Ramírez, a young ex-guerrilla leader, as their mayor in 1992. Ramírez's election platform had emphasized citizen participation and organization, rural development, health, education, gender equity, and administrative accountability. Hope for the future of local politics surged again in 1995 when Bolívar's municipal government under Ramírez's leadership organized the first municipal assembly to be held in Ecuador and brought together over three hundred residents from the canton's fifty-six mostly rural communities for three days of workshops to elaborate a development plan for the canton (Municipalidad de Bolívar 1997).

Images of Bolívar's municipal administration in the national press and NGO circles were also very positive, and Mayor Ramírez received much praise for his efforts to incorporate participatory decision-making processes into the municipal administration and for promoting gender awareness and social and economic development. In 1999 the director of a Quito-based NGO described the municipality as the "foremost" in the country among mestizo-populated cantons for its promotion of citizen participation. Another NGO, CARE International, identified the positive attitude of Mayor Ramírez as one of the key factors that led CARE to select the municipality as its first partner for pilot projects with municipalities in the areas of preventative health care and economic development.

However, despite initial enthusiasm, local support for municipal efforts to promote citizen participation steadily declined over the course of Ramírez's eight years as mayor. Many of those who endorsed the mayor's fresh ideas about participation in 1992 became frustrated and angry with the lack of municipal public works in the canton, especially in the town center. In contrast to Cotacachi, Bolívar's experience with citizen participation was not accompanied by any tangible increase in municipal public works that might have helped to build legitimacy for the new administrative practices and developmental agenda. In fact, Ramírez deliberately shifted municipal spending away from traditional public works such as street paving to less tangible programs intended to improve local health care, education, and agricultural production, with important increases in attention to rural communities.

Although these programs might have helped to reduce poverty in Bolívar had they been maintained for a longer time period, the mayor failed to secure active support from either the residents of rural communities or the town center for this shift from traditional municipal practices. Town residents were generally not interested in changing either municipal administrative practices or the local development agenda, as the town center had long been the privileged focus of municipal spending. By shifting the emphasis of the municipal government from the town center to the rural sector and away from traditional public works, Ramírez alienated large numbers of town dwellers, including the local clientelist elites, that felt even further threatened by movement toward participatory municipal planning which limited their discretionary access to municipal resources. However, there were also no strong organizations of peasants in Bolívar's rural communities that might have actively supported the nascent participatory process or the municipal development initiatives that were intended to benefit them.

Seeing few tangible results from local participatory processes, opponents of Mayor Ramírez asserted that the process of organizing the municipal assembly in 1995 and producing the local development plan in 1997 were a waste of municipal resources that they would not repeat. Municipal councilors, in fact, refused to support efforts by Ramírez to organize a second municipal assembly. Criticisms of Ramírez also went beyond poor administration to nepotism and corruption. The mayor's failure to put a halt to racist discrimination by municipal employees against the canton's Afro-Ecuadorian population also undermined possibilities of generating support for his initiatives in the canton's seven Afro-Ecuadorian communities, which represented roughly 20 percent of the local population.

Opposition to Ramírez's leadership reached a peak shortly after his reelection in September 1996. The mayor was arrested on charges of corruption and was held in a provincial jail for forty-four days, although the Superior Court of the province of Carchi did not find sufficient evidence to try him. The personal political ambitions of certain municipal councilors who enjoyed support from other members of the town elite as well as from important political allies at the provincial level played key roles in this scandal. Whether or not the accusations of corruption leveled against the mayor were true, the scandal seriously discredited both his image and that of the municipality as an institution, and it seriously divided the local population. After 1996 the mayor was unable to initiate any significant changes in municipal administrative practices or any important public works projects. The municipality's efforts to promote gender equity also largely collapsed after the mayor and his wife (who had directed those efforts) divorced and she left the canton in 1996. By 1999 most residents had few expectations of either Ramírez or the municipal government and widely characterized the efforts to promote participatory planning in their canton as a failure. Ramírez did not run in the May 2000 municipal elections, which saw the former vice-mayor, representing a coalition of six populist and right-wing political parties, assume the office of mayor. In that new political context attempts to promote local participatory politics quickly ended.

The failure of participatory and developmental initiatives in the municipality of Bolívar resulted not only from strategic errors on the part of Mayor Ramírez but also from the local balance of socioeconomic power, a legacy of the particular process of agrarian transformation in the province of Carchi. The widespread sale of *hacienda* lands to small- and medium-scale producers in Bolívar and other parts of Carchi after the 1940s meant that the distribution of agricultural land was not as unequal as in many other parts of highland Ecuador (see Barsky 1984b; Lehman 1986a, 1986b; Miño Grijalva 1985).[9] Large *haciendas* had almost completely disappeared from Bolívar by the early 1970s. However, the historical absence of external organizing agents in rural Carchi also meant that local power relations were marked by a striking lack of peasant organizations and the political dominance of medium-scale agricultural producers and commercial intermediaries. The lack of peasant organizations coupled with the lack of any indigenous population also meant that few NGOs were attracted to the province (see the next section).

Few social contexts could have been less propitious for Mayor Ramírez's efforts to promote citizen participation and socioeconomic development. Not only was there no base of organized support for the mayor's initiatives or history of participation in local organizations, but the relative lack of interest on the part of external development actors also meant that the municipality did not have the resources to invest in public works that might have helped to legitimate and generate political support for the mayor's agenda. In that setting even the most politically astute strategies for undermining the political dominance of the local clientelist elite and implementing more democratic forms of municipal governance would likely have failed. When the opposition aroused by Mayor Ramírez's corruption scandals was added to other political forces in Bolívar, efforts to democratize politics in the canton were doomed.

MAKING SENSE OF PARTICIPATORY
AND DEVELOPMENTAL MUNICIPAL GOVERNMENTS

The success or failure of a particular rural municipal government in developing participatory institutions and administrative practices affects a relatively small number of people. More important for rural development and democratization is the question of whether conditions exist that would allow successful cases of participatory and developmental governance to emerge on a broad scale. The experiences of Guamote, Cotacachi, and Bolívar suggest that four variables are central to the relative success of efforts to develop participatory institutions with strong regulatory capacities in rural municipalities: (1) an equitable distribution of productive assets, particularly agricultural land; (2) strong local peasant-indigenous organizations; (3) high levels of external technical and financial support; and (4) economic marginality. This section examines the relative presence and absence of these four factors in the three cantons and highlights the widespread absence of the first three factors in most other rural cantons in Ecuador.

Distribution of Agricultural Land and Socioeconomic
Power Relations

Evidence from Guamote and Cotacachi suggests that there is an important connection between the distribution of agricultural land and corresponding socioeconomic power relations, on the one hand, and the degree of democratic participation and the regulatory capacity of rural municipal governments, on the other hand. In the case of Guamote, agrarian reform was a crucial precursor to the emergence of local participatory institutions. The intense struggles involved in the reform process succeeded in breaking the power of the landowning elite that had previously controlled local politics in the canton and opened the political space for local indigenous-peasant organizations to democratize municipal politics.

However, although agrarian reform created opportunities for political development in Guamote, it did not lead to any significant economic improvements. Because land in the canton was of very poor quality, and the rural development programs that accompanied agrarian reform were poorly funded, inappropriately designed, and often subjected to political manipulation, the canton's population continued to live in extreme poverty. Moreover, local opportunities for nonagricultural employment and income generation were minimal. The *hacienda* owners, who dominated Guamote's economy until the late 1970s, had consistently taken profits out of the canton, with the result that there was very little investment in local nonagricultural production that might have sparked broader processes of economic development (Sylva 1986, 22). At the end of the 1990s there were still very few economic resources in the canton that might have been used to create either local employment or a demand for the growth of local service industries. Thus, while agrarian reform was a necessary precondition for the emergence of a participatory municipal administration in Guamote, it failed to address the resource void that continued to stand in the way of local economic development.

It is also important to recognize that by the 1990s the amount of land owned by indigenous peasants varied significantly, with important consequences for the distribution of political power in the canton. A considerable number of local indigenous leaders in Guamote, including the first indigenous mayor, came from a relatively small group of families that had acquired comparatively large parcels of land during and after the implementation of agrarian reforms. Ownership of larger plots of land not only enabled those families to provide their children with good educations but also meant that those children—Guamote's current crop of leaders and politicians—did not need to migrate as frequently in search of employment and could remain in their communities. As a result, they were able to forge strong social relations and, with much higher than average levels of education, to become involved in NGO-funded development projects and to lead local OSGs, which in turn enabled them to acquire important management and leadership skills (see Bebbington 1990, 167–85; 2000, 517). Reinforcing the connections between land ownership and access to political power in Guamote, cultural traditions in the area generally prevent indigenous peasants who do not own land from occupying senior positions in peasant organizations, as they are not considered to be full members of their communities (see Cervone 1996, 77–78). Similarly, the economic, legal, and cultural obstacles to landownership by women in Guamote and other rural cantons help to explain their relative lack of socioeconomic power and continued political marginalization even in municipalities that have become more inclusive in ethnic and class terms.

In Cotacachi a participatory municipal administration took root without a previous process of agrarian reform. At the end of the 1990s large agricultural operations still controlled most of the canton's land, with some of them producing for global markets. While the owners of those large estates did not obstruct the participatory process in Cotacachi, they did refuse to participate in it or to be taxed or regulated by the municipality. Although the municipal government was able to develop participatory institutions involving the economically marginal majority of the canton's population, the balance of socioeconomic power in Cotacachi prevented the municipality from exercising any authority over the most powerful economic actors.

Strong Local Peasant and Indigenous Organizations

Strong local organizations were central to the development of the participatory processes in Guamote and Cotacachi. In both cantons the election of mayors representing indigenous and peasant residents was only possible through the support of local OSGs. There were two reasons for this. First, the organizations were able to mobilize rural voter support for the indigenous candidates. Second, the election of indigenous mayors in Guamote and Cotacachi followed eight and sixteen years, respectively, of work by indigenous councilors who had been nominated by and elected with the support of local indigenous organizations. Their work created a precedent for and helped to legitimate the presence of subsequently elected indigenous mayors.

The presence of strong indigenous and peasant organizations in Guamote and Cotacachi was also very important for the production of new indigenous and peasant leaders who eventually became community leaders, councilors, and mayors. In both cantons leadership in indigenous-peasant organizations was the key path to municipal political power. Indeed, all of the indigenous and peasant politicians elected in the two cantons held leadership positions in local and/or national indigenous-peasant organizations before entering municipal politics, a pattern that was also evident among the indigenous mayors elected in other cantons in Ecuador's May 2000 elections. It is crucial to note, however, that these organizations were dominated by men and that the apparently participatory forms of municipal governance that they promoted often marginalized indigenous and peasant women.

In the absence of strong local peasant organizations that might have supported participatory initiatives and held municipal politicians accountable, attempts to establish a participatory process in Bolívar failed, despite the political will of the mayor. Local elites were easily able to manipulate discontent over the lack of traditional public works under Mayor Ramírez's leadership and to put a halt to the municipality's participatory initiatives.

There is a widespread assumption in the academic literature that as a result of their pre-Hispanic heritage, social relations in indigenous communities in Ecuador and the other Andean countries are more cooperative than in mestizo communities, and that those cooperative relationships provide the basis for more participatory and egalitarian forms of social organization, economic development, and local administration. However, traditions of community-level cooperation do not necessarily translate into the capacity to manage peasant organizations effectively, let alone to govern a municipality successfully. Moreover, the assumption of harmonious and cooperative social relations often masks important inequalities in the distribution of socioeconomic and gender power within indigenous communities. There is also increasing evidence that traditional communitarian social relations in indigenous communities are breaking down under pressure from the growing frequency and duration of migratory work trips made necessary by the crisis of rural development in Ecuador (Chapter 5).

The institutional maturity, mobilization capacity, and ability to promote economic survival (if not development) of indigenous and peasant organizations in Ecuador also vary widely. Large numbers of community-based organizations exist on paper only, while many others were created by external actors in response to opportunities for development assistance and do not represent either strong community-level bonds or a capacity for proposing and managing endogenous development strategies (Chapter 5). By the mid-1990s only a small minority of OSGs in Ecuador had developed the institutional and entrepreneurial capacity to implement local development projects (Martínez 1997, 120). Moreover, only a very small group of those organizations had developed political and economic strategies aimed at the municipal level. In most cases in which OSGs existed at all, their strategies were focused on the politically and economically less significant space of the parish. Indigenous and peasant organizations in Ecuador, including in Guamote and Cotacachi, also generally continue to be dominated by men and actively marginalize women's roles in local decision-making.

It is also important to raise the question of how strong local organizations were formed. The cases examined here suggest that external agents, such as NGOs, churches, and especially the state, as well as political struggle, have important roles to play. The formation of self-organized indigenous communities *(comunas)* and OSGs in the 1970s and 1980s was in many ways a response to legal and monetary incentives to organization created by the Ecuadorian state (Sylva 1991). Although those initiatives often functioned to subsume peasant organizations within the clientelist logic of the state (see Iturralde 1980; Striffler 2002), as the developmental capacities of the central state diminished in the 1980s, some of those organizations did manage to shake off their subordinate ties. The experiences of Guamote and Cotacachi also suggest that *political struggle*, legitimated and supported by outside actors, was a central factor in the formation and consolidation of strong local organizations. Struggles against the abuses of *hacendados* and the church, struggles to see agrarian-reform legislation implemented, and struggles to take control over local development processes played important roles in the creation and strengthening of indigenous organizations in both cantons.

External Technical and Financial Support

High levels of external technical and financial support, primarily from NGOs, were decisive for the development of participatory municipal governments in Ecuador. Both the operation and the local legitimation of participatory institutions depended on external support. NGO funding also helped to increase the relative autonomy of rural municipal governments from privileged town-based constituents and enabled the municipalities to invest in certain public works, especially in rural areas, that would have generated significant opposition had the funding come from traditional sources of municipal revenue. In both Guamote and Cotacachi, NGOs also played key roles in pressuring local indigenous leaders to make municipal institutions more inclusive of women. It thus bears noting that while external support must be coordinated and regulated by democratic institutions at the local level if it is to be effective, relationships of trust between local and external actors are also critical in order for outside agents to be able to promote progressive changes in local institutions.

The high levels of technical and financial support from NGOs in Guamote and Cotacachi are neither sustainable in the long run nor replicable on a broad scale. The vast majority of municipal governments had no support from any NGOs and the few existing NGO-municipal agreements were for very small infrastructure works and projects,[10] thus calling into question the viability, at least in the Ecuadorian context, of the development model based on NGO-municipal cooperation suggested by Reilly (1995). If municipal governance is to become more democratic on a broad scale and if municipal governments are to have the resources to promote economic and social development, significant increases in state spending and a reorientation of state spending priorities to encourage and reward participatory initiatives will be vital.[11]

Economic Marginality

The cases of participatory municipal institutions presented here represent experiences of local *political* development. However, neither Guamote, nor Cotacachi, nor any other municipalities in Ecuador that promoted citizen involvement in local decision-making had any significant influence on *economic* development. There is still a big gap between the creation of a few fledgling micro-development projects or increased attention by a municipal government to rural infrastructure, on the one hand, and, on the other hand, real processes of local economic development that might begin to curb outward migration by creating local employment opportunities and generating broad improvements in people's capacities and standards of living.

Indeed, whether significant local economic development is possible *at all* in any small rural cantons within the context of the macroeconomic policies that prevail in Ecuador in the early twenty-first century is highly questionable (Chapters 2–5). Without state policies and action aimed at both the local and national levels to support small-scale rural agricultural as well as nonagricultural producers, it is unlikely that even those cantons with strong indigenous or peasant organizations, democratic governance, high levels of NGO support, and established community-based commercial enterprises will experience significant economic development. Even in the few cantons with substantial external assistance, NGOs recognized that they knew little about how to make local development actually happen. Moreover, in Guamote, Cotacachi, and other cantons with indigenous and peasant mayors, municipal governments found that they had neither the power nor the technical knowledge to regulate local enterprises to make them less exploitative of local producers and consumers.

It was no coincidence that participatory processes emerged and indigenous and peasant mayors were elected in some of the poorest cantons in highland Ecuador. The ability to capture municipal power was conditional on either the absence of powerful economic actors (Guamote) or the confidence on the part of economic elites that a new municipal administration could not threaten their interests (Cotacachi). Unfortunately, the socioeconomic contexts within which municipal governments in the two cantons became participatory and attentive to the needs of their indigenous and peasant populations also presented significant obstacles to efforts to promote processes of equitable economic development (poor land resources and a lack of capital in Guamote, and powerful economic elites in Cotacachi).

Elections in May 2000 in Ecuador produced some significant victories for indigenous and peasant politicians at both the municipal and provincial levels. However, these victories remained confined primarily to economically peripheral areas. Indigenous and peasant representatives were also elected as mayors in some urban centers with more dynamic economies, but the crucial challenge for these newly elected politicians will be their capacity to reorganize political institutions and to regulate local economic development, that is, to reshape local power relations in ways that benefit rather than exclude and exploit the majority of their constituents.

CONCLUSION

Comparison of efforts to develop participatory municipal institutions in Guamote, Cotacachi, and Bolívar suggests a number of preconditions necessary for the emergence of participatory and developmental local governments. In Guamote, a relatively equitable distribution of agricultural land, strong OSCs, extensive external financial and technical support, and economic marginality emerged as key factors behind the relative success of participatory processes. The experience of Cotacachi showed that an equitable distribution of agricultural land and other assets was not necessary for participatory municipal institutions to operate. However, municipal governments operating in such contexts may have little capacity to regulate or tax powerful local elites and may only be able to operate as small participatory islands in much greater oceans of highly unequal economic and social power relations. The capacity of rural municipalities to promote and regulate processes of local development remains dependent on a favorable balance of local power relations, which in rural settings is based primarily on equitable patterns of landownership and strong indigenous-peasant organization.

The conditions needed for rural municipal governments to become more participatory and to exercise greater control over local development processes are not widely present in Ecuador. Not only is the number of strong indigenous-peasant organizations with political strategies aimed at attaining municipal power quite limited, but NGO resources to support participatory efforts even in those cantons with strong civil societies are insufficient. Moreover, indigenous-peasant organizations in Ecuador remain highly patriarchal institutions that often marginalize women from local decision-making. Landownership in most rural highland cantons also continues to be dominated by large agricultural enterprises that will not be regulated or integrated into the local development efforts of participatory municipalities without significant conflict. Thus, the number of rural municipalities where participatory processes can be expected to develop and flourish remains seriously restricted by the structure of landownership and the prevailing macro-policy framework as well as by the political capacity of indigenous and peasant organizations. From a public policy perspective, the minimum conditions needed for rural municipal governments in Ecuador to become more democratic and to have the power to regulate and promote processes of economic development are a more equitable distribution of agricultural land, macroeconomic policies favorable to peasant agriculture, and state support and incentives for municipal governments to become more inclusive, in socioeconomic, ethnic, *and* gender terms. In the absence of such a policy framework, the vast majority of rural municipalities in Ecuador will likely remain weakly democratic and largely ineffective as agents of rural development.

Notes

[1] The indigenous population of Ecuador is most reliably estimated at 20–25 percent of the national total (12.8 million). Indigenous peoples represent a majority or significant minority in 35 of Ecuador's 215 municipalities (Ramón 1998, 26).

[2] The municipality is the administrative level of government that corresponds with the geographic area of the canton *(cantón)*. Cantons are divided into parishes *(parroquias)*, which are administered by parish councils *(Juntas Paroquiales)*, elected since May 2000. Rural cantons generally include a town center *(cabecera)* and surrounding rural communities, which might number anywhere between 30 and 120 per canton.

[3] Field research was based on in-depth interviews with elected municipal officials and bureaucrats, leaders of local civil society organizations and businesses, and NGO staff in each of the three municipalities.

[4] On the impact of agrarian reform in Ecuador, see Barsky 1984a; Handelman 1981; Haney and Haney 1989; Redclift 1978; Striffler 2002; Zevallos 1989.

[5] Land sales to peasants often occurred only under significant organized peasant pressure on large landowners—including land seizures and other extra-legal tactics—and with financial assistance from NGOs.

[6] The extent to which the 121 *cabildo* presidents who made up the parliament actually represented their respective communities remained to be investigated. Guamote's development plan identified authoritarian leadership as a problem in many communities (Municipalidad de Guamote 1999, 28). The fact that in 2002 there were still only three female members of the parliament also indicated that women's interests were not well represented.

[7] By 1999 the municipality dedicated 47 percent of its investment budget to rural areas. By 2002 that proportion had increased to 60 percent.

[8] Direct funding from NGOs and aid agencies to the municipality of Cotacachi increased from zero prior to 1996 to an average of US$525,000 per year between 1996 and 1998, equivalent to 29.2 percent of the annual municipal budgets during those years. In 1999, the year of the worst financial crisis in Ecuador's history, NGO support surged to US$665,000, equivalent to 42 percent of the municipal budget, and enabled the municipality to continue operating in an economic context that paralyzed many other small municipalities.

[9] As in Guamote, those land sales often took place only in the context of extra-legal pressures from those seeking to purchase land.

[10] Survey conducted jointly by the author and AME (1999) on NGO-municipal cooperation. Fifty-one of 214 municipalities responded to the 1999 survey on NGO-municipal cooperation. Thirty-five of those municipalities had no support from any NGOs. Of the remaining sixteen municipalities, NGO support was concentrated in seven municipalities, including Guamote, Cotacachi, and Bolívar.

[11] Although Ecuador's Congress passed formal legislation in 1996 to increase transfers to municipal governments to 10.5 percent of central government budgets, in practice, those transfers were often much smaller than legally mandated and often arrived months and even years later than promised, seriously undermining the daily operations of many municipal governments.

Chapter 10

Externally Induced Rural Diversification

The Communitarian Experience of Salinas

LIISA L. NORTH

Grassroots-based economic enterprises supported by NGOs in rural areas face serious obstacles that can undermine their commercial viability, redistributive impact, and capacity to improve living standards. In addition to the highly unequal distribution of land and assets that still prevails in Ecuador and elsewhere in Latin America, small rural producers generally lack extension services and access to credit while they face highly volatile and monopolistic or oligopolistic markets. Moreover, experienced NGO personnel are among the first to recognize their own limited entrepreneurial capacities. NGO know-how has developed in the provision of services, with little attention dedicated to generating expertise in marketing and the institutional design of productive activities. If all this were not enough, the regulatory framework in Ecuador, as in other countries of Latin America, is highly skewed in favor of large

This chapter draws extensively on interviews conducted from January 1998 to October 2001 in Salinas, at FEPP-Guaranda, and with researchers and consultants at institutions in Quito. Altogether, forty-nine persons (or small groups) were interviewed concerning the history of the parish and its community enterprises. The interviewees included enterprise and community organization leaders and managers, the staff of the Salesian Mission, and foreign volunteers and consultants. Analyses of 1997 research in Quito that preceded the field work have been published in Spanish in North 1999 and 2001 and in English in North and Cameron 2000.

commercial producers. In an interview in April 1998 in Quito, a senior official of the UNFAO with many years of experience in Ecuador said, "Agrarian legislation [in the country] was and is designed to prevent small producers from organizing themselves for commercial purposes."

Yet, despite many obstacles and setbacks, some notable successes in rural diversification and development have taken place. Prominent among the endogenously generated success stories in Ecuador is the growth of family-owned textile enterprises in the canton of Pelileo and in some other highland regions (Chapter 11). Among the externally induced and NGO-supported local development programs, the "communitarian" agro-industrial diversification of the parish of Salinas, in the canton of Guaranda in the province of Bolívar, stands out. It was initiated by a land-redistribution program carried out by the Catholic church in the 1960s and then, from the early 1970s up to the present, it was assisted by the Salesian Mission and the country's largest rural development NGO, the church-linked FEPP (Chapter 8). Together, the Salesian Mission, the FEPP, and other church-linked institutions provided assistance for the organization of community-owned enterprises that socialized profits and for the foundation of participatory institutions that, little by little, democratized political power relations. They also helped channel sub-stantial amounts of foreign assistance—including IDB funding in the 1990s—and an impressive number of national and foreign volunteers to the parish. In effect, these institutions led a complex and multifaceted social and economic development program of micro-regional dimen-sions. It spanned an entire parish with a highly dispersed population of about five thousand in 1974 and eighty-five hundred in 1996.

The opening section of this chapter provides a brief summary of the conditions that prevailed in Salinas prior to the arrival of the external development agents and outlines the foundations for change that were laid there by a Catholic church–led land-redistribution program. It also briefly notes contrasts between Salinas and the endogenous development process in Pelileo (Chapter 11) in order to identify the social and eco-nomic structures and relationships that may be conducive to or act to prevent economic diversification and social progress. The next section examines the economic activities that were sponsored by the Salesian Mission and the FEPP. The impact of those programs on employment creation, poverty alleviation, and social change (including gender rela-tions) are discussed in the following section, and questions related to institutional design and sustainability in the fourth section. The con-cluding section addresses the impact of neoliberal policies and the role of the state and NGOs in Salinas from a comparative perspective. Rather than an exhaustive analysis, the chapter is intended to highlight princi-pal achievements, problems, and challenges in this very complex and dynamic history of transformation.

ORIGINAL CONDITIONS
AND THE FOUNDATIONS FOR CHANGE

The economic, social, and political conditions under which community-based enterprises were established in Salinas in the 1970s were not conducive to endogenous transformation. In addition to their extreme poverty, the mestizo and indigenous residents of the parish had lived under the oppressive power of the Cordobez family since the second half of the nineteenth century. Great *latifundistas*, the Cordobeces, in addition to owning *haciendas* in Salinas and other parts of the highlands, had rented lands owned by the Catholic church in the parish, thus controlling from one-half to two-thirds of its territory. In addition, the family possessed exclusive rights to the exploitation of the natural salt deposits from which the parish derives its name.

Subject to the seigniorial domination of the Cordobeces, most of the parish population was trapped in the types of servile social relations that, wherever they have been present, suppress the capacity for individual initiative and risk-taking, reduce self-esteem, and limit the possibilities of collective action. Servility, moreover, tends to take on particularly oppressive and pernicious forms in situations where ethnic cleavages and racial discrimination prevail, as in highland Ecuador.[1] It should be noted that about half of the parish hamlets were considered indigenous at the end of the 1990s by a FEPP-employed social promoter resident in the *cabecera* (head town)[2].

The parish of Salinas had also been isolated from national commercial networks and lacked even basic transportation and communication infrastructure in the early 1970s. It is located in a geographic space that, in the opinion of local residents, is "violent" and suffers from an "infernal" climate. Its *cabecera* sits 3,550 meters above sea level, with some of the smaller hamlets located at even higher altitudes where agriculture is a precarious activity. Meanwhile, the parish's semitropical lowland regions drop to altitudes of only 600 meters. At the turn of the twenty-first century, during the peak of the rainy season, communities were frequently cut off from each other and from paved highways by massive landslides that blocked transport for days and even weeks at a time. All this, along with the fact that the Cordobeces had pretty much controlled social relations and marketable surpluses, meant that the local population lacked both organizational and market experience in addition to entrepreneurial know-how.

The foundations for change in Salinas were laid when the diocese of Guaranda decided to conduct an agrarian reform on its estates in the parish. Between 1959 and 1964 the Catholic church provided low-interest credit to approximately seven hundred peasant families, who bought the church's fifteen thousand hectares (more than one-third of the parish's forty thousand hectare area) in lots of fifteen to thirty hectares in the highlands and up to fifty hectares in the lowlands (interview, José Tonello, director, FEPP, April 1998; León and Tobar 1984, 49). During the following decades the Cordobez family also sold parts of its properties to individual peasants or to community groups that benefited from the credit made available and activities sponsored by the Salesian Mission, which arrived in the parish in 1971, and the FEPP, which was established in Quito in 1972. Meanwhile, the indigenous commune of Matiaví Salinas, whose legal status as a corporate political and landowning institution dated back to the Spanish colonial period, remained in control of about one-third to one-half of the parish territory (in theory collectively but in practice increasingly under private "titles" granted to commune members).

In sum, a parish where the Catholic church had rented its estates to a powerful landlord family that controlled labor and markets was transformed during the 1960s and 1970s into an area of small and medium property owners, with support services provided by progressive sectors of the church. However, the transformation of the land-tenure structure was neither peaceful nor rapid. In addition to the resistance of the Cordobez family, the parish was crisscrossed by complex inter-ethnic and intra-ethnic conflicts. Indeed, between 1959 and 1964 confrontations between commune members and peasants who purchased church lands became so violent that one parish area was baptized the "plain of war" *(pampa de la guerra)* (Polo 1993, 37; interview, FEPP director José Tonello, April 1998). In the early 1980s the commune's lands were still subject to "multiple law suits and conflicts" (León and Tobar 1984, 44). Even twenty years later some land conflicts between communities remained unresolved, creating a far-from-ideal situation for the organization of community-based enterprises.

The end result of the church-sponsored land reform, nevertheless, was that by the early 1980s medium-sized properties dominated the Salinas countryside, although some land remained under communal ownership and a few large estates were still present (León and Tobar 1984, 48). The latest phase of land transfers took place during 1991–95 as part of a FEPP-administered debt-for-land swap program (Chapters 6 and 8). The potential for economic diversification and social progress was thus laid with the redistribution of land. Nevertheless, prior to the arrival of the Salesian Mission in 1971, the efforts of the new landowning families in the town of Salinas (the name of the *cabecera* as well as of the parish) to organize community-based economic activities had failed. This was the case with an attempt in 1962 to market salt from local natural deposits and with an effort in 1967 to organize a savings-and-credit cooperative (SCC). It is not clear to what extent these failures stemmed from rivalry among resident families, opposition of the Cordobeces, lack of knowledge and resources, or conflicts deriving from the extreme poverty and other conditions briefly described above.

Whatever the case may be, the possibilities of endogenously generated collective action and socioeconomic progress in the parish appeared unlikely. Land reform may have been a necessary condition for such advance. However, it was not a sufficient condition for the five thousand or so historically oppressed people, mostly isolated from one another and from the rest of the country in the parish's dispersed hamlets. Without external intervention and support, traditional family loyalties and feuds (which remain present in Salinas), as well as other obstacles, would probably have prevailed over shared community interests. Clearly, church-linked external agents of recognized moral authority could provide assistance in conflict resolution, ensure compliance with mutually agreed upon norms, and reduce the risks and fear involved in embarking on new activities.

The contrast was striking between the conditions that prevailed in Salinas and those that characterized Pelileo, where family textile enterprises started to grow in the mid-1970s without external assistance (Chapter 11). In that latter canton no large landlord class or servile social relations were present. Rather, a class of mestizo *minifundistas* owned most of the fertile land and had been involved in market production since the late nineteenth century. Located close to Ambato, a principal trade center since colonial times, the free peasantry of the area had participated in a lively system of local *ferias* (markets) and had developed commercial know-how and connections over a long period of time. In addition, both primary and secondary schooling had been available to Pelileo residents since the beginning of the twentieth century. And finally, Pelileo was served first by a railroad and later by good roads and electricity in contrast to the nearly nonexistent infrastructure of Salinas. In short, prior to the 1970s the conditions of popular access to assets, markets, and know-how as well as infrastructure were just about polar opposites in Salinas and Pelileo.

SOCIAL CHANGE, ECONOMIC DIVERSIFICATION, AND INSTITUTIONAL DEVELOPMENT

With the arrival of the Salesian Mission in 1971, under the charismatic leadership of Venetian Father Antonio Polo, and with support from Italian volunteers of the Organización Matto Grosso, an SCC was established in the *cabecera* in 1972. Then, step by step, SCCs were set up in both the highland and lowland hamlets where about 90 percent of the parish population lived. Low-interest loans from the SCCs played an important role in deconcentrating landownership and in the purchase of sheep and cattle by the new peasant proprietors. Moreover, since the

SCCs did not pay interest on savings accounts, their profits could be used for investment in community works and productive enterprises that generated employment. Not paying interest amounted to a tax on the population, and it was made possible by the region's isolation from national markets and formal banking institutions as well as the low inflation rates of the times.

At the same time that SCCs were established in most parish hamlets in the 1970s and 1980s, the Salesian Mission and the FEPP promoted education, encouraged economic diversification, attempted to ensure food security, and worked to provide a basic road infrastructure, effectively taking on the role of a developmental state.

The establishment of a primary school in the *cabecera* was followed by the extension of primary education to most hamlets. While these schools were later incorporated into the country's public education system, it was the Salesian Mission that provided the original impetus and the resources. Similarly, the *cabecera* high school was set up by the Mission and functioned as a night school from 1974 to 1984, when its basic financing was assumed by the Ministry of Education. With an agro-pastoral specialization, by the mid-1990s the high school was attracting students—mostly boys but also a few girls—from other parts of the country, some with small scholarships from the Salesian Mission and the possibility of residence at a Mission-run "home."[3] Interestingly enough, however, by then some *cabecera* residents were sending their children to study in more "prestigious" high schools in nearby cities, and it was the hamlet residents' children who attended the Salinas high school.

To help ensure the viability of new productive activities, the Salesian Mission and the FEPP also organized a great variety of training courses for adults, ranging from basic accounting in the 1970s to training in veterinary medicine in the 1990s. They also provided scholarships for specialized short courses and university studies in Ecuador and abroad.

In the realm of economic diversification, the Mission and the FEPP supported the genetic improvement of sheep and cattle and initiated the organization of various collectively owned and, in many cases, mutually interlinked small enterprises that provided employment to both men and women. In the *cabecera*, by the first years of the twenty-first century, these enterprises included a cheese plant and a sausage plant, a mushroom drying enterprise, a wool spinning mill, a hostel, a tourism office, a weaving cooperative, a carpentry shop, a communal store, a bakery, a ceramics workshop, and a marmalade "factory." (With the exception of the spinning mill, which employed forty to fifty workers in good times, these were small enterprises; most factories (*fábricas*) in Salinas, in fact, were small workshops with three or four workers.) In the hamlets the Mission and the FEPP sponsored economic activities that included cheese plants, bakeries, small mushroom-drying installations, and women's groups involved in raising chickens and pigs.

In order to generate investment capital for further economic diversification and local employment generation, the Salesian Mission and the FEPP promoted internal economic linkages between the highland and lowland regions of the parish. To sustain these linkages, the greater part of the local road infrastructure was constructed by parish organizations with guidance and support from the Salesian Mission and the FEPP, both of which helped channel foreign donor resources and some Ecuadorian government funding for these purposes.

Among the small enterprises it was the cheese plants, first established with Swiss government assistance in 1978, that made the parish famous all over Ecuador. The high quality aged cheeses (Parmesan, Dambo, Gruyere, and so on) were sold directly through the Salinas enterprises' own outlet and, by the mid-1990s, also through one of the country's principal supermarket chains. From the vantage point of work and incomes, the plants provided a secure market for local milk producers who had acquired land and cattle in the previous years. By 1997 plants functioned in twenty of the parish's then twenty-three hamlets; in 1998–99 the *cabecera* plant was purchasing from three to eighty liters of milk per day from each of more than two hundred producers. All together, these producers owned about five hundred mostly Brown Swiss cows, purchased with credit made available by the SCCs, the FEPP, and the Salesian Mission. Almost every household in the *cabecera* and its immediate environs owned at least a couple of cows and sold milk to the cheese plant, which employed eight people in 1998. It was the *cabecera* plant, given its location in the cool highlands and its better access to the national road network, that also provided aging facilities for cheese from the hamlets (which made up about 60 percent of total production).

As a result of the organizational efforts of the 1970s and the establishment of common norms and standards by the Salesian Mission, the FEPP, and other church-linked agencies such as Guaranda's Promoción Humana, the cheese plants that were set up in the parish in the 1980s functioned better than those organized in other parts of the country under the aegis of the same Swiss assistance program (Freire, Purschert, and Rhon 1991, 5).

Due to environmental problems created by the increasing size of cattle herds, reforestation programs were undertaken in 1981, particularly in the highland areas, and they were greatly expanded in the following years. Quite unexpectedly, edible mushrooms began to grow in the pine plantations, providing the resource base for yet another local industry—dried mushrooms. They were collected for the most part by women and children from the poorest highland hamlets and, as of 1998, dried in small family-owned or community-owned installations in the hamlets in addition to the larger drying plant that was set up in the *cabecera* in 1991 (air drying for commercial purposes had begun in 1985). Although some mushrooms were sold in the country's urban markets, by the late 1990s most were exported to Europe to purchasers found by Father Polo and the FEPP.[4] In addition to the mushrooms, little by little the reforested areas began to provide income from lumber harvests and firewood from pruning, a resource much appreciated by women near the reforestation areas.

During the initial years of diversification, enterprises were owned and managed by the SCCs; when the cheese plants were set up, the principle of "communitarian redistribution" of profits, originally established by the SCCs, was extended to them (Ramón and Ortiz 1995, 15).[5] Later, the Fundación Juvenil (Youth Foundation) and the FUNORSAL—established in 1977 and 1982 respectively—also became enterprise proprietors. The FUNORSAL, in addition, functioned as the general service provider and coordinating body for parish enterprises and groups. It must be emphasized, however, that all enterprises were started under the umbrella of the Salesian Mission. Most were designed to be transferred to the above-named organizations after achieving profitability, but others—such as a chocolate "factory"—were designed to remain in Mission hands as a source of income for its programs.

Beyond communitarian redistribution, another guiding principle in enterprise organization involved the priorization of social efficiency over economic efficiency (an option discussed by Lefeber in Chapter 2). For example, external evaluators who analyzed the cheese plants from a narrow economic-efficiency perspective recommended centralization of production in the *cabecera* (Bloemkolk and Salinas 1994, 26). However, the Salesian Mission and the FEPP insisted on a large number of small plants in as many hamlets as possible in order to ensure incomes for milk producers all over the parish, provide training and employment to dairy workers in each hamlet, and sustain a sense of community ownership (interviews with FEPP director, José Tonello, April 1998, and Father Antonio Polo, March 1998).

One more point regarding general principles must be highlighted. In addition to promoting income-earning commercial activities, the Salesian Mission and the FEPP worked to improve food security. And they did so successfully, at least in the *cabecera*, where all enterprise workers appeared to have garden plots and raise small animals for their own consumption, in addition to selling milk to the cheese plant. This *combination* of commercial and subsistence activities turned out to be essential for maintaining nutritional standards during the economic crises of 1999–2001, when some lost their jobs and others had to go on reduced time (as discussed below).

Women, however, were not given priority in enterprise creation. Nor, until recently, were they to be found among the leaders and managers of enterprises or community organizations. Indeed, a 1984 evaluation of the cheese plant found obvious discrimination against women who earned "less than men, even . . . [for] the same work" and were excluded from "decision-making" and "the management of money," while men reserved for themselves "those activities that carry power and confer a certain social status" (Meier and Rhon Dávila 1984, 32). Nevertheless, women's needs were not entirely ignored. For example, the artisan center TEXAL, which was set up to produce hand-knitted sweaters and accessories for the national market and for export, provided part-time employment and incomes, albeit small and quite unstable, to a substantial but declining number of women: sixty-five in 1976–1977, forty-five in 1998–1999, and twenty-five in 2001. At the time of its establishment in 1974, according to its manager, Gladys Salazar, TEXAL provided the "only [paid] work available" to women in the *cabecera* and liberated them from household "slavery" because their new earning capacity encouraged "greater respect at home." However, TEXAL's knitters identified Father Polo rather than the SCC, which owned the enterprise, as their chief source of support—specifically, as the person who taught them basic accounting skills and sought out export markets for their products.

By the late 1990s many more opportunities were available to women in the *cabecera*. In addition to the possibility of attending primary and secondary school, at least some had been able to take advantage of new educational opportunities created by FEPP-administered scholarships for specialized technical training and university studies. Thus, some women were beginning to occupy managerial positions in the community enterprises and umbrella organizations. However, it was only in 1998 that FUNORSAL established the principle of equal pay for equal work. By then some poor women were also receiving credit from the Salesian Mission for setting up small private enterprises. As for the hamlets, women's groups—some of which owned and managed small-scale income-generating activities—functioned in thirteen at the end of the 1990s.

In sum, the Salinas experience began with land reform and proceeded to the establishment of SCCs, the foundation and expansion of an educational system, and the construction of basic infrastructure. It involved the promotion of small-scale and decentralized rural agro-pastoral and industrial diversification; experimentation with new lines of production by the Salesian Mission,[6] the socialization of the profits of much of the new economic activity through parish organizations; a step-by-step transformation of social and gender relations that eventually created greater opportunities for women; the continuing presence of authoritative external agents in addition to the ever present charismatic leadership of Padre Antonio; and significant amounts of assistance from a great variety of foreign NGOs, governments, and international institutions.[7] The Salesian Mission and the FEPP provided some programmatic coherence to all the resource flows.

SOCIAL PROGRESS, EQUITY, AND SOCIAL RELATIONS

To what extent were the objectives of social progress and equity achieved? In 1995

> the 98 productive projects [and administrative activities] in the parish *cabecera* and the hamlets . . . generated 519 new jobs and the majority of the population [almost five thousand in 1990 and about eighty-five hundred in 1996] [was] indirectly incorporated into those activities through the supply of primary materials like milk, wool, [and] mushrooms. (Ramón and Ortiz 1995, 8)

Half of these jobs were created in the outlying hamlets (Ramón, Ortiz, and Naranjo 1995, 18). Other observers agreed that a remarkable transformation had taken place in the *cabecera*, manifested visibly in the cement-block and brick houses with sanitary facilities that had replaced the *chozas* (earthen shacks) that provided just about the only kind of housing at the beginning of the 1970s. However, there is much less consensus about the extent of poverty alleviation in the hamlets and the degree of distributional equity in the parish as a whole.

To begin with the question of poverty, by the late 1980s and early 1990s the new opportunities created in the *cabecera* had induced the return of many former emigrés, a unique phenomenon in rural Ecuador (Bebbington et al. 1992, 55). Nevertheless, in 1990—some fifteen years after the programs of the Salesian Mission and the FEPP were launched—on a ranking from 1 (lowest) to 10 (highest) based on that year's (not necessarily reliable) census data, the parish still registered 6 on indigence and 8 on poverty (Larrea et al. 1996, 46). Such extreme levels of poverty may have been relieved by the time that Ramón and Ortiz conducted their study, a plausible proposition in light of the large number of income-generating activities that became consolidated as enterprises in the *cabecera* and were launched in the hamlets in the early 1990s by the Salesian Mission, the FEPP, the FUNORSAL, and others.

Evidence of increased opportunities that had appeared even in the poorest outlying areas of the parish by the mid-1990s comes, for example, from women in the highland hamlets who, in group sessions organized as part of a study on gender and development, singled out their appreciation of income from mushroom collection and timber harvests and the possibility of selling wool to the spinning mill or *Hilandería*. Meanwhile, brick houses were beginning to replace *chozas* in some hamlets and even in the countryside as residents' incomes improved and the FEPP, together with the government's Ministry of Housing, provided credit and technical advice for house construction.

Nevertheless, the experiences of Dr. Gina Echenique, the Ministry of Health–employed physician who provided services to the *cabecera* and the highland hamlets, are cause for concern. Her records indicated that while malnutrition had been just about eliminated in the *cabecera*, it remained at low to moderate levels (as measured by weight/age) among 30 percent of highland hamlet children between one to four years of age during most of the year and increased to 50 percent during August and September. During those months the school lunch supplement (an oatmeal drink with a cracker) was not available to school-age children, and hence families had to distribute whatever food they had among a greater number of members.

Despite this evidence of continued extreme poverty, the physician's data have to be weighed by reference to the situation prior to the arrival of the Salesian Mission and the generally high levels of malnutrition that characterize Ecuador's rural highlands. Indeed, infant mortality in the *cabecera* was reduced by 76 percent between 1970 and 1990 (Bebbington et al. 1992, 54), and according to the World Bank, the average level of malnutrition in the rural highlands within the one-to-four age group, at 48.5 percent, is higher than it is in Salinas (World Bank 1995, 22). Nevertheless, in light of the highly visible economic and social development programs in the parish and the elimination of malnutrition in the *cabecera*, the physician's data imply that the benefits of those programs had not been as widely shared as the most enthusiastic observers suggest. (The earlier-mentioned differences in the amount of milk sold to the cheese plant by local producers, ranging from three to eighty liters, were certainly indicative of significant social differences in the *cabecera*, as was the *cabecera* residents' recently acquired habit of sending their children to high schools in the neighboring cities.)

Why might some have benefited much more than others from the programs launched in the parish? The degree to which people in different parts of the parish could improve their living conditions was, of course, influenced by the geographic and infrastructural conditions described earlier. However, among the combination of social factors that may account for persistent poverty and increased inequality, first of all, lies the decision of the Salesian Mission to work with the local elite, that is, with the members of the most important mestizo families of the pre-Salesian barter economy who were "recognized as the center of local power" in the *cabecera* (Bebbington et al. 1992, 40). Consisting of six extended families, they subsequently dominated the leadership of community organizations and enterprises; one family in particular exercised virtual veto power over the decisions of those organizations during the 1990s. As the leaders of the Grameen Bank of Bangladesh and other institutions that have successfully raised the living standards of the very poor have discovered, development programs that rely on local elites tend to concentrate power and resources in their hands (Bornstein 1996, 115).

This raises questions about the strategies of the principal external development promotion agents. Why did the Salesian Mission choose to work with the parish elite? First of all, it has to be noted that the church's developmental work was and is based on a philosophy of class and ethnic conciliation (interview, Father Antonio Polo, March 12, 1998). Second, some observers argue that it made sense to work with the families with greater commercial (albeit mostly barter economy) experience, especially in light of the low levels of social differentiation at the time that the Mission arrived. For example, even the members of the group with which Father Polo founded the *cabecera* SCC had no more than three years of primary education. The same observers also emphasize that, despite the land conflicts discussed earlier, an important degree of social solidarity did exist in the parish, and that it prevailed even in the relations between the indigenous and mestizos, given their common experience of oppression under the *hacienda* regime (Bebbington et al. 1992, 36, 39; Ramón and Ortiz 1995) or, in the words of Father Polo, their lives as "serfs of the Codobeces."

Although the arguments concerning solidarity may be somewhat overdrawn, it is true that the leading families of the *cabecera* were poor. They lived in the same kinds of *chozas* as the indigenous people of the highland hamlets. They were also apparently willing to work with the Salesian Mission in projects that potentially could incorporate the entire community. Moreover, in light of the violent conflicts over land that had erupted between the church and the indigenous commune of Matiaví Salinas in the 1960s, the Salesian Mission may have had few alternative partners available.

It also bears noting that development initiatives focused on the indigenous poor in situations of sharp ethnic divisions and acute poverty can carry their own dangers. For example, in evaluating the destructive impacts of Guatemala's ethnically charged civil war on its agricultural development projects in that country in the early 1980s, the NGO World Neighbors concluded that it "should probably have devoted more effort to building bridges and mechanisms for conflict resolution between the majority (Indians) and the [mestizo] minority" in order to prevent or at least attenuate the violence that erupted at the site of what had been a remarkably successful project with regard to improving indigenous living standards (Krishna and Bunch 1997, 151).

Although the precise extent to which wealth and power were concentrated in Salinas remains unclear,[8] the visible inequalities in distributional impacts were also certainly influenced by a history of discrimination against women (see below); initially very low levels of education among the parish population, which inhibited their effective participation in decision-making; and the historical legacy of highly personalistic, paternalistic, authoritarian, and family-loyalty-based social relations that encouraged favoritism and inhibited open debate and grassroots involvement. As late as 2000–2001, not only FEPP staff and foreign consultants but also some members of the younger generation of FUNORSAL leaders repeatedly referred to lack of self-esteem and self-confidence (especially among women), as well as paternalistic attitudes on the part of leaders and led alike. All this provided the social context within which some local leaders could act as if they owned the cooperative enterprises and umbrella organizations, skewing the distribution of benefits to favor some families and groups.

At least some of the historically grounded and inequity-generating attitudes and social relationships mentioned above were changing by the turn of the century. Most remarkably, in February 2001 the hamlets revolted, so to speak, against the *cabecera* during the course of the country's nationwide *levantamiento indígena* (indigenous uprising)—the sixth since 1990. The residents of the nearby hamlets occupied the Salinas plaza and demanded FUNORSAL support for the uprising as well as a democratization of decision-making processes in parish institutions. Both the fact that the revolt took place—reflecting a new self-assertiveness on the part of the poorer sectors—and the fact that the occupation ended in dialogue and new agreements augured well for the evolution of the parish economy and society. It should be noted that if the Salesian Mission and the FEPP had followed the earlier mentioned external evaluator's narrowly economic efficiency-based recommendation that cheese production be centralized in the *cabecera*, inequalities would have become even greater, with the consequent possibility of greater and more acrimonious social and ethnic conflict.

SUSTAINABILITY AND INSTITUTIONAL DESIGN

Whatever the problems deriving from the historical evolution of social relations in the parish may have been, the Salesian Mission and the FEPP appear to have paid insufficient attention to the design of institutions that could ensure participation and control mechanisms that could prevent community organization and enterprise managers from utilizing them as a base for advancing their private or family interests. Of course, all the issues raised above are interrelated, and even the best designed of institutions might have been captured by the leading families. But the question remains: In addition to insisting on as much enterprise decentralization as possible in order to promote income-generating activities across the parish, could the Salesian Mission and the FEPP have attempted to design institutions in a way that promoted greater distributional equality? Might this have been done by, for example, finding mechanisms to ensure more extensive participation in decision-making and in monitoring enterprise managers and social organization leaders? Might greater social progress have been achieved, especially with regard to children's nutrition and health and sanitary conditions, by seeking greater involvement on the part of women?[9]

Although no definitive answers can be provided, it repeatedly has been found, for example, that credit and income controlled by women have a greater impact on the improvement of family living conditions than credit and income managed by men (see, for example, Camacho and Prieto 1997, 47). Moreover, various donor-agency evaluations of the parish's enterprises have expressed concern about lack of worker participation in decision-making and management. For example, a 1994 evaluation proposed that steps be taken to organize women mushroom collectors (many of them among the poorest in the parish) to address health problems arising from picking mushrooms in the frigid and humid highland conditions (Bloemkolk and Salinas 1994, 33). Still, in 1999, when asked about the possibilities of extending health and other services to these women and their children, a leading member of the Grupo Juvenil, the community organization that owns the drying plant in the *cabecera*, simply responded that the group was thinking of organizing a yearly *fiesta* for the collectors. Although his response may have represented an extreme case of paternalism, it was not out of line with the attitudes of other community-enterprise and organization heads and staff, especially (but not only) members of the older generation. Such individuals, in tune with the authoritarian and paternalistic social relations of the *hacienda* system, tended to think in terms of providing gifts and organizing celebrations instead of establishing secure channels for participation that might lead not only to a different social distribution of enterprise profits and external funding but also to better enterprise performance.

In fact, variations in the profitability and efficiency of enterprises were related to the quality of social relations within them (Merino Salom 1998). The smaller of them, such as the cheese and sausage plants which had a simple division of labor and had benefited from sustained technical assistance, were profitable and for the most part well run by the mid-1990s. At the opposite end of the spectrum, the *Hilandería* (which was established in 1987 and employed up to forty or fifty workers during good times), had a very checkered history. It had closed and been reorganized under external managerial assistance on two occasions, and it was again in a difficult process of transition toward local management in 1999–2001, thirteen years after its foundation.

In the opinion of the Quebecois cooperant who had been called upon to reorganize the *Hilandería* on two occasions, its fundamental problems did not derive from a lack of technical capacity, which, in his experience, "can be easily transmitted"; rather, they derived from the social relations within the factory and from its relations with the community organization that owned it, the FUNORSAL. In his opinion these relations included authoritarian styles of administration (a tendency to "crush the other"); the absence of negotiated and transparent rules within the factory and between it and the FUNORSAL (for example, with regard to the division and uses of profits for distribution vs. investment); lack of confidence in the administrative team on the part of the workers who tended to consider only outsiders "knowledgeable"; and lack of commercial experience, particularly with regard to the need to engage in research and innovation to respond to changing market conditions and demand. As the largest of the parish enterprises, the *Hilandería* had special problems deriving from its complex division of labor, hierarchies based on specializations, relatively large salary differences, and so forth; nevertheless, its problems were shared, to varying degrees, by the other, smaller community-owned enterprises.

In comparison with the cooperant's analysis, external evaluations of the *Hilandería*, conducted in the midst of its second major crisis in the mid-1990s were much harsher in their critiques of its administrative, technical, commercial, and financial management (Bloemkolk and Salinas 1994; Naranjo Bonilla 1995). Naranjo Bonilla, in particular, stressed the alienation of the workers who openly "manifested their discontent, argued that they do not participate in decision-making, are not listened to nor given consideration." Economic efficiency, she also argued, had been sacrificed to the creation of employment and the generation of incomes, especially for a certain group of families. These problems and others persisted in 2001, and they manifested themselves in alienation from a sense of ownership among its workers—an attitude of "what does it matter to me?" in the words of the *Hilandería* administrator.[10]

The divisive issues in the *cabecera*, mutatis mutandis, found their parallels in some hamlets, with profound consequences for the sustainability of a FUNORSAL-administered credit program that was capitalized by the IDB from 1992 to 1996. By October 2001 its capital had been reduced to one-fifth of the original US$250,000. The reasons for decapitalization were many, and they varied from one hamlet to another. At least seven of the thirty-four groups of borrowers in the hamlets suffered from serious internal conflicts and/or corruption among their leaders. One community simply refused to pay, arguing that 2000 was a Jubilee year and that the FUNORSAL should follow the precedent of state banks that had forgiven debts in the past. Other communities were willing to pay the principal but rejected interest payments.

Of course, the generalized economic crisis of the country during the second half of the 1990s did not create propitious conditions for the economic activities that were financed by the loans. Nevertheless, rather than attributing the problems to national economic conditions beyond their control, some FUNORSAL administrators pointed to a lack of feasibility studies, technical assistance, and coherent follow-up and education on the FUNORSAL's part (at least partly caused by pressure to spend according to rigid schedules established by the IDB). Others pointed to the presence in the parish of charitable NGOs that, by providing donations, undercut credit-repayment discipline. And finally, in

2000, the exchange rate adopted by the Ecuadorian government for conversion to the dollar cut the value of the fund in half.

In short, Salinas is not the communal paradise that some have claimed it to be, and the continued presence of high poverty levels derives in part from problems internal to the communitarian system. Overall, however, the programs sponsored there have created new skills and capacities, probably improving opportunities for a majority of the population. The parish economy and institutions were healthy enough to incorporate young people, who continued to return home after completing higher studies in nearby cities. Donors also continued to fund old and new programs because, as a consequence of the foundations laid by the church-sponsored agrarian reform and the work done by the Salesian Mission and the FEPP, development assistance in Salinas tended to yield "visible results" that could be presented attractively in reports to donors. At the same time, resentment on the part of those who, to different degrees, felt excluded from benefits appeared to be counterbalanced by a sense of pride in the achievements of the parish and satisfaction with at least some of the programs sponsored by the community organizations and the Salesian Mission. Not least in sustaining that pride was the steady stream of visitors from poor communities in highland Ecuador who came to see the accomplishments of the Salinas cooperatives in order to learn and possibly replicate.

Equally important for the sustainability of the communitarian experience, Salesian Mission and FEPP staff, as well as members of the younger generation among the parish's leading families who occupy managerial positions within the FUNORSAL, were conscious of the problems identified above, some of them acutely and vocally so. Beyond continued work on improving management and marketing, they were attempting to establish greater transparency and fairer work incentives; ensure a broader distribution of benefits; encourage higher levels of participation, especially among women; further decentralize community-based economic activities; and provide new kinds of opportunities through the establishment of small family enterprises. Employment policies, the division of profits between enterprises and their collective owners, and the relative costs and benefits of maintaining the staffs of the latter—especially the FUNORSAL, where salaries for its thirty-six to forty employees tripled between 1991 and 1997—remained delicate issues.

ADJUSTMENT PROGRAMS
AND THE ROLES OF THE STATE AND NGOS

Although it seems that more could have been done in Salinas with the resources available from various external agents, factors outside the control of parish organizations and principal external support agents also played a role in limiting poverty alleviation and economic diversification. Beyond the problematic historical legacy and related patterns of social relations in the parish, the modus operandi of some of the charity-inspired external agents has not been entirely helpful. Also, some fifteen years of reductions in government spending on public health, education, and infrastructure have clearly hurt.

Local resources and donor contributions were insufficient to compensate for enormous cutbacks in what had always been deficient state support. Under IMF pressure the proportion of public expenditure in GDP fell from 20.5 percent to 11 percent between 1982 and 1992, and then remained at low levels throughout the 1990s. With regard to health conditions in Salinas, the physician cited earlier singled out reductions in the quality of lunch supplements, the elimination of stipends for community health workers, and lack of attention to the provision of potable water among the causes of the incapacity of the poorest to provide adequate nourishment for their children. The lack of support for hamlet health workers, moreover, had induced some of "the best" among them to emigrate to nearby provincial capitals. Meanwhile, the capacity of the *cabecera* clinic to provide services was also reduced. For example, in the midst of the 1999 economic crisis, largely provoked by the corrupt deregulation and collapse of the country's financial system (Chapter 1), the contraceptives that the clinic had provided free of charge to poor women who had begun to practice birth control were no longer available from the Ministry of Health.

As for infrastructure, the deplorable state of parish roads increased the costs of marketing and the maintenance of vehicles. Since uncleared rainy-season landslides cut off hamlets from their markets for days and even weeks at a time, perishable products spoiled. Periodic electrical outages also caused spoilage, especially in the workshops and "factories" of the hot and humid lowlands, and sharp fluctuations in voltage damaged machinery, increasing repair and maintenance costs and reducing enterprise profits. Operating costs were further inflated by the corruption of the state and its customs services in particular; the *Hilandería*, for example, wound up paying dearly to extract the used machinery donated by a Quebecois industrialist from the port of Guayaquil.

Nevertheless, the impacts of adjustment programs on the profitability of parish enterprises, through 1998, were contradictory. The enterprises that directed their output to high-income markets (the cheese, sausage, and mushroom plants) were even able to expand production. On the other hand, the women weavers of TEXAL (approximately forty-five persons in mid-1998) found themselves competing in saturated and insecure markets—with the sweater production of dozens of women's groups that had been organized over the previous decade in Ecuador and other Andean countries. Then, in 1999, the bank crisis that was associated with a 9 percent drop in the country's per capita income, as might

be expected, had serious adverse impacts on just about all parish enterprises. In the fall of 2001 it appeared that many productive activities
were beginning to be hurt by competing imports that were made cheap
by the overvalued currency that had resulted from the adoption of the
US dollar. With regard to the impact of dollarization on agricultural and
dairy activities, a resident German cooperant laconically observed: "The
prices of veterinary products have gone through the ceiling while the
prices of *campesino* products have gone through the floor."

The massive emigration that was taking place from many regions of
the country at that time, however, found no parallel in Salinas, although
some individuals did abandon the parish (such as the health workers la-
mented by Dr. Echenique). However, Salinas did not escape the sharp
increases in criminal activity that created insecurity all over the country
during the 1980s and 1990s. During 2000–2001, parish institutions and
enterprises began to suffer from both petty and major thefts, a source of
great consternation to all community leaders.

Beyond the specific effects of Ecuador's socioeconomic crisis of the
1990s and from a broader comparative economic history perspective,
it can be argued that the Salesian Mission and the FEPP substituted
for the absence of a developmental state; that is, they acted as state-
like authoritative external agents that carried out policies similar to
those suggested by Lefeber (Chapter 2). First of all, an extensive
land-redistribution program provided the foundation for economic diversification and social progress. As the Quebecois cooperant who worked
in the *cabecera* during the 1990s pointed out, in the worst moments of the
1999 crisis—when some were laid off (for example, twelve from the
Hilandería) and others were forced on half time (thirty-one at the same
enterprise)—agriculture and animal husbandry ensured subsistence
among the town's people, because all had access to some land and owned
a few animals. Then, as *Hilandería* sales declined again in mid-2001, that
subsistence base cushioned the impact of another round of half-time work.

Second, on the foundation of land reform, the Mission and the FEPP
established a local macroeconomic policy framework, so to speak, by
extending infant-industry protection through a variety of subsidies that
provided time for experimentation and learning. As the German
cooperant noted, "Salinas is based on continuing subsidies, but so then is
European agriculture." Third, in addition to credit programs, extension
services, and other supports, the FEPP and the Salesian Mission sought
out domestic and export markets for parish enterprises. Fourth, they promoted primary and later secondary and higher education in addition to
providing courses on specialized topics. Fifth, to ensure a broader distribution of the surplus, they focused on the generation of employment
(including employment for women), promoted commercial linkages
among the hamlets, and encouraged the formation of institutions that

could socialize some of the profits of new economic activities. Finally, once the damage caused by growing cattle herds became evident, the FEPP and others took action to reverse environmental degradation.

Overall, the initiatives taken by the Salesian Mission and the FEPP can be viewed as a miniature version of the basic elements of the rural development policies pursued by the East Asian NICs following World War II, that is, rural diversification based on agrarian reform and the organization of economic institutions that could socialize profits. (Of course, the policies of the NICs included elements that even the most resource rich and capable of NGOs could not possibly replicate, not even in a relatively small and isolated area like Salinas.) To use Taiwan as an example, agrarian reform was implemented through farmers' associations that enjoyed extremely broad mandates, which included agricultural credit and insurance; reforestation; arbitration of rural disputes; the provision of agricultural marketing and extension services; and the warehousing, processing, and manufacturing of farm products (Yager 1988, 133). Indeed, they were granted monopolies in marketing the most important agricultural products of their members and were able to socialize the gains made from agricultural and other forms of rural growth and diversification (Stavis 1974, 61). Along with agrarian reform, the promotion of labor-intensive rural industry and public works played a critical role in generating employment, narrowing the income gap between urban and rural families, stimulating the growth of domestic demand, and slowing down rural-to-urban migration.

In sum, both traditional political power relations and asset distribution were profoundly transformed in the course of industrialization in the East Asian NICs. Although the FEPP and the Salesian Mission created a micro-regional version of such policies in Salinas, they pursued them within a national political and economic context that, in all fundamental respects, was the opposite of that which had prevailed in the East Asian NICs. In Ecuador, land concentration remained extremely high; public investment in education and health increased in the 1970s but decreased dramatically in the 1980s and 1990s; and the capacity of the state to provide direction to economic development—problematic at best even in the past—was gutted in the 1980s and 1990s. That national context, in turn, was to an important degree structured by the neoliberal adjustment programs demanded by IFIs and donors, USAID in particular.

Finally, it is ironic that the IDB, while providing assistance to the FUNORSAL, also insisted on the adoption of the Agrarian Development Law of 1994 (Treakle 1998). It brought agrarian reform to an end and therefore cut off possibilities of the type of asset redistribution on which economic diversification and social progress in Salinas were based. Even before the law was passed, the likelihood of replicating the Salinas experience was very low. It was difficult to imagine how the large amounts of external resources and technical assistance that the parish received could be pulled together in another location. However, the 1994 law made replication even more unlikely (see also Chapters 4 and 5).

Notes

[1] For an analysis of the social consequences of servility in the indigenous highlands of Ecuador, see Casagrande 1981. Cervone examines racism in day-to-day relations between mestizos and Indians in the small towns of Chimborazo (Cervone 1999), and de la Torre Espinosa focuses on the racism confronted by today's middle-class Indians, including difficulties in obtaining credit for their businesses (de la Torre Espinosa 1996).

[2] The response to the question "Who is an Indian?" is far from straightforward, with estimates ranging from a low of 6 percent to a high of 40–45 percent. For a discussion of these issues, see Muratorio 1994; Whitten 1981; Casagrande 1981; Cervone 1999; de la Torre Espinosa 1996.

[3] By the twenty-first century one to two years of high school were available in five hamlets also.

[4] By 2001 the mushrooms had obtained a German sanitary seal and a Swiss green seal.

[5] The *cabecera* cheese plant capitalized its owner, the town's SCC, which, among services to its 485 members in 1998, provided low-interest loans for purchasing cows, low-cost tractor rental for preparing pasture, and full coverage of funeral costs (interview with SCC president, Ernesto Lopez, April 1998). Three and a half years later, the number of members had grown to 715, partly as a result of assistance provided by Swiss Contact for turning the SCC into the "financial center" of the parish (Interview, SCC president Fabian Vargas, October 2001).

[6] In 2001 the Mission ran at least seventeen enterprises and promotional activities.

[7] In addition to the IDB and donors mentioned above, these included CEBEMO and Mensen in Nood from Holland; Borederlijk from Belgium; Agro Acción and Bread for the World from Germany; the IAF and the Peace Corps from the United States; CESI and the Fondo Ecuatoriano-Canadiense from Canada; Mani Tese from Italy; and Ayuda en Acción from Spain.

[8] Father Polo emphasizes that there were only ten surnames in *cabecera* when he arrived in the early 1970s. He also believes that the social ascent of families from outlying areas was reflected in the fact that quite a few of them had taken residence in the *cabecera*, with the number of surnames in that head town tripling by the year 2000 (interview, Father Antonio Polo, October 2001; see also Polo 2002).

[9] Whyte and Whyte, and Holcombe, provide illuminating discussions of the institutional design of the Mondragón cooperatives and the Grameen Bank, respectively (see Whyte and Whyte 1988; Holcombe 1995).

[10] In this respect, Korovkin's study of three cotton cooperatives established by Peru's 1969 agrarian reform found that the best economic performance was achieved by the enterprise that employed the simplest technologies, was characterized by lowest levels of social differentiation, and had a long history of union organization that had cemented solidarity among the coop members (Korovkin 1990, 136–51).

Chapter 11

Endogenous Rural Diversification

Family Textile Enterprises
in Pelileo, Tungurahua

LIISA L. NORTH

In its 1995 report on Ecuador the World Bank singled out the "blue jeans" industry of the town of Pelileo as an example of the entrepreneurial potential of small-scale producers and of the possibilities of rural diversification and social progress. The Bank attributed the town's prosperity to the growth of hundreds of small family-owned-and-operated jeans tailoring workshops (World Bank 1995, 18). Indeed, Pelileo—located about twenty kilometers from Ambato, the capital of the central highland province of Tungurahua—had acquired by then an almost mythical status in Ecuador as the *ciudad azul* (blue city), named for the color of the denim cloth on which its social and economic advance appeared to have been built.

INSOTEC, an NGO that received funding from the IBD in 1993, provided services to the micro- and small-scale enterprises in Pelileo and several other Ecuadorian cities. In the mid-1990s it identified three

The following discussion draws heavily on interviews conducted from March 1998 to October 2001 in Ambato and Pelileo in the province of Tungurahua. Altogether, seventeen individuals—heads of various chambers of production, bank officials, municipal officials, small producers, and others—were interviewed in Ambato (the capital of the province), and twenty individuals or couples, including fifteen jeans producers, were interviewed in Pelileo. Prior to the field work, secondary sources were consulted and interviews were conducted in Quito during 1997. An interpretation of the data can also be found in Martínez 2000a, 67–108; Luciano Martínez was involved in most aspects of the research in Ambato and Pelileo.

hundred workshops that were dedicated to manufacturing denim cloth-ing—jackets, shirts, children's overalls, and the like, in addition to jeans—in the parish of Pelileo, that is, in the head town or *cabecera* of the same name (population six thousand in 1995) and its rural environs (popula-tion eleven thousand) (Dávalos 1996, 12). In fact, there may have been as many as six hundred to seven hundred such mostly informal (that is, not legally registered) household enterprises in the overwhelmingly rural canton of Pelileo (total pop. 38,000) where the town is located.

Altogether, according to the highest estimates, the industry provided full-time or part-time work to as many as eight thousand persons, about 20 percent of the population of the canton in the early 1990s; about half of those employed in the industry were women (García, Eugenio, and Navarette 1993, 53–54, 90). The majority of the enterprises were very small, employing three to six people, mostly family members, including the proprietor, who was a woman in 22.5 percent of the 217 firms sur-veyed by INSOTEC (Dávalos 1996, 17, 14). Quite a few, however, had a dozen or more workers (engaged in piecework on the enterprise pre-mises or in their own homes), and a few were small factories, employing as many as thirty or forty laborers.

Clearly, not only the town's prosperity but also the prosperity of the surrounding parish and canton depended largely on the ups and downs of this textile industry. It had "taken off" in the mid-1980s, but its origins dated to the late 1960s.The first Pelileo jeans were apparently stitched together by César Paredes in 1968 or 1969 on pedal-operated machines in a small workshop that employed three or four workers. His workshop, located on the outskirts of the *cabecera*, eventually turned into a small factory that had employed as many as sixty workers but was operating with thirty-five in April 2000. When he first started to expand produc-tion, Paredes paid to have the town's electrical services extended to his workshop. However, by the early 1970s, at the beginning of the petro-leum boom and the height of ISI, all the rural areas around the *cabecera* began to be electrified, making the production of jeans and other types of artisan products feasible across the countryside of the canton.

Income from the denim-clothing industry brought significant improve-ments in living standards, highly visible in the new, well-constructed, and roomy houses that dotted much of the canton's countryside in the 1990s. On a ranking from 1 (lowest) to 10 (highest), based on 1990 cen-sus data, the parish of Pelileo was among the most prosperous rural par-ishes in the highlands, registering 3 on indigence and 4 on poverty (Larrea et al. 1996, 61). However, a closer examination of this micro-region dem-onstrates that the origins of its economic diversification and compara-tive well-being cannot be derived simply from the growth of jeans manu-facturing. Rather, they lay in earlier historical periods, in a set of mutually interacting and reinforcing socioeconomic and political relations and struc-tures that included a relatively broad distribution of land; the presence of highly productive small properties or *minifundios* that were involved in market as well as subsistence production; longstanding favorable access to nearby urban markets; the precocious expansion of the educational system; and the early construction of transportation and communication infrastructure (Ibarra 1987; Martínez 1994, 35–61).[1]

In fact, the conditions under which family operated small-scale enterprises took off in Pelileo were polar opposites of the conditions in which the Salesian Mission and the FEPP began to promote rural diversification in the parish of Salinas (Chapter 10). Similarly, whereas the church and NGOs played a critical promotional role in Salinas, the role of the NGO service provider in Pelileo was marginal to the evolution of the industry. That NGO, INSOTEC, established its offices in Pelileo in 1992, quite a few years after jeans manufacturing had become established, and, unlike the Salesian Mission and the FEPP in Salinas, could do little to affect the general trends in the evolution of the industry.

This chapter begins with a discussion of the historical socioeconomic relations and structures that facilitated the emergence of family-owned artisan enterprises and processes of rural diversification in Pelileo and elsewhere in the province of Tungurahua. The industry and its growth are described in the second section. The third section deals with the jeans industry's deepening crisis from the mid-1990s onward, focusing on the impact of neoliberal SAPs, including the adoption of the US dollar as the official currency of the country in January 2000. The concluding section discusses the roles of the state and NGOs, not only with reference to Pelileo but with regard to the broader developmental issues raised by Lefeber and Grinspun (Chapters 2 and 3).

FACILITATING CONDITIONS FOR THE EMERGENCE OF THE JEANS INDUSTRY

Artisan production in the canton of Pelileo, as elsewhere in the province of Tungurahua, dates to the middle of the nineteenth century, if not earlier (Ibarra 1987; Martínez 1994, 64; Forster 1990, 42), and the production of pants and shirts for local markets had begun already in the 1920s (Dávalos 1996, 2).[2] The artisans were both town dwellers and *minifundistas*, that is, smallholding free peasants who could dispose of their own labor and sell their agricultural and artisan products either directly in the vibrant system of local *ferias* (markets) or indirectly through merchants who contracted them to produce a variety of commodities for urban outlets. Small agricultural holdings were prominent in the areas adjacent to Ambato by the middle of the nineteenth century (Bromley 1980, 89), and *minifundistas* who owned fertile valley lands formed a prominent segment of rural society in the province of Tungurahua, including Pelileo, by the late nineteenth century (Martínez 1994, 50–59).

Indeed, they, rather than the large-estate owners who reigned over the countryside in Salinas (Chapter 10), Chimborazo (Chapter 7), and most other parts of Ecuador (Chapters 5 and 6), may have dominated provincial trade in domestic food products at that time (Ibarra 1987; Forster 1990, 39–58). Later, the land base of small producers was augmented through purchases, the construction of irrigation works, and to some extent by the modest agrarian reform laws of 1964 and 1973 (Forster 1990, 303–7).

In addition to selling in local *ferias*, rural and urban artisans were contracted by merchants, especially from the provincial capital, Ambato. Since colonial times this city had occupied a strategic location in the national commercial and transportation grid between the coast and the highlands, between regions of the northern and central highlands, and between all these regions and central Amazonian areas. Not only is Pelileo located only twenty kilometers from Ambato, but the principal route from the central highlands to the Amazonian region passes through the town. Within the hub of principal transportation routes, the independent *minifundistas* and artisans in areas adjacent to Ambato were in a position to participate in the growing commercial exchange between the coast and the highlands generated by the coastal cacao export boom of the 1860s-1920s. In addition to selling their agricultural and artisan goods, they became merchants in the "pack trade" between the coast and highlands (goods were transported on precarious trails solely by pack animals and on the backs of porters). The pack trade also opened access to relatively cheap credit and expanded opportunities for petty capital accumulation that could be used to purchase more land. Although a railroad that connected the coast with the highlands was completed in 1908 and arrived in Pelileo in 1918, the pack trade remained viable through the 1930s (Forster 1990, 61–62).

Along with the railroad, the early extension of electrification to Pelileo provided yet another stimulus to commercial development and, later, to the participation of *minifundistas* in the production and marketing of artisan goods. Electricity reached the *cabecera* in 1927 (Guevara 1945, 382), and more than 85 percent of households in this primarily rural canton enjoyed electric service by the mid-1990s.

The widespread ownership of land by *minifundistas*—that is, the presence of a free, landholding peasantry—was clearly among the critical elements that made it possible for the rural population of Pelileo specifically, and much of Tungurahua generally, to take advantage of commercial opportunities. Or, to state it conversely, the absence of large-estate dominance and servile social relations facilitated forms of commercial growth in which important segments of the population could earn incomes and benefit. In Tungurahua, the *huasipungo*—Ecuador's version of servility—"was practically insignificant" (Martínez 1994, 52).[3]

Ownership of even very small parcels of land could provide the resource base for participating in market exchange, for the time and effort needed to acquire new skills, for the formal and informal guarantees required by moneylenders and lending institutions, and for risk-taking because the produce of the parcel could guarantee or partly guarantee the satisfaction of the family's basic subsistence needs when markets turned sour. And successful participation in artisan production and commercial activity by landless or land-short urban and semi-urban workers could raise capital for the purchase of more land. In turn, the growth of a class of merchants, or "groups of intermediaries," to whom both rural and urban small producers could sell, had been historically favored by the presence of large numbers of *minifundistas* who sold their produce in the many small town *ferias* that were and remain typical of the areas surrounding Ambato (see Bromley 1980, 90).

In effect, a number of mutually reinforcing factors—involving widespread landownership, social freedoms (including, importantly, freedom of movement), and ready access to markets—facilitated processes of rural diversification. They also created a social context in which education and knowledge of new technologies relevant for expanding market production came to be valued. As early as 1869 the Cantonal Council of Pelileo sought to establish primary schools for the "aboriginal children who had been disadvantaged from the benefits of education since the most remote of times," and the first efforts to establish a secondary school in the *cabecera* dated to 1897 (Guevara 1945, 347, 354).[4]

Still, in the period 1998–2001, when one could expect the textile-manufacturing sector to have separated entirely from its agricultural ties and origins, ten of the fifteen jeans producers interviewed in Pelileo and the adjacent parish of Huambaló were engaged in agricultural and pastoral activities and/or raising small animals. These artisans sold tree tomatoes, onions, potatoes, and fruit, as well as milk, chickens, eggs, guinea pigs *(cuyes)*, and pigs. Moreover, among some of those who dedicated their time entirely to jeans tailoring, savings from raising animals had provided at least part of the capital for setting up the enterprise. And land and animals, for subsistence or sale, provided a measure of security in the midst of the 1999–2000 crisis that followed the collapse the country's private banking system and then the impacts of the adoption of the US dollar as Ecuador's official currency.

The interview results from 1998–2001 are consistent with the findings of a survey of 455 Tungurahua artisans conducted in 1990 by Luciano Martínez. His respondents came from parish *cabeceras* and did not include enterprise owners from the surrounding countryside, where many family enterprises are also located. Martínez nevertheless found that almost half of even the *cabecera*-based artisans owned some agricultural land, most of them less than one hectare, and 42 percent declared that their incomes derived from more than one occupation, with agriculture and commerce being the most frequently mentioned other activities (Martínez 1994, 122, 106–7). Forty of the 455 artisans in that 1990 survey were jeans producers from El Tambo, an urbanized section of the town of Pelileo, and even among them, 37.7 percent owned some land (Martínez 2000a, 68 n. 21).[5]

The connections between the agricultural and artisan worlds were brought out also in an interview with the president of the Artisan Chamber (Cámara Artesanal) of Tungurahua, a provincial association of the larger enterprises. He thought that up to 20 percent of the chamber's then more or less eight hundred members were rural and owned some land. He also reported that about thirty members were engaged in greenhouse agriculture.

THE GROWTH AND CONSOLIDATION
OF THE JEANS INDUSTRY

Although the fifteen enterprises whose evolution we followed during 1998–2001 cannot be considered a representative sample of the industry, they do allow us to identify and probe certain of its principal facets. With regard to the exceptional characteristics of the enterprises included in this study, first of all, all but one of their owners used or had used some or all of the services available from INSOTEC which, at the time, had about eighty to ninety clients among the jeans producers, that is, less than one-third of the 271 included in its survey. (That survey, it should be recalled, may have covered only half of the actual number of enterprises.) In addition, two of the fewer than a dozen or so small factory-scale producers in Pelileo were among the fifteen interviewed in 1998–2001. Moreover, female proprietors were clearly over-represented: five out of the fifteen were women, in comparison to the 22.5 percent that INSOTEC found in its survey, and a sixth woman became the sole owner of an enterprise upon the accidental death of her husband. In general terms, the group interviewed represented somewhat larger producers; they were among the 30 percent of jeans manufacturers who owned more than five sewing machines.[6] It also seems that the fifteen were among some of the best managed and most solidly established. All but perhaps one appeared to have survived both the acute economic crisis of 1999–2000 and at least the initial impacts of dollarization, albeit with difficulties, when many of their neighbors did not.

Although members of a small and nonrepresentative sample, the fifteen Pelileo enterprise owners' stories nevertheless provide insights into the growth and evolution of the jeans industry. They illustrate and provide specific examples of the general trends identified in historical studies and larger surveys (Martínez 1994; Dávalos 1996; García, Eugenio, and Navarette 1993), various newspaper articles (see *Hoy* 1997; Centero 1998), and the observations of the bank and credit program managers, artisan chamber leaders, municipal officials, INSOTEC staff, and others who were interviewed during 1998–2001. The interviews also provoke questions for further research concerning the industry's origins and evolution. In particular, they call attention to the prominent role that women have played in the industry—a phenomenon which previous studies have certainly mentioned but have not attempted to analyze. For example, in 1990 Martínez found that 51 percent of the 455 artisan entrepreneurs in his survey were women, and that percentage increased to 56.2 among the smaller workshop owners (Martínez 2000a, 56). Finally, they emphasize that conditions in the industry were highly volatile during the 1990s, in particular, and as a consequence, the predominant trends of any one moment could change quite dramatically or even be reversed at the next moment.

By 1970 "the production of slacks in the canton of Pelileo was very important both with regard to their quality and the diversity of styles," attracting merchants from all over Tungurahua and neighboring provinces to contract local artisans as home-based pieceworkers (García, Eugenio, and Navarette 1993, 47). It was at the beginning of that decade of rapid domestic market growth and subsidized ISI, fueled by the petroleum boom (1972–82), that the road from Ambato to Pelileo was paved, shortening the trip to the *cabecera* for merchants from the provincial capital to about thirty minutes. In the conditions of rapidly growing domestic demand, those merchants were increasingly attracted by the large numbers of skilled artisans available among the "many poor peasant families" in the canton (García, Eugenio, and Navarette 1993, 47). Moreover, according to Sergio Llerena, president of a Pelileo tailors' association, the textile factories that were established in Quito and elsewhere in Ecuador at that time "wanted to hide their workers [in their homes in the countryside] in order to avoid labor legislation."

However, at least some of the town-based artisan producers began to yearn for independence from the merchants and to seek direct access to markets. In this regard, Llerena recounted: "We realized that we were workers—we tailored for others even though we also hired workers. We realized that we could not sell directly and began to ask ourselves why the big commercial houses took our money, because they were the ones who kept the capital." Thus, sometime in the early 1970s, a nucleus of artisans from Pelileo participated in efforts by artisans from various parts of the country to obtain permission from the municipal authorities in Quito to establish sales posts in the colonial center of the city. "And that's how Pelileo began to rise to prominence," according to Llerena. "Some went to Quito; others to Riobamba and Guayaquil, where they also had to get permits. And that's how people began to go out and sell directly," although, at first, they were "very few."

Nevertheless, although direct sales by jeans entrepreneurs may have increased in quantity, throughout the 1970s, perhaps "80 percent of production was contracted by merchants who represented certain factories [and] institutions, or who simply sold in the markets in different parts of the country as well as in neighboring countries" (García, Eugenio, and Navarette 1993, 47). Even in the 1980s and 1990s a large but varying proportion of production continued to be sold to wholesale merchants and contracted by various types of intermediaries, despite the growth of direct sales to individual consumers and retailers at *ferias* in highland cities and at Pelileo's own Saturday jeans *feria*, which was established in 1993. The Saturday *feria* stretched along the highway that passed through El Tambo and led to the town of Baños, a popular health resort that attracted much weekend tourism from Quito and other cities. By 2000 the temporary sales posts of the early 1990s were largely replaced by a dozen or more permanent "boutiques" that sold other clothing as well as locally produced jeans.

All the historic social-and-economic factors, processes, and trends identified above combined in different, complex, and changing ways in the evolution and operation of individual jeans and denim clothing enterprises.[7] In particular, both the importance of merchant capital and access to even tiny amounts of land emerged clearly from the stories told by many of the fifteen workshop proprietors, as did the role of women in enterprise ownership and management.

To provide a few examples, one of the workshop owners—a married woman with six workers, four of them family members—had learned her trade from her artisan parents in the 1950s. They, together with her grandmother, had manufactured wool *(casimir)* and polyester slacks, sweaters, lined jackets, and children's overalls for an Ambato-based merchant, who used to come and pick up the goods with pack mules. The production from her own workshop, which was established in 1991 in an urban location within Pelileo town limits, was sold by her husband and daughter at the Saturday *feria* in Ambato and at the Monday market in Quito. Although she initially stated that her time was dedicated solely to jeans production, it turned out that her backyard was large enough to raise chickens for home consumption and then, in the midst of the 1999–2000 economic crisis, to start raising geese. Their eggs fetched what she considered an "attractive price" at a time when her carpenter husband was finding it difficult to obtain work, and their noisy aggressiveness eliminated the need to keep dogs to guard the house.

Another woman, who had separated from her husband but owned and operated a jeans tailoring workshop that they had established in the *cabecera* in 1977, learned the trade over a period of ten years as a pieceworker in Quito. One of the eight children of an indigenous peasant family, she inherited "too little land" to live from agriculture, and apparently it was her own and her former husband's savings and connections from their piecework experience that allowed them to establish their own enterprise, or "become independent," as many of the enterprise owners in Pelileo liked to say. On Tuesdays and Saturdays she traveled to Quito to sell to retailers and also directly from a post in the colonial center of the city. Nevertheless, the "too little land" that she had inherited was sufficient to raise pigs for sale.

A couple who owned a textile enterprise in the countryside combined the manufacture of children's clothing with fruit and vegetable production (apples, tomatoes, and onions) and animal husbandry (chickens, pigs, and a cow). They had purchased land with earnings from the textile workshop that they established in the late 1970s. (The possibility of purchasing small amounts of land in the canton and elsewhere in Tungurahua was favored by the fact that it was an area of *minifundistas* rather than large estates, which, when put on the market, were normally sold intact.) When the husband died in an accident in December 1999, the wife continued to run the business and seemed to be weathering the economic crises of the time more successfully than many of the other fifteen producers.

In all, either wives, mothers, or older daughters were present at all but two of the fifteen enterprises where interviews were conducted. Moreover, it was often the wives who responded to the questions—either their co-proprietor husbands were absent at the time, or the husband simply sat back and listened to his wife explain the history and operations of their enterprise. In addition, investment and other decisions appeared to have been taken jointly. Women appear to have been integrated into this artisan economy in a "non-subordinated" fashion (Martínez 1994, 90). How this came about remains to be studied, but clues and a point of departure for such a study may be found in the analysis provided by Forster. She found that trade and work opportunities in the coastal region during the cacao boom years of the late nineteenth and early twentieth centuries induced so many men from parts of Tungurahua to migrate to the coast, at least temporarily, that women enjoyed unusual freedom and economic opportunities. For example, landowners in the province "had to settle for women sharecroppers to get the work done" (Forster 1990, 277). Thus it appears that the control of economic assets and decisions on the part of women may also have had their origins in the particular historical characteristics and evolution of the smallholder or *minifundista* agrarian structure of Tungurahua and its linkages to the dynamic labor and commodity markets of earlier periods.

Although all fifteen manufacturers interviewed for this study learned their skills as jeans producers on the job—from parents and other relatives, as pieceworkers, or, in their own words, simply by "imitating"— and most started their businesses with savings accumulated from piecework, the sale of animals, the assistance of relatives, and/or credit for the purchase of sewing machines provided by merchants, other patterns of learning and capitalization were also identified by observers of the industry. Somewhat fewer than half of the respondents in the 1996 INSOTEC survey had sought and obtained credit from banks and cooperatives: about 14 percent from private banks, another 14 percent from the BNF, about 10 percent from cooperatives, and only 4.6 percent from NGOs (calculated from figures provided by Dávalos 1996, 33–34). Most had clearly relied on their own savings, on their families, and/or on merchants who extended credit for the purchases of sewing machines and cloth. Although support institutions were not entirely lacking in the area, in fact, little in the way of institutional support for the industry and its evolution emerged from the interviews with the producers (INSOTEC's role will be discussed below).

When asked about their best years of sales and profits, the owners of the oldest enterprises—those established in the late 1970s and early 1980s—all agreed that the 1980s were their best years because demand was rising and there were, compared to the mid-1990s, few producers. All producers agreed that the years following 1995 had been extremely difficult, not only due to declining demand and cheap imports, but also because, in the words of a BNF official, by the late 1990s competition was "reaching absurd levels," given the increasingly limited size of the market and the numbers of new people who had entered the sector. Moreover, by then, according to industry leaders and local bankers, this was the situation that prevailed in all sectors of production in Tungurahua.

THE CRISIS OF THE JEANS INDUSTRY AND ADJUSTMENT PROGRAM IMPACTS

How did Pelileo jeans producers fare in the course of 1990s SAPs, trade liberalization policies, and dollarization? As noted, INSOTEC began to provide technical services to Pelileo jeans producers in 1992, quite a few years after the industry had taken off. However, INSOTEC's support programs were not able to prevent or reverse the deepening crisis that the sector confronted from the mid-1990s onward. First of all, in March 1998 the head of the INSOTEC office in Ambato reported that the average number of workers employed by jeans enterprises that used the NGO's services was falling steadily (from about six or seven to four) and that many small units in the area had been forced into bankruptcy. Already the crisis of the industry was such that the producers had formed a "debtors' club,"[8] and the staff of the BNF, which had provided credit to some of the larger enterprises, did not dare to enter Pelileo due to fear for their personal safety.

A year later, in March-May 1999, Pelileo's workshops—along with just about all other enterprises in the country—were practically paralyzed by the fiscal crisis of the state and the meltdown of the country's private banking system, which were both manifestations and causes of the country's catastrophic economic crisis. Only one of the producers reported having lost her savings in the financial system bankruptcies, but just about all complained of getting stuck with bad checks or delayed payments by intermediaries. In overall terms the crisis led to a dramatic decline in demand as the country's per capita income declined by 9 percent, after a 1 percent decline in 1998 (Larrea and Sánchez 2002, 14–15). By March 2000 at least some of the jeans enterprises that had managed to survive the 1999 crisis were beginning to recover slowly, but the estimates of the number of establishments that had disappeared range from a low of 25 percent to a high of 40 and even 50 percent of producers. One producer thought that the stabilization and slight increase in his sales by April 2000 was a consequence of the very large numbers of other manufacturers who had gone bankrupt. In any case, the brief recovery following the adoption of the US dollar at the beginning of that year was followed by currency overvaluation, which in turn led to increasing amounts of clothing imports, especially from Peru, but also from Colombia and Panama. In October 2001 all ten jeans entrepreneurs who were interviewed on that occasion reported decreased sales and/or decreased profits per unit, trends that, according to Alba Chavez, the head of the INSOTEC office in Pelileo, only worsened in 2002.

The causes of the jeans producers' problems were multiple and interrelated, and they were shared—in different degrees and ways—by other sectors of industry in Tungurahua and elsewhere in the country. They included the effects of the early 1995 war with Peru (which closed borders to trade with that country); widespread and frequent electricity outages in 1995 and 1996 in Tungurahua, in particular; and loss of sales on the coast (where about half of the country's population resides) as a consequence of the devastating floods caused by El Niño in 1998 and continuing heavy rains in 1999. However, one special aspect of economic liberalization—that is, increasing imports of used clothing and, according to some, also liquidation stocks imported under the used-clothing label—had begun to wreak havoc among the artisan textile industries of the canton in the early 1990s. At the same time, imports of used shoes devastated small-scale industry in neighboring cantons and trade liberalization led to the import of Brazilian bus and truck parts, which left the Ambato-based metal and mechanical industries reeling,[9] reducing local employment and incomes and therefore the demand for the jeans manufacturers' wares. As more than one of the jeans producers interviewed put it: "How can you expect people to buy clothing when they can't afford to eat?"[10] According to the president of the Chamber of Small Industries of Tungurahua, membership in his association dropped from approximately 1,200 in 1994 to 157 in 1999 due to bankruptcies and reductions in the scale of operations from "small industry" to the "artisan" category, which brought lower taxes and other benefits to the producer.

In more general terms, increased nationwide unemployment and underemployment provoked by neoliberal policies and the incapacity of a weakened state to maintain electrical infrastructure or respond with employment and reconstruction programs to disasters like El Niño, restricted the purchasing power of the low-income and low-to-medium-income consumers who formed the jeans producers' markets.[11] In this respect it is relevant to note that while Ecuador's average per capita income, according to World Bank data, reached US$1,600 per year in 1994, median income remained below US$700; in other words, more than half the population subsisted below the poverty line in the mid-1990s (see Chapter 4), and that very high incidence of poverty increased during the following years.

Finally, almost incessant political protests against different aspects of the neoliberal policy package during the 1990s—blockages of the country's principal highways, teachers' strikes, doctors' and nurses' strikes, indigenous uprisings, and much more—also took their toll on the economy. At the same time, the meltdown of the private banking system in 1999 was in significant part induced by the deregulation of the financial system demanded by international banks and donors. In effect, a vicious cycle of mutually reinforcing economic and political decay set in during the 1990s.

By 1998–1999, even Pelileo, the historically prosperous and dynamic zone of small-scale private entrepreneurship, was reeling from the sharp contraction of low- and middle-income markets while confronting competition from very cheap imports of used clothing. Significantly, in the midst of the spring 1999 crisis, unable to sell their accumulated stock, two of the fifteen jeans producers interviewed turned their attention entirely to agricultural activities; two others who had previously engaged in agriculture only for household consumption began to produce for the market; another wondered about the wisdom of his past decision to invest in the purchase of more sewing machines instead of acquiring more land; and yet others were pleased to have pigs, chickens, or eggs available for sale.

As noted above, the estimates of the percentage of enterprises that disappeared during 1999–2000 ranged from 25 percent to 40 and even 50 percent, with the higher percentages mentioned more frequently in 2000 and by small producers. A clothing-store owner estimated that "during the past six months, two thousand people [in the canton] were left without work." Which kinds of enterprises went bankrupt and which survived? With regard to the bankruptcies, both producers and observers agreed that it was the smallest units, with the least capital and the highest levels of dependence on credit, that had to close their doors.

However, some also identified among the casualties medium-sized producers who had been in business for a long time. The large- and medium-sized enterprise owners who were interviewed reported temporary closures and decapitalization in order to survive; among other things, they sold their trucks or some of their sewing machines to cover debts and raise money.

With respect to those who succeeded in staying in business, the president of the Artisan Chamber of Tungurahua identified ownership of land as a key factor in survival; the others, according to him, were up-to-date technology and administrative capacity. In the same vein, one of the jeans-producer families involved in agricultural production considered itself extremely lucky in comparison to city-based artisans who had no access to land. Another manufacturer family that was simply attempting to sell accumulated stock said that it would not be eating if it were not for the food that family members could produce for themselves and the little bit of income they were earning from raising chickens, guinea pigs, and pigs for the market. Meanwhile, Alba Chavez, the head of the INSOTEC office in Pelileo, thought that perhaps 20 percent of the NGO's eighty-two clients were involved in agricultural production for the market in 1999. The following year, her assistant, the daughter of a successful female jeans entrepreneur, thought that many rural manufacturers had turned entirely to agriculture and, of those who remained in the jeans sector, 20–25 percent were "also farmers now."

Toward the end of 2001 one of the two producers included in this study who owned factory-sized enterprises in Pelileo reported that he had purchased a dairy farm with ten milk cows and ten calves. Largely as a consequence of the steadily increasing imports that resulted from the overvaluation of the currency following dollarization, his profit margin on jeans had descended to the point where he feared that he would have to close his factory. Thus he sold some property in Pelileo, drew on dollar savings that he had accumulated in better times, and purchased the farm in a neighboring canton. He also built a "shopping center," where he rented space and sold more and more cheap imported clothing and less and less of his own and fellow Pelileo producers' denim goods. Local products were getting priced out of the market as a consequence of the effects of dollarization.

But farming and commerce were not options available to all. Moreover, the overvalued currency was encouraging the importation of vegetables, fruit, pork, and chicken meat from Peru, in particular. Thus, in late 2001 the farmers among the jeans producers found it "better to eat than to sell" whatever they produced, because the sales prices were barely covering the costs of production.

In these circumstances various producers and chamber heads referred to artisans who had become taxi or truck drivers (in markets that were also saturated), said that "a few are in debtors' jail," or, most frequently of all, identified people (especially young people between the ages of twenty and thirty) who had emigrated to Spain or elsewhere. By 2000 just about everyone interviewed in Pelileo and Ambato told stories of emigration, confessed that they themselves had entertained the idea, or turned the interview around to ask about job opportunities in Canada. One producer stated in April 2000 that, of the ten people he knew who had gone bankrupt, three had emigrated.

In effect, according to a BNF official, emigration was the most frequent response to bankruptcy among the small producers in the Ambato area because "there are no opportunities in any part of the country." According to him, the exodus from Tungurahua began around 1996–1997 and, since the BNF was involved in receiving the payments for passports, he could certify that in Ambato alone the number of requests peaked at three hundred per day and reached two thousand per month during certain moments in 1999–2000. At the Banco Solidario of Ambato, which provided credit to micro- and small enterprises in the city, some clients went to Spain without paying their debts, "shoemakers and woodworkers" especially among them, "but in the majority of cases, the family members . . . [later came] to pay the debts with the money that the emigrants [were] sending from Spain." A textile merchant also reported that he was receiving money from Spain from former clients who had gone bankrupt.

Thus, a province that had been historically characterized by low levels of emigration because its intensively cultivated *minifundios* and labor-intensive artisan enterprises generated employment for the new generations of workers became a region of massive outflows of human talent in the course of neoliberal adjustment programs and their associated political-economic crises of the 1990s. Viable rural and small-town livelihoods based on the creative combination of different types of economic activities were effectively destroyed. Emigration from the country as a whole reached such great proportions that in 2000 remittances became "the second most important earner of foreign exchange after oil," totaling almost 10 percent of GDP (*The Economist* 2001, 8).

As Jenny Perez, the head of the INSOTEC office in Ambato, put it, the crisis of 1999–2000 could not be "compared to any of the previous crises during which the producers, in one way or another, could keep their businesses going. . . . Everyone now wants to leave the country; in this situation, there is no possibility of saving or investing. People simply consume everything they earn." A year and a half later, Perez reported more bankruptcies, fewer workers in the enterprises that had survived, and continued if not increased emigration. The possibility of exporting to Colombia, an alternative that INSOTEC had been pursuing, she declared, "was dead—killed by terrorists, guerrillas, and bandits who robbed the merchandise, and then finished off by dollarization."

STATES AND NGOS

It remains unclear how much INSOTEC contributed to the development of the jeans industry and the extent to which it was able to provide assistance to Pelileo producers during the crisis years. To be sure, its technical services—low-cost access to specialized machines for finishing details like button holes—improved the quality and presumably the prices of producers' goods and induced some private merchants to begin providing similar services. Reasonably priced credit for the purchase of fabric from the INSOTEC outlet may also have kept down the interest rates of private suppliers. These were important contributions and, in better macroeconomic circumstances, they might have laid the basis for advance on programs that the NGO had began to explore, such as cooperative export marketing and the reduction of severe levels of environmental pollution created by the jeans bleaching process (Weigel and Weininger 1996). However, no movement on either front took place during the course of this study. The producers did express interest in the possibilities of cooperative marketing, but crisis management clearly crowded out the organizational and other efforts required for long-term planning, both at INSOTEC and among the jeans producers. As for the environment, the producers either ignored or denied the problems of contamination. Their reactions, although lamentable, were understandable; since the mid-1990s the energy and time required to cope with wild rides in the market have left little room for tackling other complex and potentially costly problems.[12]

INSOTEC did achieve some progress, albeit problematic, on reducing the pirating of brand names, thereby protecting producers against lawsuits. The jeans industry grew in the 1970s and 1980s by using the most popular labels on the international market—Levi, Wrangler, and so on—without license. This eventually led to litigation by the transnational corporations against the larger Pelileo producers, and the lawsuits were won, as was to be expected, by the corporations. Thus, by the late 1990s, with INSOTEC assistance in some cases, the larger manufacturers were producing under their own labels, and the NGO was encouraging the medium-sized and smaller entrepreneurs to do the same. However, in the course of the study it became clear that at least some of the merchants who purchased from medium-sized and smaller producers were insisting that they continue to use the internationally recognized brand names. Meanwhile, in the "boutiques" of Pelileo, jeans and other clothing were often displayed with no labels at all; the customer chose the brand name that he or she liked the most and had it sewn into the clothing.

Overall then, INSOTEC's role appears to have been marginal to the evolution of the jeans economy. First of all, to reiterate, it established a service center in Pelileo only in 1992, at least a decade after the industry had "taken off." Neither the origins nor the growth of this manufacturing sector can be explained with reference to NGO initiatives or support; rather, the industry emerged, over a lengthy period of time, from a set of mutually reinforcing conditions that included, most prominently, the presence of a smallholding peasantry, artisan traditions, and access to markets. Many artisan producers, moreover, sustained themselves in good part through a combination of subsistence and income-generating activities, similar to the textile workers of the *Hilandería* in Salinas (Chapter 10). In fact, rural poverty had declined and entrepreneurial capacities had developed in Pelileo and Tungurahua prior to the flowering of the jeans industry as, indeed, they had in other micro-regions of *minifundistas* around important market centers in Ecuador (Martínez 2000a; Solomon 1981).

The connection between manufacturing development and smallholder agriculture can be found in other parts of the world as well, in places as distant and different from one another as nineteenth-century Sweden, northern Italy, and post–World War II East Asia. There, the most successful NICs developed on the basis of labor-intensive rural industrialization that accompanied profound agrarian reforms.

In short, when INSOTEC started to provide services in Pelileo, an entire historical process had already resulted in the accumulation of physical capital; the presence of educated human talent; the emergence of an entrepreneurial ethos and commonly shared business norms; widespread knowledge of markets and how they functioned in different parts of the country and its frontiers; and even access to credit (albeit most frequently through family and merchant channels rather than the formal banking system). The people of Pelileo, and indeed of Tungurahua, were movers and doers. There is no evidence for the image often presented in critiques of the ISI phase of the hemisphere's economic history of a population spoiled by a populist state, waiting on government to provide subsidies and handouts.

In this context a NGO could certainly make contributions to the development of the jeans-manufacturing sector, as INSOTEC did. However, the sector's overall health—like that of other artisan and small scale industries in the province and elsewhere in the country—depended on broader macroeconomic conditions rather than on technocratic interventions. Those conditions, in turn, depended on the evolution of international markets; the policy pressures emanating from the IFIs with regard to the implementation of adjustment programs; and the capacity of the Ecuadorian government to sustain a minimum of economic stability and social well-being in order to ensure the maintenance of domestic demand, which made up 87 percent of the market for the country's manufacturing industries (Larrea 1998b).

The IFIs, of course, directed the Ecuadorian government toward balancing its budget to pay its foreign debt by cutting back on public services; relying on market forces, and therefore gutting the state planning institutions that had begun to develop capacity in the 1970s, if not somewhat earlier; deregulating financial markets, a policy that, as pointed out earlier, led to the meltdown of the country's banking system and formed a key component of the massive crisis of 1999–2000; securing property rights and therefore, among other things, terminating all efforts to pursue land reform despite an extremely high concentration of rural property and ongoing land conflicts that generated political instability and human rights violations in the countryside (Chapter 6); and liberalizing trade in a country where the local manufacturing sector was extremely weak and vulnerable to international competition.

The Ecuadorian state itself was so closely tied to the interests of a narrow set of regionally based and, for the most part, export-economy-linked elites that all these policies were pursued with amazing disregard for popular welfare and little concern for sustaining productive sectors that were not controlled by those elites and their allied foreign investors (Larrea and North 1997). Within this national and international correlation of political forces and power, trade liberalization was pursued with total contempt for small producers, whose organizations, within the elite dominated political and associational systems of Ecuador, as in many other third world countries, were simply too weak to have their voices heard by those who wielded power. As one of the industry association heads in Ambato put it, "The political panorama has been terrible since [President] Duran [1992–96] and [his minister of finance] Armijos. . . . The government does not respond to us; it is only interested in the large enterprises" (March 1999).[13]

Meanwhile, balancing the budget was given priority over, for example, creating employment through public investment in urgently needed water control and transportation projects on the coast, where El Niño struck in 1998. Such publicly financed infrastructure programs can play an important role in sustaining lower-class incomes, and therefore local demand and decentralized productive economic activities, which, in turn, can provide tax income for sustaining government programs (Chapter 4). Later, during the financial crisis of 1999–2000, the interests of those who had engaged in massive corruption were protected—both those of the bankers and of the large agricultural interests of the coast—according to one of the industry leaders interviewed in Ambato (March 1999).

The corruption and waste at the pinnacles of economic and political power, in turn, bred cynicism and contributed to the breakdown of the understandings and norms—or informal institutional arrangements—that had allowed the artisan and small-business sectors to develop. Producers in Pelileo started to get stuck with "bad checks" from merchants during the second half of the 1990s; workers started stealing from their employers, a phenomenon that one of the workshop proprietors in Ambato said she understood because the real purchasing power of the wages she was able to pay were "pitiful"; Pelileo, like other towns, was hit by so many robberies that its residents in 2000 organized citizen "brigades" for night patrols; and the eight hundred members of the Tungurahua debtors' club, according to the head of the organization, who was also a member of the Ambato City Council, saw no reason why they should pay the accumulated interest on their loans when the richest men in the country were bailed out by the government to the tune of hundreds of millions of dollars. In his view, Ecuador had been "assaulted by a financial sector . . . controlled by twenty families." In this situation of palpable hatred of banks and bankers, it is quite amazing that at least some emigrants were attempting to pay back loans that they had incurred from local financial institutions—like the Banco Solidario—with the moneys that they were earning abroad.

Briefly then, Ecuador's economy and society were devastated by the ways in which SAPs were pursued. With few exceptions, such as the FEPP in the highly unusual circumstances of the parish of Salinas (Chapter 10), NGOs could do little to counteract the overwhelmingly destructive impacts of those policies on productive activities and living standards. In fact, INSOTEC , which was supposed to be a model NGO that would recover costs and even grow by charging fees for technical services provided to productive sectors, was forced to close down three of its six service centers in the first few months of 2002. If public policy had been focused on maintaining domestic market demand and employment, NGO support programs for micro- and small enterprises might have yielded quantitatively and qualitatively better results.

Notes

[1] In his illuminating article on non-farm employment as a route out of poverty in rural Ecuador, Lanjouw identifies a positive relationship between rural economic diversification, on the one hand, and market proximity and the expansion of education and infrastructure, on the other, but he fails to probe the influence of landownership patterns, although he does mention them (Lanjouw 1998, 19).

[2] According to Pelileo historian Dario Guevara, textile production in the area dates back to the colonial period (Guevara 1945, 139; see also 87, 140–41).

[3] Similarly, in the neighboring province of Cotopaxi a significant amount of commercial development took place around Saquisili, where, as in Tungurauhua, small-property holders dedicated themselves to local commercial activity (Bromley 1980).

[4] The relationship between literacy and landownership patterns merits research. It is notable that in Costa Rica, with a large class of small coffee producers, over half of the population was literate by 1905 (Booth 1990, 391).

[5] Our interview results and Martínez's data are contradicted by the findings of the 1996 INSOTEC survey, in which only sixteen of the 217 jeans producers stated that they had another business and only three declared that they were involved in farming (Dávalos 1996, 10). We are convinced that the INSOTEC survey did not capture the actual diversity of the producers' income sources because the artisans do not consider farming a business. In the course of our interviews, landownership and agricultural and commercial activities came to light, in most cases, only upon probing; the principal income—except in two cases—came from denim-clothing production, at least most of the time.

[6] The INSOTEC survey found that 70 percent of producers owned one to five sewing machines, 23 percent owned six to ten, 4.6 percent owned eleven to fifteen, and 2.3 percent owned more than fifteen (Dávalos 1996, 25).

[7] An "act of God," the virtual destruction of Old Pelileo in the earthquake of 1949, may have further loosened social relations in the town and its surrounding areas in ways that left room for the emergence of entrepreneurial talent. The New Pelileo, today's *cabecera*, was built on what was considered more secure higher ground.

[8] The debtors' club in Pelileo formed part of the provincial debtors' club which had been established in 1997, and the latter formed part of a national debtors' club.

[9] According to the president of the Chamber of Small Industries of Tungurahua, between 1994 and 1999, 60 percent of small metal and mechanical industry plants in the province "disappeared or passed into the category of artisan enterprise" in order to take advantage of the more favorable tax legislation available to the smaller artisan units. During the same period, half of shoe manufacturers also "disappeared." The fact that the Artisan Chamber reported an increase in membership during this time provides corroboration for his observations regarding the conversion of some small industrial plants into artisan enterprises.

[10] A BNF official stated: "The food intake levels of the people have gone down to the point that we are seeing the reappearance of illnesses, tuberculosis in particular . . . and we are also seeing students abandoning school."

[11] With regard to sustaining employment, incomes, and living standards through employment programs in the aftermath of natural disasters, see Dreze and Sen 1989.

[12] As the prices of textiles and other inputs, exchange rates, and interest rates rose precipitously, the most often expressed wish of the jeans producers was for a minimum of market stability. This is why they initially favored dollarization. However, nine out of the ten producers interviewed in October 2001 were either convinced or beginning to think that the dollar had become their greatest problem.

[13] In 2001, when imports started to undercut sales and profits, a group of the larger and most successful textile producers in Pelileo discussed the possibility of seeking help from the national Congress. However, they ultimately decided that it would be useless to attempt this because most of the deputies in Congress were involved in import businesses.

Bibliography

Abers, Rebecca. 2000. *Inventing Local Democracy: Grassroots Politics in Brazil.* Boulder, Colo: Lynne Rienner.

Acosta, Alberto. 2002. "Ecuador: un modelo para América Latina?" *Boletín ICCI-Rimai* (monthly publication of the Scientific Institute of Indigenous Cultures, Quito) 4, no. 34 (January).

Acosta, Alberto, and José E. Joncoso, eds. 2000. *Dolarización: Informe Urgente.* Quito: ILDIS and Abya-Yala/UPS.

Adams, Dale W., and J. D. Von Pischke. 1992. "Microenterprise Credit Programs: Déja Vu." *World Development* 20, no. 10.

Almeida, José, et al. 1993. *Sismo Etnico en el Ecuador.* Quito: CEDIME/Abya-Yala.

Altimir, Oscar. 1999. "Desigualdad, empleo y pobreza en América latina: efectors del ajuste y del cambio en el estilo de desarrollo." In *Pobreza y desigualdad en América latina,* edited by Víctor E. Tokman and Guillermo O'Donnell. Buenos Aires-Barcelona-México.

Alvarado, Javier. 1994. "Transacciones de tierras y crédito en la pequeña agricultura comercial." *Debate Agrario* (Lima) 20.

Arcos Cabrera, Carlos. 2001. *Ecuador: cooperación para el desarrollo, balance de una década.* Quito: Abya-Yala.

Arcos Cabrera, Carlos, and Edison Palomeque Vallejo. 1997. *El Mito al Debate: Las ONGs en Ecuador.* Quito: Abya-Yala.

Arrobo Rodas, Carlos, and Mercedes Prieto. 1995. "La Participación Campesina en Proyectos de Desarrollo Rural: El Programa Nacional de Desarrollo Rural (PRONADER) y otros casos ecuatorianos." Quito: IICA. Mimeo.

Bailey, Michael. 2000. "Agricultural Trade and the Livelihoods of Small Farmers." Discussion Paper for DFID Toward Development of a White Paper on Globalisation. Oxford, UK: Oxfam GB.

Baloyra, Enrique. 1983. "Reactionary Despotism in El Salvador: An Impediment to Democratic Transition." In *Trouble in Our Backyard: Central America and the United States in the Eighties,* edited by Martin Diskin. New York: Pantheon.

Banco Central del Ecuador. 1985. *FODERUMA: Informe semestral.* Quito.

———. 1988. *Boletín estadístico de la provincia de Chimborazo* (Quito) 4.

Barragan, Valeria, and José L. Velasquez. 2000. "Continúa el drama migratorio." *Tiempos del Mundo* (March 16).

Barrera, Augusto, ed. 1999. "Ecuador: un modelo para [des]armar: descentralización, disparidades regionales y modo de desarrollo." Quito: CIUDAD.

227

Barril, Alex. 1980. "Desarrollo tecnológico, producción agropecuaria y relaciones de producción en la sierra ecuatoriana." In Osvaldo Barsky et al., *Ecuador: Cambios en el agro serrano*. Quito: FLACSO.

Barsky, Osvaldo. 1984a. *La reforma agraria ecuatoriana*. Quito: Corporación Editora Nacional.

———. 1984b. *Acumulación campesina en el Ecuador: Los productores de papa del Carchi*. Quito: FLACSO.

Barsky, Osvaldo, and Gustavo Cosse. 1981. *Tecnología y el cambio social*. Quito: FLACSO.

Bebbington, Anthony. 1990. *Indigenous Agriculture in the Central Andes: The Cultural Ecology and Institutional Conditions of Its Construction and Change*. Ph.D. dissertation, Clark University, Worcester, Massachusetts.

———. 1997a. "New States, New NGOs? Crises and Transitions Among Rural Development NGOs in the Andean Region." *World Development* 25, no. 1.

———. 1997b. "Reinventing NGOs and Rethinking Alternatives in the Andes." *Annals of the American Academy of Political and Social Science* 554.

———. 1999. "Capitals and Capabilities: A Framework for Analyzing Peasant Viability, Rural Livelihoods and Poverty." *World Development* 27, no. 12.

———. 2000. "Encountering Development: Livelihood Transitions and Place Transformations in the Andes." *Annals of the Association of American Geographers* 90, no. 3.

———. 2001. "Globalized Andes? Livelihoods, Landscapes, and Development." *Eucemene* 8, no. 3.

Bebbington, Anthony, et al. 1992. *Actores de Una Década Ganada: Tribus, Comunidades y Campesinos en la Modernidad*. Quito: COMUNIDEC.

Bebbington, Anthony, and Graham Thiele, with Penelope Davies, Martin Prager, and Hernando Riveros. 1993. *Non-governmental Organizations and the State in Latin America: Rethinking Roles in Sustainable Agricultural Development*. New York: Routledge.

Bebbington, Anthony, and Thomas Perrault. 1999. "Social Capital, Development, and Access to Resources in Highland Ecuador." *Economic Geography* 79, no. 4.

Beck, Scott H., and Kenneth Mijeski. 2001. "The *Pachakutik* Political Movement and the 1996 and 1998 Elections: A Closer Examination of the Effects of Regionalism and Ethnicity." Paper presented at the 2001 meetings of the Latin American Studies Association, Washington, D.C., September 6–8.

Bello, Walden, and Anuradha Mittal. 2001. "The Meaning of Doha." Bangkok: Focus on the Global South.

Berry, Albert. 1997. "The Income Distribution Threat in Latin America." *Latin American Research Review* 32, no. 2.

———, ed. 1998. *Poverty, Economic Reform, and Income Distribution in Latin America*. Boulder, Colo.: Lynne Rienner.

Bienefeld, Manfred. 1988. "Dependency Theory and the Political Economy of Africa's Crisis." *Review of African Political Economy* 14.

Birdsall, Nancy, and Richard Sabot. 1994. "Inequality as a Constraint on Growth in Latin America." *Development Policy.* Washington, D.C.: IDB (September).

Bloemkolk, Eric, and Jorge Salinas. 1994. "Las Empresas Comunitarias de Salinas: Una evaluación socio-económica." *Salinas, Ecuador: SNV Servicio Holandés de Cooperación al Desarrollo y Banco Interamericano de Desarrollo (January). Mimeo.

Bolens, Rutgard. 1995. "La nueva política de riego en el Ecuador." *Ecuador Debate* (Quito) 36.

Booth, John A. 1990. "Costa Rica: The Roots of Democratic Stability." In *Democracy in Developing Countries: Latin America*, edited by Larry Diamond, Juan J. Linz, and Seymour Martin Lipset. Boulder, Colo.: Lynne Rienner.

Bornstein, David. 1996. *The Price of a Dream: The Story of the Grameen Bank and the Idea That Is Helping the Poor to Change Their Lives.* New York: Simon & Schuster.

Boyce, James K., and Manuel Pastor Jr. 1996. "Macroeconomic Policy and Peace Building in El Salvador." In *Rebuilding Societies After Civil War*, edited by Krishna Kumar. Boulder, Colo.: Lynne Rienner.

Bretón Solo de Zaldívar, Victor. 2001. *Cooperación al desarrollo y demandas étnicas en los Andes ecuatorianos.* Quito: FLACSO Ecuador.

Bridges. 2001. "At Long Last, Implementation Debate Receives a Nudge." *Bridges Between Trade and Sustainable Development* 5, no. 5.

Bromley, Rosemary D. F. 1980. "El papel del comercio en el crecimiento de las ciudades de la sierra central del Ecuador, 1750–1920." *Revista Interamericana de Planificación* 14.

Brownrigg, Leslie Ann. 1972. "The Nobles of Cuenca: The Agrarian Elite of Southern Ecuador." Ph.D. dissertation, Columbia University.

Burki, Shahid Javed, and G. E. Perry. 1998. *Beyond the Washington Consensus: Institutions Matter.* Washington, D.C.: The World Bank.

Burns, E. Bradford. 1980. *The Poverty of Progress: Latin America in the Nineteenth Century.* Berkeley and Los Angeles: University of California Press.

CAAP (Centro Andino de Acción Popular). 1991. *Pre-diagnostico y estrategia de desarrollo de Cotacachi.* Quito: CAAP.

Camacho, Gloria, and Mercedes Prieto. 1997. Género y Desarrollo Rural: Manual de autocapacitacíon para operadores de proyectos." Quito: Dirección de la Mujer-MBS (Ministerio de Bienestar Social).

Camacho, Patricia. 1991. *Programa Regional Riobamba: Evaluación del crédito.* Quito: FEPP.

Cameron, John D., and Liisa L. North.1997. "Las asociaciones de granjeros y el desarollo agrícola en Taiwan." *Ecuador Debate* (Quito) 42.

Carrasco, Hernán. 1990. "Migración temporal en la sierra: Una estratégia de recampesinización." In *El campesinado contemporaneo*, edited by Fernando Botero. Bogota, Colombia: CEREC (Centro de studios de la Realidad Colombiana).

———. 1991. "Indígenas serranos en Quito y Guayaquil: relaciones interétnicas y urbanización de migrantes." *América Indígena* 51, no. 4.

————. 1997. "Población indígena, población mestiza y la democratización de los poderes locales en Chimborazo, Ecuador." In *Pueblos indígenas y poderes locales*, edited by Sebastian Cox. Santiago de Chile: Red Interamericana de Agricultura y Democracia.

Carroll, Thomas. 1992. *Intermediary NGOs: The Supporting Link in Grassroots Development*. West Hartford, Conn.: Kumarian Press.

Carroll, Thomas, and Anthony J. Bebbington. 2000. "Peasant Federations and Rural Development Policies in the Andes." *Policy Sciences* 33.

Carter, M., B. Bradford, and D. Mesbah. 1996. "Agricultural Export Booms and the Rural Poor in Chile, Guatemala and Paraguay." *Latin American Research Review* 31, no. 1.

Casagrande, Joseph B. 1981. "Strategies for Survival: The Indians of Highland Ecuador." In *Cultural Transformations and Ethnicity in Modern Ecuador*, edited by Norman E. Whitten Jr. Urbana, Ill.: University of Illinois Press.

Cassidy, J. 1997. "The Return of Karl Marx." *The New Yorker* 73 (October), 20–27.

Centero, Pablo 1998. "Fin del milagro del jean." *Hoy* (March 27).

Cervone, Emma. 1996. *The Return of Atahualpa: Ethnic Conflict and Indian Movement in Ecuadorian Andes*. Ph.D. dissertation, St. Andrews University (Scotland).

————. 1999. "Racismo y vida cotidiana: las tácticas de la defensa étnica." In *Ecuador Racista: Imágenes e identidades*, edited by Emma Cervone and Fredy Rivera. Quito: FLACSO.

CELA (Centro de Estudios Latinoamericanos de la Pontificia Universidad Católica del Ecuador). 2001. "Evaluación de los Impactos Económicos y Sociales de las Políticas de Ajuste Estructural en el Ecuador, 1982–1991." Quito: SAPRI [Structural Adjustment Participatory Review Initiative]-Ecuador (February). Mimeo.

CESA. 1997. *El campesinado de Chimborazo: situación actual y perspectivas*. Quito: CESA.

Chiriboga, Manuel. 1988. "La reforma agraria ecuatoriana y los cambios en la distribución de la propiedad rural agricola, 1974–1985." In *Transformaciones agrarias en el Ecuador*, edited by Pierre Gondard et al. Quito: Geografia Básica del Ecuador.

————. 1995. "Las ONGs y el desarollo rural en los países andinos: Dilemnas y desafios." In *Desarrollo rural en los Andes*, edited by Manuel Chiriboga. Quito: CAAP.

————. 2001. "El levantamiento indígena ecuatoriano de 2001: una interpretación." *Iconos: Revista de FLACSO-Sede Ecuador* 10 (April).

Chiriboga, Manuel, et al. 1999. *Cambiar se puede: Experiencias del FEPP en el desarrollo rural del Ecuador*. Quito: FEPP/Abya-Yala.

CIDA (Comité Interamerican de Desarrollo Agricola). 1965. *Tenencia de la tierra y desarrollo socio-economico del sector agricola: Ecuador*. Washington, D.C.: Unión Panamericana.

Cismondi, Oscar. 1994. "Conclusiones del Seminario." *Debate Agrario* (Lima) 20.

Clarke, Tony, and Maude Barlow. 1997. *MAI: The Multilateral Agreement on Investment and the Threat to Canadian Sovereignty.* Toronto: Stoddart.

Colburn, Forrest D. 1993. "Exceptions to Urban Bias in Latin America: Cuba and Costa Rica." *The Journal of Development Studies* 29, no. 4.

Conaghan, Catherine M. 1988. *Restructuring Domination: Industrialists and the State in Ecuador.* Pittsburgh: University of Pittsburgh Press.

———. 1996. "A Deficit of Democratic Authenticity: Political Linkage and the Public in Andean Politics." *Studies in Comparative International Development* 31, no. 3 (Fall).

Conaghan, Catherine M., and James M. Malloy. 1994. *Unsettling Statecraft: Democracy and Neoliberalism in the Andes.* Pittsburgh: University of Pittsburgh Press.

Crespo, Carlos, and Peter Bischof. 1991. *Informe de evaluación. Programa Regional Riobamba. Primera Fase.* Quito: FEPP. Mimeo.

Cueva, Augustin. 1982. *The Process of Political Domination in Ecuador*, trans. Danielle Salti. New Brunswick, N.J.: Transaction Books.

Dandler, Jorge. 1999. "Indigenous Peoples and the Rule of Law in Latin America: Do They Have a Chance?" In *The (Un)Rule of Law and the Underprivileged in Latin America*, edited by Juan E. Méndez, Guillermo O'Donnell, and Paulo Sérgio Pinheiro. Notre Dame, Ind.: University of Notre Dame Press.

Dávalos, M. V. 1996. "Censo Empresarial en Pelileo. Documento Elaborado como Parte del Estudio 'Pelileo, un Distrito Empresarial.'" Quito: INSOTEC (December). Mimeo.

de Janvry, Alain. 1982. *The Agrarian Question and Reformism in Latin America.* Baltimore, Md.: Johns Hopkins University Press.

———. 1994. "Reformas en las áreas económica y social: el desafío de un crecimiento equitativo en la agricultura de América Latina." *Políticas Agrícolas* 1, no. 0.

de Janvry, Alain, and Elisabeth Sadoulet. 2000. "Making Investment in the Rural Poor into Good Business: New Perspectives from Rural Development in Latin America." Paper presented to the Conference on Developing the Rural Economy and Reducing Poverty in Latin America and the Caribbean, annual governor's meeting of the IDB, New Orleans, March 24.

de Janvry, Alain, Elisabeth Sadoulet, and Linda Wilcox Young. 1989. "Land and Labour in Latin American Agriculture from the 1950s to the 1980s." *Journal of Peasant Studies* 16, no. 3.

Demery, Lionel, and Michael Walton. 1998. "Are Poverty Reduction and Other Twenty-first Century Social Goals Attainable?" Washington, D.C.: The World Bank.

de la Torre Espinosa, Carlos. 1996. *El racismo en el Ecuador: Experiencias de los indios de clase media.* Quito: CAAP.

DCTR *(Denuncias de conflicto de tierra rural).* 1990–2001, various. Quito: Comisión Ecuménica de Derechos Humanos.

DDP, *Derechos del Pueblo.* Various 1990–2001. Quito: Comisión Ecuménica de Derechos Humanos.

Donnelly, Jack. 1984. "Human Rights and Development: Complementary or Competing Concerns?" *World Politics* 36, no. 2 (January).

Dourejeanni, A. 1993. "No a la privatización de la propiedad del agua." *Agronoticias* (Lima) 160.

Dreze, Jean, and Amartya Sen. 1989. *Hunger and Public Action.* Oxford: Clarendon Press.

Dubly, Alain, and Alicia Granda. 1991. *Desalojos y despojos (Los conflictos agrarios en Ecuador 1983–1990).* Quito: Editorial El Conejo/CEDHU.

Echeverría, Rubén G. 2000a. "Un creciente interés en lograr mercados de tierras rurales más efectivos." *Políticas Agrícolas* (Bogota).

———. 2000b. "Opciones para reducir la pobreza rural en America Latina y el Caribe." *Revista de la CEPAL* 70 (April).

Ecofuturo. 1990. *Diagnóstico social, económico y físico: Provincia de Chimborazo.* Mimeo.

The Economist. 2001. "Patches of Light: Special Report on Agricultural Trade" (June 9). 81–83.

Economist Intelligence Unit. 2001. "Country Forecast: Ecuador" (June).

Edwards, Michael, and David Hulme. 1995. *Non-Governmental Organizations—Performance and Accountability.* London: Earthscan/Save the Children.

Einarsson, Peter. 2000. "Agricultural Trade Policy as if Food Security and Ecological Sustainability Mattered." Stockholm: Church of Sweden Aid, Forum Syd, and the Swedish Society for Nature Conservation.

Escobal, Javier. 1994. "Impacto de las políticas de ajuste sobre la pequeña agricultura." *Debate Agrario* (Lima), 20.

Escobar, Arturo. 1995. *Encountering Development: The Making and Unmaking of the Third World.* Princeton, N.J.: Princeton University Press.

Evans, Peter. 1987. "Class, State, and Dependence in East Asia: Lessons for Latin Americanists." In *The Political Economy of the New Asian Industrialism,* edited by Frederic C. Deyo. Ithaca, N.Y.: Cornell University Press.

———. 1996. "Government Action, Social Capital and Development: Reviewing the Evidence on Synergy." *World Development* 14, no. 6.

Fajnsylber, Fernando. 1990. "The United States and Japan as Models of Industrialization." In *Manufacturing Miracles: Paths of Industrialization in Latin America and East Asia,* edited by Gary Gereffi and Donald L. Wyman. Princeton, N.J.: Princeton University Press.

FAO (United Nations Food and Agriculture Organization). 1995. *El desarrollo agrícola en el nuevo marco macro-económico de América Latina.* Santiago de Chile: FAO.

———. 1996. *Rome Declaration on World Food Security.* Rome: FAO.

———. 1999. "Experience with the Implementation of the Uruguay Round Agreement on Agriculture—Developing Country Experiences." Paper presented to the FAO Symposium on Agriculture, Trade, and Food Security: Issues and Options in the Forthcoming WTO Negotiations from the Perspective of Developing Countries, Geneva, September 23-24.

———. 2001. The State of Food and Agriculture. Rome: FAO.

————. 1987. *Programa Regional Riobamba. Apoyo al autodesarrollo campesino.* Riobamba, Ecuador: FEPP. Mimeo.

————. 1992. *Programa Regional Riobamba. Segunda Fase.* Riobamba, Ecuador: FEPP. Mimeo.

————. 1995. *Programa Regional Riobamba. Segunda Fase. Informe de evaluación final.* Riobamba, Ecuador: FEPP. Mimeo.

————. 1996a. *Proyecto de desarrollo agropecuario, pequeña agroindustria y uso racional de la tierra adquirida por organizaciones campesinas de Guamote y Tixán en la provincia de Chimborazo.* Riobamba, Ecuador: FEPP. Mimeo.

————. 1996b. *Proyecto de desarrollo agropecuario y pequeña agroindustria en las tierra adquiridas por los campesinos de Chimborazo y Tungurahua.* Riobamba, Ecuador: FEPP. Mimeo.

————. 1999a. *Informe anual 1998.* Quito: FEPP.

————. 1999b. *Informe de evaluación Proyecto Desarrollo agropecuario y pequeña industria en las tierras adquiridas por los campesinos de Chimborazo y Tungurahua.* Riobamba, Ecuador: FEPP. Mimeo.

Fei, John C. H., Gustav Ranis, and Shirley W. Y. Kuo. 1979. *Growth with Equity: The Taiwan Case.* London: Oxford University Press.

Fishlow, Albert, et al. 1994. *Miracle or Design? Lessons from the East Asian Experience.* Washington, D.C.: Overseas Development Council.

FLACSO-IICA. 1994. *Los Andes en cifras.* Quito: FLACSO/IICA.

Flora, Cornelia B. 1995. "Social Capital and Sustainability: Agricultural Communities in the Great Plains and Corn Belt." Journal Paper No. J16309. Ames, Iowa: Iowa Agriculture and Home Economics Experiment Station.

Flores, Ruben. 1996. "Diagnostico de los Gremios de Productores Agropecuarios: Una Propuesta de Trabajo para el Fortelecimiento de los Mismos." *Programa Sector Agricola.* Quito: FLACSO.

Forster, Nancy R. 1989. "*Minifundistas* in Tungurahua, Ecuador: Survival on the Agricultural Ladder." In *Searching for Agrarian Reform in Latin America*, edited by William C. Thiesenhusen. Boston: Unwin Hyman.

————. 1990. "Struggle for Land and Livelihood: Peasant Differentiation and Survival During the Agrarian Transition in Tungurahua, Ecuador." Ph.D. dissertation, University of Wisconsin.

Fox, Jonathan. 1994. "Latin America's Emerging Local Politics." *Journal of Democracy* 5, no. 2.

Fox, Jonathan, and L. David Brown, eds. 1998. *The Struggle for Accountability: The World Bank, NGOs, and Grassroots Movements.* Cambridge, Mass.: The MIT Press.

Freire, Segundo, Oskar Purschert, and Francisco Rhon Dávila. 1991. "Proyecto Queserías Rurales: diagnóstico ex-post." Final report for the FEPP. Quito (March-April).

FUNDAGRO. 1996. *Regularización, tenencia de tierras y aguas.* Final conference report. Quito. Mimeo.

Galli, Rosemary E. 1981. "Rural Development and the Contradictions of Capitalist Development." In *The Political Economy of Rural Development*, edited by Rosemary Galli. Albany, N.Y.: State University of New York Press.

Gangotena, Francisco, et al. 1980. "Apreciaciones preliminares sobre la incidencia de la disolución de la hacienda tradicional en la estructura agraria: el caso Guamote." *Revista de la Universidad Catolica* (Quito) 8, no. 26.

García, Fernando S. 2001. "Un levantamiento indigena mas? A proposito de los sucesos de febrero 2001." *Íconos—Revista de FLACSO—Ecuador* (Quito) 10 (April).

García, Nancy, María Eugenio, and Nancy Navarrete. 1993. "Producción y comercialización del jeans en el canton Pelileo y su incidencia en los ambitos de su geografía económica." Bachelor's thesis, Technical University of Ambato, Ecuador.

Gobierno del Ecuador. 2001. *Ley de Desarrollo Agrario*. Quito: Corporación de Ediciones y Publicaciones.

Gonzalez de Olarte, Efrain. 1988. Modernización a paso de tortuga. Economía campesina en el Perú. *Nueva Sociedad* 96 (Caracas).

Green, Duncan, and Shishir Priyadarshi. 2001. "Proposal for a 'Development Box' in the WTO Agreement on Agriculture." London: Catholic Fund for Overseas Development.

Griffin, Keith. 1983. "Sistemas de control laboral y probreza rural en Ecuador." In *Concentración de Tierras y Pobreza Rural*. México: Fondo de Cultura Económica.

———. 1989. *Alternative Strategies for Economic Development. Economic Choices for the Developing Countries*. London: MacMillan with OECD Development Centre.

Grindle, Merilee S. 1986. *State and Countryside: Development Policy and Agrarian Politics in Latin America*. Baltimore, Md.: Johns Hopkins University Press.

Grinspun, Ricardo, and Robert Kreklewich. 1994. "Consolidating Neoliberal Reforms: 'Free Trade' as a Conditioning Framework." *Studies in Political Economy* 43 (Spring).

Grundmann, Gesa. 1995. *De peones a propietarios. Hacia un mejor aprovechamiento de los recursos y potenciales por grupos campesinos en Guamote, provincia de Chimborazo, Ecuador*. Berlin: Center for Advanced Studies in Rural Development, University of Humbolt.

Grunenfelder-Elliker, Barbara. 2001. "Exclusion to the Point of Attrition. Gendered Emigration from Ecuador at a Crossroads." Paper presented at the Twenty-Third International Congress of the Latin American Studies Association, Washington, D.C., September 6–8.

Grzybowski, Cándido. 1990. "Rural Workers and Democratization in Brazil." *Journal of Development Studies* 26, no. 4.

Gudynas, Eduardo. 2001. "Multifuncionalidad y desarrollo agropecuario sustentable." *Nueva Sociedad* (Caracas) 174.

Guerrero, Andrés. 1983. *Haciendas, capital y lucha de clases andina*. Quito: El Conejo.

Guevara, Dario. 1945. *La Puerta de El Dorado: Monografía del Cantón Pelileo.* Quito: Editora Moderna.

Hamerschlag, Kari. 2001. "Echoes from a Not Too Distant, Destructive Past? US Government and International Financial Institutions' Policies and Programs in Latin America and the Caribbean: Opportunities for Influence Today." Washington, D.C.: Action Aid USA (June).

Handelman, Howard. 1981. "Ecuadorian Agrarian Reform: The Politics of Limited Change," in *The Politics of Agrarian Change in Asia and Latin America*, edited by Howard Handelman. Bloomington, Ind.: Indiana University Press.

Haney, Emil B., and Wava G. Haney. 1984. *La transformación de la estructura agraria en la provincia de Chimborazo.* Madison, Wis.: Land Tenure Center, University of Wisconsin.

———. 1989. "The Agrarian Transition in Highland Ecuador: From Precapitalism to Agrarian Capitalism in Chimborazo." In *Searching for Agrarian Reform in Latin America*, edited by William Thiesenhusen. Boston: Unwin Hyman.

———. 1990. "La transición agraria en la sierra del Ecuador. Del semifeudalismo al capitalismo en Chimborazo." In *Ecuador Debate* (Quito) 20.

Hansen, David P. 1971. "Political Decision Making in Ecuador: The Influence of Business Groups." Ph.D. dissertation, University of Florida.

Healy, Kevin. 2001. *Llamas, Weavings, and Organic Chocolate: Multicultural Grassroots Development in the Andes and Amazon of Bolivia.* Notre Dame, Ind.: University of Notre Dame Press.

Hewitt de Alcantara, Cynthia. 1993. "Introduction: Markets in Principle and Practice." In *Real Markets: Social and Political Issues of Food Policy Reform*, edited by C. Hewitt de Alcantara. London: Frank Cass.

Holcombe, Susan. 1995. *Managing to Empower: The Grameen Bank's Experience of Poverty Alleviation.* London: Zed Books.

Hoy (Quito). 1997. "Tungurahua, cae la microempresa" (April 7), 7A.

Hulme, David, and Michael Edwards, eds. 1997. *NGOs, States and Donors: Too Close for Comfort?* London: MacMillan Press Ltd.

Hulme, David, and Paul Mosley. 1996. *Finance Against Poverty.* London and New York: Routledge.

Human Rights Watch. 2002. *Tainted Harvest: Child Labor and Obstacles to Organizing on Ecuador's Banana Plantations.* New York: Human Rights Watch.

Ibarra, Hernán. 1987. "Tierra, mercado y capital comercial en la sierra central: el caso de Tungurahua (1850–1930)." Master's thesis, FLACSO, Quito.

IDB (Inter-American Development Bank). 1996. Hacia dónde vas, América Latina? *El Bid.* Septiembre-Octubre.

INEC (Instituto Nacional de Estadísticas y Censos). 1954. *Primer censo agropecuario, 1954.* Quito: INEC.

———. 1974. *Segundo censo agropecuario, 1974.* Quito: INEC.

Ingco, Merlinda D. 1996. "Progress in Agricultural Trade Liberalization and Welfare of Least-Developed Countries." Washington, D.C.: International Trade Division, World Bank.

Iturralde, Diego A. 1980. *Guamote: campesinos y comunas.* Otavalo, Ecuador: Instituto Otavaleño de Antropología.

Jaramillo, Carlos Felipe. 2000. "El mercado rural de tierras en América Latina: hacia una nueva estrategia." *Políticas Agrícolas* (Bogota).

Jokisch, Brad D. 2001. "From New York to Madrid: A Description of Recent Trends in Ecuadorian Emigration." Paper presented at the Twenty-Third International Congress of the Latin American Studies Association, Washington, D.C., September 6-8.

Jonas, Susanne. 2000. *Of Centaurs and Doves: Guatemala's Peace Process.* Boulder, Colo.: Westview Press.

Jordán Bucheli, Fausto. 1988. *El minifundio: Su evolución en el Ecuador.* Quito: Corporación Editora Nacional.

Josling, Tim. 1999. "Developing Countries and the New Round of Multilateral Trade Negotiations: Background Notes on Agriculture." Paper presented at the workshop "Developing Countries and the New Round of Multilateral Trade Negotiations," Harvard University, Cambridge, Massachusetts, November 5-6.

Kahn, Joseph. 2001. "US Scientists See Big Power Savings from Conservation," *The New York Times,* May 6, sec. 1, p. 1.

Kay, Cristóbal. 1995. "Rural Development and Agrarian Issues in Contemporary Latin America." In *Structural Adjustment and the Agricultural Sector in Latin America and the Caribbean,* edited by John Weeks. New York: St. Martin's Press.

———. 1998. "Latin America's Agrarian Reform: Lights and Shadows." *Land Reform, Land Settlement and Cooperatives* 2.

———. 2001a. "Asia's and Latin America's Development in Comparative Perspective: Landlords, Peasants, and Industrialization." Working Paper Series No. 336. The Hague: Institute of Social Studies.

———. 2001b. "Reflections on Rural Violence in Latin America." *Third World Quarterly* 55, no. 2.

Korovkin, Tanya. 1990. *Politics of Agricultural Co-Operativism: Peru, 1969–1983.* Vancouver, B.C.: University of British Columbia Press.

———. 1997. "Indigenous Peasant Struggles and the Capitalist Modernization of Agriculture: Chimborazo, 1964–1991." *Latin American Perspectives* 24, no. 3 (May).

———. 1998. "Commodity Production and Ethnic Culture: Otavalo, Northern Ecuador." *Economic Development and Cultural Change* 47, no. 1.

———. 2000. "Weak Weapons, Strong Weapons? Hidden Resistance and Political Protest in Highland Ecuador." *Journal of Peasant Studies* 27, no. 3 (April).

———. 2001. "Reinventing the Communal Tradition: Indigenous Peoples, Civil Society, and Democratization in Andean Ecuador." *Latin American Research Review* 36, no. 3.

———. 2003. "Cut Flower Exports, Female Labor, and Community Participation." *Latin American Perspectives* (forthcoming).

Kowalchuk, Lisa. 2000. "In the Eye of the Beholder: Politics and Perception in the Salvadorean Peasant Movement." Ph.D. dissertation, York University, Toronto.

Krishna, Anirudh, and Roland Bunch. 1997. "Farmer-to-Farmer Experimentation and Extension: Integral Rural Development for Smallholders in Guatemala." In *Reasons for Hope: Instructive Experiences in Rural Development*, edited by Anirudh Krishna, Norman Uphoff, and Milton J. Esman. West Hartford, Conn.: Kumarian Press.

Krishna, Anirudh, Norman Uphoff, and Milton J. Esman, eds. 1997. *Reasons for Hope: Instructive Experiences of Rural Development*. West Hartford, Conn.: Kumarian Press.

Krupa, Chris. 2001. "Producing Neoliberal Spaces: Labour and Community in Ecuador's Cut-Flower Sector." Paper presented at the 2001 meetings of the Latin American Studies Association, Washington, D.C., September 6–8.

Kuo, Shirley, Gustav Ranis, and John C. H. Fei. 1981. *The Taiwan Success Story: Rapid Growth with Improved Distribution in the Republic of China, 1952–1979*. Boulder, Colo.: Westview Press.

Kuznets, Simon. 1955. "Economic Growth and Income Inequality." *American Economic Review* 48, no. 3.

Landsberger, Henry A., ed. 1969. *Latin American Peasant Movements*. Ithaca, N.Y.: Cornell University Press.

Lanjouw, Peter. 1998. "Ecuador's Rural Nonfarm Sector as a Route Out of Poverty, Policy Research Working Paper 1904." Washington, D.C.: The World Bank (March).

Larrea, Carlos. 1992. "The Mirage of Development: Oil, Employment, and Poverty in Ecuador (1970–1990)." Doctoral dissertation, York University.

———. 1998a. "Structural Adjustment, Income Distribution, and Employment in Ecuador." In *Poverty, Economic Reform, and Income Distribution in Latin America*, edited by Albert Berry. Boulder, Colo.: Lynne Rienner.

———. 1998b. "La pequeña y mediana empresa en el contexto de la apertura comercial, ajuste y crisis en el Ecuador." Paper presented to the workshop entitled "Pequeña y mediana empresa, mercados laborales y distribución de ingreso en América Latina y el Caribe." Buenos Aires: University of Toronto. Mimeo.

Larrea, Carlos, and Liisa L. North. 1997. "Ecuador: Adjustment Policy Impacts on Truncated Development and Democratization." *Third World Quarterly* 18, no. 5.

Larrea, Carlos, and Jeannette Sánchez. 2002. "Desarrollo Humano y Políticas Sociales en el Ecuador: Una Propuesta Alternativa." Quito: PNUD.

Larrea, Carlos, et al. 1987. *El Banano en El Ecuador: Transnacionales, Modernización Subdesarrollo*. Quito: FLACSO/Corporación Editora Nacional.

————. 1996. *La Geografía de la Pobreza en el Ecuador.* Quito: Secretaría Técnica del Frente Social.

Lefeber, Louis. 1968. "Planning in a Surplus Labor Economy." *American Economic Review* 58 (June).

————. 1974a. "The Paradigm of Economic Development." *World Development* 2, no. 1.

————. 1974b. "Critique of Development Planning in Private Enterprise Economies." *Indian Economic Review,* NS no. 2.

————. 1990. Review of *The Latin American Debt,* by P. P. Kuczynski, *Economic Development and Cultural Change* (April).

————. 1992. "What Remains of Development Economics?" *The Indian Economic Review* 27.

————. 1993. "Review of the Life and Political Economy of Lauchlin Currie by Roger J. Sandilands." *Economic Development and Cultural Change* 42, no. 1 (October).

————. 1997. "Trade, Employment, and the Rural Economy." In *Ciudad y campo en América Latina,* edited by M. Yamada. Osaka, Japan: The Japan Center for Area Studies.

————. 1998. "Políticas agrícolas y desarrollo rural en el Ecuador: con referencia a Morris D. Whitaker." *Ecuador Debate* (Quito) 43.

————. 2000. "Classical vs. Neoclassical Economic Thought in Historical Perspective: The Interpretation of Processes of Economic Growth and Development." *History of Political Thought,* 21, no. 3.

Lehmann, David. 1986a. "Two Paths of Agrarian Capitalism, or a Critique of Chayanovian Marxism." *Comparative Studies in Society and History* 28, no. 4.

————. 1986b. "Sharecropping and the Capitalist Transition in Agriculture: Some Evidence from the Highlands of Ecuador." *Journal of Development Economics* 23.

León, Jorge. 1994. *De campesinos a ciudadanos diferentes.* Quito: Abya-Yala.

————. 1998. "Contexte social et cycle politique: les ONG en Équateur." In *ONG et développment. Société, économie, politique,* edited by J. P. Deler et al. Paris: Karthala.

————. 2001. "Conflicto etnico, democracia y Estado." *Íconos—Revista de FLACSO—Ecuador* (Quito) 10 (April).

León, Jorge, and Guadalupe Tobar. 1984. "Zona Salinas-Guanujo." In *La Situación de los Campesinos en Ocho Zonas del Ecuador,* vol. 2, edited by Alain Dubly. Quito: ALOP (Latin American Association of Promotion Organizations)-CESA-CONADE (National Development Council, Government of Ecuador)-FAO-MAG-SEDRI (Secretariat of Integrated Rural Development).

Lentz, Carola. 1987. *Migración e identidad etnica: la tranformación historica de una comunidad indígena en la sierra ecuatoriana.* Quito: Abya-Yala.

Levy, Santiago, and Sweder van Wijnbergen. 1992. "Maize and the Free Trade Agreement Between Mexico and the United States." *The World Bank Economic Review* 6, no. 1.

Lipton, Michael. 1977. *Why Poor People Stay Poor.* London: Temple Smith.

Llambi, Luis. 1990. "El proceso de transformación del campesinado latinoamericano." In *El campesino contemporaneo*, edited by Fernando Botero. Bogotá, Colombia: CEREC (Centro de studios de la Realidad Colombiana).

Lobe, Jim. 2001. "Learn from Cuba Says World Bank." Interpress Third World News Agency (April 30).

MacLeod, Greg. 1997. "From Mondragon to America: Experiments in Community Economic Development." Sydney, Nova Scotia: University College of Cape Breton Press.

Madeley, John. 1999. *Trade and the Hungry: How International Trade Is Causing Hunger.* Brussels: Association of World Council of Churches–related Development Organizations in Europe (APRODEV).

———. 2000. *Trade and Hunger: An Overview of Case Studies on the Impact of Trade Liberalization on Food Security.* Stockholm: Forum Syd.

MAG (Ministerio de Agricultura y Ganadería). 1983. *Guamote: estudio socioeconómico.* Quito: MAG.

Martínez Flores, Alexandra. 2001. "Voces de los pobres en Ecuador. Perspectivas de bienestar y opniones para el cambio." Quito: CEPLAES/Banco Mundial Poverty Group.

Martínez, Luciano. 1985. "Articulación mercantil de las comunidades indígenas en la sierra ecuatoriana." In *Economía política del Ecuador: Campo, región, nación*, edited by Louis Lefeber. Quito: Corporación Editora Nacional.

———. 1992. "El levantamiento indígena, la lucha por la tierra y el proyecto alternativo." *Cuadernos de la Realidad Ecuatoriana 5.*

———. 1993. "Los asalariados temporales agrícolas. El caso ecuatoriano." In *Los pobres del campo: el trabajador eventual*, edited by Sergio Gómez and Emilio Klein. Santiago, Chile: FLACSO-PREALC.

———. 1994. *Los Campesinos-Artesanos en la Sierra Central: El Caso Tungurahua.* Quito: CAAP.

———. 1995. "Tipología de productores rurales." Quito: CAAP. Mimeo.

———. 1997. "Organizaciones de segundo grado, capital social y desarrollo sostenible." *Íconos* (Quito) 2.

———. 1999. Respuestas endógenas y alternativas de los campesinos frente al ajuste: el caso Ecuador. In *Los límites del desarrollo. Modelos "rotos" y modelos "por construir" en América Latina y África*, ed. Víctor Bretón, Francisco García, and Albert Roca. Barcelona: Icaria, Institut Català d'Antropología.

———. 2000a. *Economías rurales: Actividades rurales no agrícolas en Ecuador.* Quito: CAAP.

———. 2000b. "Caracterización de la situación de la tenencia y regularización de la tierra. Informe sobre el estudio." Quito: PSA-IICA. Mimeo.

Martínez, Luciano, ed. 2000c. *Antología de Estudios Rurales.* Quito: FLACSO.

Martínez, Luciano, and Alex Barril. 1995. *Desafíos del desarrollo rural frente a la modernización económica.* Quito: IICA.

Martínez, Luciano, and Rafael Urriola. 1994. "El impacto del ajuste en el agro ecuatoriano." *Debate Agrario* (Lima) 20.

Mayoux, Linda. 1995. "From Vicious to Virtuous Circles? Gender and Micro-Enterprise Development." Occasional Paper No. 3. UN Fourth World Conference on Women (May).

McCulloch, Neil, Alan Winters, and Xavier Cirera. 2001. *Trade Liberalization and Poverty: A Handbook.* London: Centre for Economic Policy Research and Department for International Development.

McNeill, M. K. 1998. "How the West Won." *The New York Review of Books* (April).

Mead, Donald C., and Carl Liedholm. 1998. "The Dynamics of Micro and Small Enterprises in Developing Countries." *World Development* 26, no. 1.

Meier, Peter, and Francisco Rhon Dávila. 1984. "Evaluación del Proyecto Queserias Rurales en Ecuador." Final report. Quito: Cooperación Técnica del Gobierno Suizo (COTESU).

Mena, Norma. 1999. *Impacto de la floricultura en los campesinos de Cayambe.* Quito: IEDECA.

Merino Salom, Jorge Roberto. 1998. "Evaluación de la administración de cuatro agroindustrias comunitarias, en la Cabecera Parroquial de Salinas, provincia de Bolívar, Ecuador." Thesis. Honduras: Departamento de Desarrollo Rural del Zamorano.

Miller, Morris. 1986. *Coping Is Not Enough.* Oxford: Oxford University Press.

Ministerio del Frente Social. 2000. *SIISE: Sistema Integrado de Indicadores Sociales del Ecuador.* Quito. Ministerio del Frente Social.

Miño Grijalva, Wilson. 1985. *Haciendas y pueblos en la sierra ecuatoriana: el caso de la provincia de Carchi, 1881–1980.* Quito: FLACSO.

Montoya, Rodrigo. 1989. *Lucha por la tierra, reformas agrarias y capitalismo en el Perú del siglo XX.* Lima, Peru: Mosca Azul.

Moore Jr., Barrington. 1966. *Social Origins of Dictatorship and Democracy: Lord and Peasant in the Making of the Modern World.* Boston: Beacon Press.

Moreno Yañez, Segundo, and José Figueroa. 1992. *El Levantamiento Indígena de Inti-Raymi.* Quito: Abya-Yala.

Municipalidad de Bolívar. 1997. "Plan de desarrollo del Cantón Bolívar, Carchi." Quito: Asociación de Municipalidades Ecuatorianas.

Municipalidad de Guamote. 1999. "Plan participativo de desarrollo del canton Guamote." Unpublished draft (November).

Muratorio, Blanca. 1980. "Protestantism and Capitalism Revisisted in Rural Highland Ecuador." *Journal of Peasant Studies* 8, no. 1.

———. ed. 1994. *Imágenes e Imagineros. Representaciones de los indígenas ecuatorianos, Siglos SIX y XX.* Quito: FLACSO, Sede Ecuador.

Murray, Gerald F. 1997. "A Haitian Peasant Tree Chronicle: Adaptive Evolution and Institutional Intrusion." In Krishna et al. 1997.

Muyulema Calle, Armando. 1997. *La Quema de Nucanchic Huasi (1994), los rostros discursivos del conflicto social en Cañar.* Master's thesis, Universidad Andina Simón Bolívar, Quito.

Naranjo Bonilla, Mariana. 1995. "Organización, Gestión, y Administración del Modelo de Desarrollo Empresarial Comunitario de la FUNORSAL." In "Guía para el conocimiento de la organización y gestión de la

FUNORSAL," edited by Galo Ramón Valarezo, Gustavo Ortiz Hidalgo, and Mariana Naranjo Bonilla. Proyecto "Desarrollo Forestal Campesino" (DEC-FAO Holanda) y Fundación de Organizaciones de Salinas. Salinas, Ecuador (January). Mimeo.

Navarro, Wilson, Alonso Vallejo, and Xavier Villaverde. 1996. *Tierra para la vida: acceso de los campesinos ecuatorianos a la tierra, opcion y experiencias del FEPP.* Quito: FEPP.

Navas, Mónica. 1998. "Ley de desarrollo agrario y la tenencia de tierras en el Ecuador." *Ecuador Debate* (Quito) 45.

NGO Group. 2000. "Towards Reducing Hunger by Half: A Canadian NGO Proposal for Canadian Aid." Ottawa: Canadian NGO Food Security Working Group.

Nickson, R. Andrew. 1995. *Local Government in Latin America.* Boulder, Colo.: Lynne Rienner.

North, Liisa L. 1985. "Implementación de la política económica y la estructura del poder político en el Ecuador." In *Economía, Política del Ecuador: Campo, Región, Nación,* edited by Louis Lefeber. Quito: Corporación Editora Nacional.

———. 1997. "Qué Pasó en Taiwan? Un Relato de la Reforma Agraria y de la Industrialización Rural." In *El Desarrollo Sostenible en el Medio Rural,* edited by Luciano Martínez. Quito: FLACSO-Ecuador.

———. 1999. "El Programa de Salinas: Una experiencia de desarrollo microregional." In *Cambiar se puede: Experiencias del FEPP en el desarrollo rural del Ecuador,* edited by Manuel Chiriboga et al. Quito: FEPP/Abya-Yala.

———. 2001. "Estrategias comunitarias de desarrollo rural en un contexto de políticas neoliberales: el case de Salinas desde una perspectiva comparativa." In *Realidad y desafíos de la economía solidaria: Iniciativas comunitarias y cooperativas en el Ecuador,* edited by Giuseppina Da Ros. Quito: Pontificia Universidad Católica del Ecuador & Abya-Yala.

North, Liisa L., and John D. Cameron. 2000. "Grassroots-Based Rural Development Strategies: Ecuador in Comparative Perspective." *World Development* 28, no. 10.

North, Liisa L., Wade A. Kit, and Rob Koep. 2003. "Rural Land Conflicts and Human Rights Violations in Ecuador." Working Paper. Toronto: Centre for Research on Latin America and the Caribbean, York University.

ODEPLAN (Oficina de Planificación de la Presidencia de la Republica). 1999. *Desarollo social y gestión municipal en el Ecuador: Jerarquización y tipologías.* Quito: Secretaría General de la Presidencia.

Ojeda Segovia, Lautaro. 2000. *La descentralización en el Ecuador: Avatares de un proceso inconcluso.* Quito: CEPLAES.

Ortiz Crespo, Gonzalo. 2000. "Esquema de la historia económica del Ecuador en el siglo XX, second part." *Gestión* 68.

Oxfam GB. 2000. "Make Trade Work for the Poor." Position paper on UNCTAD, on the occasion of its tenth conference in Bangkok.

Pacari, Nina. 1996. "Taking on the Neoliberal Agenda." *NACLA Report on the Americas* 29, no. 5 (March-April).

Padilla, Washington. 1989. *Dioses modernos: protestantismo en el Ecuador*. Quito: Corporación Editora Nacional.

Paige, Jeffrey M. 1975. "Agrarian Revolutions: Social Movements and Export Agriculture in the Underdeveloped World." New York: Free Press.

———. 1997. "Coffee and Power: Revolution and the Rise of Democracy in Central America." Cambridge, Mass. and London: Harvard University Press.

Paniagua, Alberto. 1992. "Estado y desarrollo rural: Historia de un difícil encuentro." *Debate Agrario* (Lima) 13.

Paré, Louisa. 1990. "The Challenge of Rural Democratization in Mexico." *Journal of Development Studies* 26, no. 4.

Petras, James. 1997. "Imperialism and NGOs in Latin America." *Monthly Review* 49, no. 7.

———. 2000. *La izquierda contratada: Conflicto de clases en América Latina en la era del neoliberalismo*. Madrid: Akal.

Phillips, Wendy. 2000. *Food Security: A First Step Toward More Fair Trade*. Mississauga, Ontario: World Vision Canada.

Plant, Roger. 1999. The Rule of Law and the Underprivileged in Latin America: A Rural Perspective. In *The (Un)Rule of Law and the Underprivileged in Latin America*, edited by Juan E. Méndez, Guillermo O'Donnell, and Paulo Sérgio Pinheiro. Notre Dame, Ind.: University of Notre Dame Press.

PNUD (Programa de Naciones Unidas para el Desarrollo). 1999. *Informe sobre Desarrollo Humano, Ecuador 1999*. Quito: PNUD (November).

Polo, Antonio. 1993. "La Empressa Comunitaria Andina: Un nuevo paradigma para el desarrollo." Quito: COMUNIDEC-Fundación Interamericana.

———. 2002. "La puerta abierta: '30 años de aventura misionera y social en Salinas de Bolívar, Ecuador.'" Quito: Abya-Yala, FEPP, FAO, and DFC (Community Forestry Development).

Powell, John Duncan. 1970. "Peasant Society and Clientelist Politics." *American Political Science Review* 64, no. 2.

Priyadarshi, Shishir. 2001. *"Food Security" in the Agreement on Agriculture*. Geneva: South Centre.

Putnam, Robert D. 1993. *Making Democracy Work: Civic Traditions in Modern Italy*. Princeton, N.J.: Princeton University Press.

Ramón, Galo. 1998. *Diseñando la utopia: propuesta nacional de participación de los pueblos indios y negros*. Quito: PRODEPINE.

Ramón Valarezo, Galo, and Gustavo Ortiz Hidalgo. Part 1, 1995. "Guía para el conocimiento de la organización y gestión de la FUNORSAL." Proyecto "Desarrollo Forestal Campesino" (DEC-FAO Holanda) y Fundación de Organizaciones de Salinas. Salinas, Ecuador (January). Mimeo.

Rasnake, Roger Neil. 1988. *Domination and Cultural Resistance: Authority and Power Among an Andean People*. Durham, N.C.: Duke University Press.

Redclift, Michael. 1978. *Agrarian Reform and Peasant Organization on the Ecuadorian Coast*. London: Athlone Press.

Reilly, Charles, ed. 1995. *New Paths to Democratic Development in Latin America: The Rise of NGO-Municipal Collaboration.* Boulder, Colo.: Lynne Rienner.

Ritchie, Mark, Tim Lang, Peter Rosset, Miguel Altieri, Steven Shrybman, Al Krebs, Vandana Shiva, and Helena Norberg-Hodge. 1999. "The WTO and the Globalization of Food Insecurity." San Francisco: International Forum on Globalization.

Riviera Cusicanqui, Silvia. 1990. "Liberal Democracy and Ayllu Democracy in Bolivia: The Case of Northern Potosí." *Journal of Development Studies* 26, no. 4.

Rodrik, Dani. 2001. "The Global Governance of Trade As If Development Really Mattered." A paper prepared for UNDP (April).

Rosales, Mario. 1989. "El municipio ecuatoriano: Sintomas y razones de su fragilidad." In *Descentralización y democracía: gobiernos locales en America Latina,* edited by Jordi Borja. Santiago, Chile: CLACSO (Latin American Council of Social Sciences).

Rosset, Peter. 1999. "The Multiple Functions and Benefits of Small Farm Agriculture in the Context of Global Trade Negotiations." Oakland, Calif.: Food First/The Institute for Food and Development Policy.

Rueschemeyer, Dietrich, Evelyne Huber Stephens, and John D. Stephens. 1992. *Capitalist Development and Democracy.* Chicago: University of Chicago Press.

Saad Herrería, Pedro. 2000. *La Caida de Mahuad.* Quito: Editorial El Conejo.

Samaniego P., Pablo. 2001. "Los ponchos tenían la razón." *Gestión* 80 (February).

Sandilands, Roger J. 1990. *The Life and Political Economy of Lauchlin Currie.* Durham, N.C.: Duke University Press.

Schott, Jeffrey J. 2001. *Prospects for Free Trade in the Americas.* Washington, D.C.: Institute for International Economics.

Scott, James C. 1998. *Seeing Like a State: How Certain Schemes to Improve the Human Condition Have Failed.* New Haven, Conn.: Yale University Press.

Segarra, Monique. 1997. "Redefining the Public/Private Mix: NGOs and the Emergency Social Investment Fund in Ecuador." In *The New Politics of Inequality in Latin America: Rethinking Participation and Representation,* edited by Douglas Chalmers et al. New York: Oxford University Press.

SEL (Social Enterprise London). 2001. *Introducing Social Enterprise.* London: Social Enterprise London.

Seligson, Mitchell A. 2002. "Trouble in Paradise? The Erosion of System Support in Costa Rica, 1978–1999." In *Latin American Research Review* 37, no. 1.

Selverston-Scher, Melina. 2001. *Ethnopolitics in Ecuador: Indigenous Rights and the Strengthening of Democracy.* Miami, Fla.: University of Miami North-South Center Press.

Sen, Amartya K. 1964. "Size of Holdings and Productivity." *Economic Weekly* 16.

———. 1977. "Rational Fools: A Critique of the Behavioral Foundations of Economic Theory." *Philosophy and Public Affairs* 5.

Shapouri, Shahla, and Stacey Rosen. 2001. "Food Security Assessment: Regional Overview." *Agriculture Information Bulletin*. Washington, D.C.: USDA.

Shiva, Vandana. 2000. "War Against Nature and the People of the South." In *Views from the South: The Effects of Globalization and the WTO on Third World Countries*, edited by the International Forum on Globalization (IFG). San Francisco: IFG.

Shrybman, Steven. 1999. *A Citizen's Guide: The World Trade Organization*. Ottawa and Toronto: Canadian Centre for Policy Alternatives and James Lorimer.

SIISE (Sistema Integrado de Indicadores Sociales del Ecuador). 2001. "El saldo social de la década de 1990: aumento de la pobreza y concentración del ingreso." *Íconos: Revista de FLACSO-Sede Ecuador* 11 (July).

Smith, Ransford. 2000. "El Sur, la OMC y la nueva ronda." *Tercer Mundo Económico*, no. 141-42.

Sogge, David, ed. 1998. *Compasión y calculo. Un análisis crítico de la cooperación no gubernamental al desarrollo*. Barcelona, Spain: Icaria.

Sogge, David, and Simon Zadek. 1998. "Leyes del Mercado." In *Compasión y calculo. Un análisis crítico de la cooperación no gubernamental al desarrollo*, edited by David Sogge. Barcelona, Spain: Icaria.

Solomon, Frank. 1981. "Weavers of Otavalo." In *Cultural Transformations and Ethnicity in Modern Ecuador*, edited by Norman E. Whitten Jr. Urbana, Ill.: University of Illinois Press.

Sreenivasan, Gauri, and Ricardo Grinspun. 2002. *The Rural Poor and Food Security*. Paper 2 in the Trade and Poverty Series, Canadian Council for International Co-operation, Ottawa.

Stavis, Benedict. 1974. "Rural Local Governance and Agricultural Development in Taiwan." Ithaca, N.Y.: Rural Development Committee, Center for International Studies, Cornell University. Mimeo.

Stevens, Christopher, Romilly Greenhill, Jane Kennan, and Stephen Devereux. 2001. *The WTO Agreement on Agriculture and Food Security*. UK: Commonwealth Secretariat.

Stiglitz, Joseph E. 2000. "The Insider: What I Learned at the World Economic Crisis." *The New Republic* (April 17).

———. 2002. *Globalization and Its Discontents*. New York: W. W. Norton.

Streeten, Paul. 1993. "Markets and States: Against Minimalism." *World Development* 21, no. 8.

Striffler, Steve. 2002. *In the Shadows of State and Capital: The United Fruit Company, Popular Struggle, and Agrarian Restructuring in Ecuador, 1900–1995*. Durham, N.C.: Duke University Press.

Ströbele-Gregor, Juliana. 1994. "From Indio to Mestizo . . . to Indio: New Indianist Movements in Bolivia." *Latin American Perspectives* 21, no. 2.

Stumpf, Joseph. 1999. *Informe de evaluación desarrollo agropecuario, pequeña agroindustria y uso racional de la tierra adquirida por organizaciones campesinas de Guamote y Tixán en la provincia de Chimborazo, Ecuador*. Ickiling, Germany: DWH (Deutsche Welthungerhilfe/German AgroAction). Mimeo.

Swift, R. 1977. "Interview with A. Alvarez Cerda," *New Internationalist* (December).

Sylva, Paola. 1986. *Gamonalismo y lucha campesina: Estudio de la sobrevivencia y disolución en un sector terrateniente, el caso de la provincia de Chimborazo, 1940–1979.* Quito: Abya-Yala.

———. 1991. "La organización rural en el Ecuador." Quito: CEPP (Center for Popular Education and Promotion)/Abya-Yala.

Tendler, Judith. 1997. *Good Government in the Tropics.* Baltimore, Md.: The Johns Hopkins University Press.

Thompson, Ginger. 2001. "An Exodus of Migrant Families Is Bleeding Mexico's Heartland." *The New York Times* (June 17).

Thorp, Rosemary. 1998. *Progress, Poverty, and Exclusion: An Economic History of Latin America in the Twentieth Century.* Washington, D.C.: The Johns Hopkins University Press for the IDB and the European Union.

Thorp, Rosemary, and Geoff Bertram. 1978. *Peru 1890–1977: Growth and Policy in an Open Economy.* New York: Columbia University Press.

Thrupp, Lori Ann. 1994. *Challenges in Latin America's Recent Agro-Export Boom.* Washington, D.C.: World Resource Institute.

Todd, Helen. 1996. *Women at the Center: Grameen Bank Borrowers After One Decade.* Boulder, Colo.: Westview Press.

Toledo, Victor. 1995. "Campesinidad, agroindustrialidad, sostentabilidad: los fundamentos ecológicos e historicos del desarrollo." Inter-American Group for Sustainable Agricultural and Natural Resource Development (Mexico). Working paper no. 3.

Tonello, José. 1995. "Acceso a la tierra con fondos de la deuda externa." In Chiriboga 1995.

———. 1997. "Las operaciones con la deuda externa y sus impactos sobre una OGN." In *Fondos de deuda externa y de contravalor para el desarrollo.* Quito: ALOP, FOLADE, and FEPP.

Torres, Victor Hugo. 1999. "Guamote: el proceso indígena de gobierno municipal participativo." In *Ciudadanias emergentes: Experiencias democráticas de desarrollo local,* edited by Mauro Hidalgo et al. Quito: Abya-Yala.

Treakle, Kay. 1998. "Ecuador: Structural Adjustment and Indigenous and Environmentalist Resistance." In *Fox and Brown* 1998.

Trueblood, Michael, and Shahla Shapouri. 2001. "Implications of Trade Liberalization on Food Security of Low-Income Countries." *Agriculture Information Bulletin.* Washington, D.C.: USDA.

Uggen, John Forrest. 1975. "Peasant Mobilization in Ecuador: A Case Study of Guayas Province." Ph.D. dissertation, University of Miami.

United Nations. 1994. *An Agenda for Development.* Document A/48/935.

UNDP (United Nations Development Program). 1996. *Human Development Report 1996.* New York and Oxford: Oxford University Press.

———. 1999. "Human Development Report 1999—Globalization with a Human Face." New York: UNDP.

———. 2001. "Human Development Report 2001—Making New Technologies Work for Human Development." New York: UNDP.

UN-Habitat and Municipality of Dubai. 2000. "Best Practices Database: Democratization of Municipal Management for Equitable and Sustainable Development." Bestpractices.org website.

UNECLAC (United Nations Economic Commission for Latin America and the Caribbean). 2000. *Statistical Yearbook 2000*. Santiago, Chile: UNECLAC.

Uphoff, Norman, Milton J. Esman, and Anirudh Krishna, eds. 1998. *Reasons for Success: Learning from Instructive Experiences in Rural Development*. West Harford, Conn.: Kumarian Press.

US Government. 2001. *National Energy Policy: Report of the National Energy Policy Development Group*. Washington, D.C.: U.S. Government Printing Office.

Vallejo, Alonso, Wilson Navarro, and Xabier Villaverde. 1996. *Tierra para la vida: Acceso de los campesinos ecuatorianas a la tierra: opción y experiencias del FEPP*. Quito: FEPP.

Van Cott, Donna Lee. 1994. "Indigenous People and Democracy: Issues for Policymakers." In *Indigenous Peoples and Democracy in Latin America*, edited by Donna Lee Van Cott. New York: St. Martin's Press.

Velasco, Fernando. 1979. *Reforma agraria y el movimiento indígena campesino en la Sierra*. Quito: El Conejo.

Vogelgesang, Frank. 2000. "Tierra, Mercado y Estado." *Políticas Agrícolas* (Bogota).

Vos, Rob. 1987. *Industrialización, empleo y necesidades básicas en el Ecuador*. Quito: Corporación Editora Nacional and FLACSO.

———. 1988. "Producción, Empleo y Tecnología." In *El Problema Agrario en el Ecuador*, edited by Manuel Chiriboga. Quito: ILDIS (Latin American Institute of Social Research).

Wade, Robert. 2001. "Showdown at the World Bank." *New Left Review* 7 (second series).

Wallerstein, Immanuel. 1979. "The Rural Economy in Modern World Society." In *The Capitalist World-Economy*. Cambridge: Cambridge University Press.

Waridel, Laure. 2001. *Coffee with Pleasure: Just Java and World Trade*. Montreal: Black Rose Books.

Waterbury, Ronald. 1999. "'Lo Que Dice el Mercado': Development Without Developers in a Oaxacan Peasant Community." In *Globalization and the Rural Poor in Latin America*, ed. William M. Loker. Boulder, Colo.: Lynne Rienner.

Weigel, Stefan, and Jurgen Weininger. 1996. "Impacto Ambiental de la Industria del Jean en Pelileo." Quito: INSOTEC.

Weisbrot, Mark, Dean Baker, Egor Kraev, and Judy Chen. 2001. "The Scorecard on Globalization 1980–2000: Twenty Years of Diminished Progress." Briefing Paper. Washington, D.C.: Center for Economic and Policy Research (July).

Weisbrot, Mark, Dean Baker, Robert Naiman, and Gila Neta. 2000. "Growth May Be Good for the Poor—But Are IMF and World Bank Policies Good for Growth?" Briefing Paper (draft). Washington, D.C.: Center for Economic and Policy Research.

Whitaker, Morris D. et al. 1996. *Evaluación de las Reformas a las Políticas Agrícolas en el Ecuador.* 2 volumes. Quito: IDEA (Institute of Agriculture and Livestock Strategy).

Whitten Jr., Norman E., ed. 1981. *Cultural Transformations and Ethnicity in Modern Ecuador.* Urbana, Ill.: University of Illinois Press.

Whyte, William Foote. 1995. "Learning from the Mondragón Cooperative Experience." *Studies in Comparative International Development* 30, no. 2.

Whyte, William Foote, and Kathleen King Whyte. 1988. *Making Mondragón: The Growth and Dynamics of the Worker Cooperative Complex.* Ithaca, N.Y.: New York State School of Industrial and Labor Relations, Cornell University.

Winn, Peter, and Lilia Ferro-Clerico. 1997. "Can a Leftist Government Make a Difference? The Frente Amplio Administration in Montevideo, 1990–1994." In *The New Politics of Inequality in Latin America,* edited by Douglas A. Chalmers, Carlos M. Vilas, Katherine Hite, Scott B. Martin, Kerianne Piester, and Monique Segarra. New York: Oxford University Press.

Winson, Anthony. 1989. *Coffee and Democracy in Modern Costa Rica.* Toronto, Ont.: Between The Lines.

Wolf, Eric. 1955. "Closed Corporate Communities in Mesoamerica and Java." *Southwestern Journal of Anthropology* 13, no. 1.

———. 1969. *Peasant Wars of the Twentieth Century.* New York: Harper & Row.

Wood, Geoff. 1997. "States Without Citizens: The Problems of the Franchise State." In Hulme and Edwards 1997.

World Bank. 1995. *Ecuador Poverty Report.* Part 1, *Components of a Poverty Alleviation Strategy.* Draft, "yellow" version. Washington, D.C.: World Bank.

———. 1997. *World Development Report 1997: The State in a Changing World.* New York: Oxford University Press.

———. 2000. *World Development Report 2000/2001.* New York: Oxford University Press.

Yager, Joseph A. 1988. *Transforming Agriculture in Taiwan: The Experience of the Joint Commission on Rural Reconstruction.* Ithaca, N.Y.: Cornell University Press.

Younger, Stephan, et al. 1997. *Incidencia distributiva del gasto público y funciones de demanda en Ecuador.* Quito: FLACSO.

Zamosc, León. 1989. "Peasant Struggles of the 1970s in Colombia." In *Power and Popular Protest: Latin American Social Movements,* edited by Susan Eckstein. Berkeley and Los Angeles: University of California Press.

———. 1993. "Protesta agraria y el movimiento indígena en la sierra ecuatoriana." In *Sismo étnico en el Ecuador,* edited by Andrés Guerrero et al. Quito: CEDIME and Abya-Yala.

———. 1994. "Agrarian Protest and the Indian Movement in the Ecuadorian Highlands." *Latin American Research Reivew* 29, no. 3.

————. 1995. *Estadística de las areas de predominio étnico de la Sierra ecuatoriana.* Quito: Abya-Yala.

Zappata, Alex C. 2000. "Participación social en la evaluación y diseño de políticas económicas: una experiencia en el Ecuador." Quito: SAPRI [Structural Adjustment Participatory Review Initiative]-Ecuador (October). Mimeo.

Zeitlin, Maurice, and Richard Earl Ratcliff. 1988. *Landlords and Capitalists: The Dominant Classes in Chile.* Princeton, N.J.: Princeton University Press.

Zevallos L. José Vicente. 1989. "Agrarian Reform and Structural Change: Ecuador Since 1964." In *Searching for Agrarian Reform in Latin America,* edited by William C. Thiesenhusen. Boston: Unwin Hyman.

About the Contributors

Victor Bretón Solo de Zaldívar is professor of social anthropology at the University of Lleida in Spain and a member of the university's Grupo Inderdisciplinar de Estudios de Desarrollo y Multiculturalidad (GIEDEM). His research and publications have focused on rural development and peasant economies, with special reference to Cataluña and Ecuador. His recent books include *Capitalismo, reforma agraria y organización comunal en los Andes: Una introducción al caso ecuatoriano* (1997); *Tierra, Estado y Capitalismo: La transformación agraria del occidente catalán, 1940–1990* (2000), and *Cooperación al desarrollo y demandas étnicas en los Andes ecuatorianos: Ensayos sobre indigenismo, desarrollo rural y neoindigenismo* (2001).

John Cameron is a Ph.D. candidate in the Department of Political Science at York University and a graduate research associate of York's Centre for Research on Latin America and the Caribbean (CERLAC). His doctoral thesis deals with municipal democratization in Ecuador in comparative Andean perspective, with reference to Bolivia and Peru. Before embarking on his doctoral studies, he conducted research on urban social movements in Chile and worked as a legislative assistant with the provincial Government of Yukon in Canada. He has presented papers at numerous scholarly conferences and published articles in *Ecuador Debate* and *World Development*.

Ricardo Grinspun is associate professor of economics at York University and a fellow of York's Centre for Research on Latin America and the Caribbean (CERLAC), where he has directed several large-scale international development projects organized with partner institutions—both universities and NGOs—in Latin America. His research has focused on questions of development and international trade, hemispheric integration, and globalization in the Americas. He has written numerous technical reports and co-edited and co-authored four books on these issues, the latest of these on the participation of civil society in the Central American integration process. His most recent research has dealt with the linkages between international trade rules and global poverty. His numerous articles have been published in *Latin American Research Review*, *NACLA Report on the America*, *Nueva Sociedad* (Caracas), *Studies in Political Economy*, and *Review of Radical Political Economics*, among other journals.

Wade Kit completed the Ph.D. in history at Tulane University. His doctoral dissertation focused on land tenure, labor relations, and Kekchí-finquero society in Alta Verapaz, Guatemala. He has published articles on the political economy of the Guatemalan coffee economy in the *Canadian Journal of Latin American and Caribbean Studies* and *The Americas*. Since completing a master's of business administration at York University's Schulich School of Business, he has worked as a financial analyst in the Loan Syndications Department of Scotiabank Inverlat Capital Markets in Mexico City.

Robert B. Koep is a Ph.D. candidate in the Department of Political Science at York University. His doctoral thesis research has focused on the programs of Maquita Cusunchic-Comerciando entre Hermanos (MCCH), an Ecuadorean fair-trade organization.

Tanya Korovkin is associate professor of political science at the University of Waterloo and a fellow of York University's Centre for Research on Latin America and the Caribbearn (CERLAC). She has published books, book chapters, and articles on the politics of agricultural development and cooperativism in Chile and Peru. Her articles on indigenous politics, land conflicts, communal traditions, and local government in Ecuador have appeared in the *Latin American Research Review*, *Journal of Peasant Studies*, *Economic Development and Cultural Change*, and *Latin American Perspectives*, among other scholarly outlets. Her current research focuses on the developmental and social impacts of the cut-flower and petroleum-export industries in the highland and Amazonian regions of Ecuador, respectively.

Louis Lefeber is professor emeritus of economics at York University and a fellow of York's Centre for Research on Latin America and the Caribbean (CERLAC), as well as its founding director. He has been a consultant to numerous governments (Nepal, India, Venezuela, Puerto Rico, Greece) and international organizations, including the UN Industrial Development Organization (UNIDO), the UN Economic Commission for Latin America and the Caribbean (UNECLAC), and the Organization of American States (OAS). He is the author of numerous reports, books, and book chapters on theoretical issues of development, regional and development planning in South and Southeast Asia, and issues of development and democratization in Ecuador and elsewhere in Latin America. His articles have been published in *The American Economic Review*, *World Development*, *Indian Economic Review*, *Desarrollo Económico*, *International Journal of Political Economy*, *Ecuador Debate*, and *History of Political Thought*, among other journals.

Luciano Martínez is professor of political economy in the Faculty of Economics of the Central University of Ecuador and at the Ecuador seat of the Latin American Faculty of Social Sciences (FLACSO) in Quito. He has been a consultant to the United Nations Economic Commission for Latin America and the Caribbean (UNECLAC), the World Bank, UNICEF, the International Labor Organization (ILO), and the Instituto Interamericano de Cooperación Agrícola (IICA). He has published numerous books on rural poverty and development, peasant and indigenous society, and rural artisan production, and he is currently working on issues related to social capital formation and land markets. His articles have appeared in *Ecuador Debate*, *Debate Agrario* (Peru), *Revista de Estudios Latinoamericanos* (Holland), *Revista Latinoamericana de Sociología Rural*, and *ICONOS*, the quarterly journal of FLACSO Ecuador.

Liisa L. North is professor of political science at York University and a fellow of York's Centre for Research on Latin America and the Caribbean (CERLAC), where she has headed several international cooperation programs organized with the Latin American Faculty of Social Sciences (FLACSO) and various Andean NGOs. She has published monographs, book chapters, and articles on party politics, civil-military relations, and development processes in Chile, Peru, and Ecuador; on the civil wars, United Nations' peacekeeping missions, and human rights and refugee crises in El Salvador and Guatemala; and on Canadian–Latin American relations, with particular reference to Central America and the Organization of American States (OAS). Her articles have appeared in *Studies in Political Economy*, *Latin American Perspectives*, *Third World Quarterly*, *Ecuador Debate*, and *World Development*, among other journals. She has collaborated in various capacities with NGOs, including the former Jesuit Centre for Social Faith and Justice in Toronto, OXFAM-Canada, and the Fondo Ecuatoriano Populorum Progressio (FEPP) in Quito.

Index

Acosta, Alberto, 13
Africa, sub-Saharan, 27
Agrarian Development Law. *See* Agricultural Development Law (1994)
Agreement on Agriculture (WTO). *See* AoA
Agricultural Development Law (1994), 13, 17, 89, 91, 110, 117, 121, 137, 205–6
Agricultural Promotion Law (1979), 136, 137–38
agriculture (*see also* AoA [Agreement on Agriculture]; *haciendas*): Amazonian region colonization for, 109, 133; biological diversity for, 49; (large) commercial, 2, 11, 13, 14, 42, 43, 49–51, 54, 55, 63, 75–76, 77, 87, 88, 89, 91, 99, 103, 109, 127–28, 130, 170, 174–75, 179, 184, 185n5, 210; developed countries support of, 9, 61, 65nn20–21; double feminization and, 90; Eastern Asia (land) reforms for, 15–16, 44n1, 88, 205; environmental concerns from, 51, 64n8, 75, 77, 84n19, 158, 205; exports for, 2, 11, 50, 63, 64n5, 69, 72, 109, 122; failure of improvement in, 2, 11; flower, 72, 89–90, 105n13, 123; food security and, 53–55; free market displace of indigenous, 36–37, 39–40, 51, 52–53, 60; GNP's share for, 72, 85; government regulatory power weakened by trade liberalization for, 52–53, 57–58, 98; government's role in, 70–71, 77, 80–82, 83n12; growth of, 87; growth's decline for, 72; imports for, 60; ISI negative influence on, 11, 109; labor conflicts in, 128; land conflicts,

human rights violations declined in, 119–23; land conflicts, human rights violations escalated in, 111–13, 114t–115t, 116–19, 121, 128, 137–38, 139–40, 152, 156, 184; land conflicts, reform failure, landlord power and, 2, 11–13, 19, 64n4, 99, 107, 108–19, 121–22, 123n3, 130, 133, 135–36, 137, 145, 170, 179, 184, 185n5, 190, 205–6; land markets and, 91, 103, 110; land ownership unequally concentrated for, 99–100, 105nn14–16, 110; land percentage as small farm for, 99–100, 105nn14–16, 134; land purchases by peasants for, 12, 17, 120, 135–37, 144, 146, 149–57, 153t, 163nn9–10, 163nn12–15, 168, 177, 185n9, 188, 189–90, 209–10, 215; land reform, distribution and, 12, 14–15, 17–18, 38, 42, 55, 78–79, 84n14, 103, 127–28, 130–31, 133–34, 149–57, 165, 167, 170, 178–80, 185n5, 210; land titles for, 137; large v. small scale, 49–51, 54, 75–76, 77, 84n19, 87, 91, 92–93, 99, 104; livestock/dairy, 134–35, 136, 138, 146, 155, 159–60, 192–94, 195, 200, 205, 206n5, 215, 219; *maquila* industries of, 50; marginal lands used in, 28, 74–75, 78, 91–92, 134, 138; *minifundistas*, 209–10, 215, 218, 219, 222; modernization of, 50–51, 127–28, 130, 134; (European) multifunctional role of, 48–49; mushroom, 193–94, 200, 206n4; 1973 land reform for, 133–34, 137, 152, 167, 170; organic/ecology business, 97, 162; peasant-based civil wars, negotiated peace and failure of

253

Also from Kumarian Press...

Global Issues

Going Global: Transforming Relief and Development NGOs
Marc Lindenberg and Coralie Bryant

Inequity in the Global Village: Recycled Rhetoric and Disposable People
Jan Knippers Black

Running Out of Control: Dilemmas of Globalization
R. Alan Hedley

Sustainable Livelihoods: Building on the Wealth of the Poor
Kristin Helmore and Naresh Singh

Trapped: Modern-Day Slavery in the Brazilian Amazon
Binka Le Breton

Where Corruption Lives
Edited by Gerald E. Caiden, O.P. Dwivedi and Joseph Jabbra

Conflict Resolution, Environment, Gender Studies, Globalization, International Development, Microfinance, Political Economy

Advocacy for Social Justice: A Global Action and Reflection Guide
David Cohen, Rosa de la Vega, Gabrielle Watson for Oxfam America and the Advocacy Institute

Better Governance and Public Policy
Capacity Building and Democratic Renewal in Africa
Edited by Dele Olowu and Soumana Sako

Confronting Globalization
Economic Integration and Popular Resistance in Mexico
Edited by Timothy A. Wise, Laura Carlsen, Hilda Salazar

The Humanitarian Enterprise: Dilemmas and Discoveries
Larry Minear

Pathways Out of Poverty: Innovations in Microfinance for the Poorest Families
Edited by Sam Daley-Harris

War and Intervention: Issues for Contemporary Peace Operations
Michael V. Bhatia

Worlds Apart: Civil Society and the Battle for Ethical Globalization
John D. Clark

Visit Kumarian Press at **www.kpbooks.com** or
call **toll-free 800.289.2664** for a complete catalog.

Kumarian Press, located in Bloomfield, Connecticut, is a forward-looking, scholarly press that promotes active international engagement and an awareness of global connectedness.